For my mother and father,
Mary Jane and Charleston Fields

PART ONE

"When to comes to marriage, men are in the driver seat."

Belinda Oliver

1

I fed Max, sexed him, and when he fell asleep, I left him. My friends call me Gabby to my face, and crazy behind my back. I've put up with Max's philandering ways for four years, but don't get it twisted. I didn't leave in the middle of the night because I stopped loving him. I left because I love him too much for my own good. Max was sleeping like a hibernating bear when I eased out the bed. He stirred in his sleep. I kissed his sweet lips, and whispered calming words while I rubbed his back like a mother sooths a baby. That was all it took to lure him back to sleep. I swept my eyes over all six feet four inches of his naked, muscular, dark chocolate, fineness tangled in his sky-blue sheets. I dressed quickly, grabbed my keys, and tiptoed out the bedroom before I could talk myself out of leaving. My car was already packed for my escape. Leaving him was not easy. The man can put it down, plus he gave me everything I dreamed of and more. I'm just not sure if I can give him the one thing he wants the most.

Max's parents brought him a comfortable contemporary style house with four-bedrooms, five bathrooms, a huge kitchen, and a peanut-shaped swimming pool. I loved making his house our home. He had chosen the house because he knew I would love it. He begged me to marry him when I moved in with him. He wanted me to fill the house with love, and lots of babies.

I'm the youngest of my mother's eleven children. I'm what she calls her menopause miracle baby. Slap me and my mama, but I'm determined to make something more out of myself than a baby mama. I want children. They just aren't on my short to do list. The University of Mississippi offered me a full scholarship plus a cost of living stipend to attend dental school. I would be a damn fool if I didn't accept it. Leaving Max to pursue my own dreams was the second hardest decision I've ever had to make.

After driving all night, my first stop was the office of diversity and minority student affairs. I needed a place to stay, and a student roommate to help pay the bills would be ideal. It made sense to see if anyone was looking for a roommate before I looked for an apartment of my own. I had made my choice to leave, now I had to put on my big girl panties, and learn to fend for myself.

Luck seemed to be on my side. A second-year medical student was in the office looking for a roommate. I accepted her offer on the spot. I agreed to share the rent before I checked the place, or her out. It was a mistake. I should have done my due diligence. Now I'm stuck in a roach infected apartment with a lying roommate named Sara, and her boyfriend Dylan. Sara tricked me into thinking Dylan was her brother. Well, I assumed that he was, and like my sister, Lorna, always says, when you assume you usually make an ass of you and me. Sara and Dylan have the same mahogany-colored skin and curly black hair. How was I supposed to know their pet names for each other were Bro, and Sis? I have five older brothers and five sisters. Our variations in skin color and hair textures confuse people all the time. When my brothers helped me, move into this dump, a truck filled with rednecks called me a n-lover. My brothers are a dark brown color like my father. I'm what they call café au lait like my mother. Big Mama says God mixes things up however he chooses. Just when I thought America was changing, some fools who don't know jack about me, called me a derogatory name that reminded me that slavery never really ended for some people in America. Most people around here are still as set in their ignorant ways as my one-hundred-year-old great grandmother.

Before I could finish unpacking, Sara and Dylan went to Sara's room, and from what I could comprehend from their argument, they were fighting about me moving in. Shortly after the fight, they filled the apartment with loud moans and groans. Their love making made my emotions as raw as live electrical wires snapped apart by a storm. I immediately second guessed my decision to leave Max. I do love him. I'll give his fine ass all the children he wants after I finish dental school.

My mother's greatest accomplishment is her eleven kids. Daddy still can't keep his hands off Mommy. Belinda is a great mother and grandmother. I look the most like her. Max can't keep his hands to himself when we are together either. I figure we won't have any problems making babies, when I'm ready. How my parents managed to raise all of us with their meager resources is commendable. Max and I wouldn't have the financial worries of my parents, but I doubt if Max is ready, or if he is even capable of committing to fifty plus years of marriage like my parents. They say, once a cheater, always a cheater. I called my mother to avoid calling Max.

"Baby girl, it sounds like you jumped out the frying pan into the fire, and a grease fire at that. You should tell your daddy he was right about Max so you can come back home."

I rolled my eyes. She couldn't see me, but if she could, she would threaten to knock me into never, never land. "Max has loved, protected and supported me since Daddy did and said those horrible things to us. We would probably be married by now if Daddy hadn't done that."

"Well, you hang in there, baby," she said. I lip-synced along with her when she said, "Your daddy just couldn't stand the thought of losing another daughter to another slick, fast-talking man like Max. You're our baby and he has high hopes for you. He loves you to death. He says there is plenty of room here if you want to come home. He's your daddy, he is always going to be in your corner."

The drive from Nashville to Jackson, and all the running around I had done, just to have a bed, and a place to rest my head had worn me out. I did it all so I wouldn't have to ask Daddy to let me come home. I'm never going back home. That's my number two goal. That is the main reason I must secure my future ability to take care of myself. The divorce rate is steadily rising. It's not like it was when Belinda and Daddy got married. The statistics say there is a fifty/fifty chance that good intentions of forevermore will end in divorce. Women need to be prepared just in case they end up on the wrong side of fifty percent. The laws have changed, and the stats say women cheat as often as men. Loving Max for his net worth was never my goal even though his mother thinks I'm a gold digger. Dental school is my opportunity. I love Daddy too much for my own good as well. What he did to me, is only one of the things that scare me about the things people do in the name of love.

Later that night, a storm roared outside. The rain sounded like it was coming down in sheets. Thunder and lightning sounded and looked like it was right over us, but it was Sara and Dylan's moans and groans that woke me up from the first real sleep I had gotten in two days. I reached for Max when Sara made a screeching sound that was followed by a tumbling sound, and a loud thump! Someone or something hit the floor hard enough to shake my bed.

"I oughta kill your sorry ass," Sara yelled!

It was hard for me to imagine those words coming from the shy innocent-looking girl I had met yesterday at the office of minority student affairs. A gold crucifix was plastered between her lovely breasts like a birthmark. She had made this dump sound great. Hardwood floors, two large bedrooms with private bathrooms, bay-windows perfect for watching the sunrise and sunset, all for a mere two-hundred-fifty-dollars a month. I didn't bother to check her, or the place out.

Her big doe-eyes filled with tears that spilled over when I said, I would take it, if I could move in right away.

Someone's footsteps sounded like cat paws pitter-patting against the wooden floor as they ran toward the kitchen. A minute later spoons, forks and knives clanged together at a frantic rate. I sat straight up in the bed when I realized I was no longer safe at home with Max. My teeth chattered like it was a frigid winter night. My imagination ran rampant when Sara ran back to her room and threatened Dylan again. Anyone who will lead their roommate to believe their boyfriend is their brother could kill Dylan, me, and herself, and make our murders look like a sorted love triangle. It was my second night in the apartment. Dylan hadn't left when I went to bed. I had made sure my door was locked. The best thing about this place my brothers had said, and they would know, was the upgraded locks on the bedroom doors. Dylan had winked at me. Maybe it wasn't a come-on, maybe he was letting me know I had been had. If I had known he was Sara's boyfriend, I would have thought twice before moving in, or at least insisted upon splitting the rent three ways. It was hard enough for me to ask Lil' Curtis to loan me the money to move in, until I get my stipend. Daddy told Max he was responsible for me the day he stepped between Daddy and me and stopped my father from hurting me more. I was already damaged emotionally. Max has given me everything I wanted and more. I couldn't ask him for money so I could leave him. Well, I could have if I had wrapped it around the right lie, sex, and food. I'm not that kind of girl even though I'm tired of being controlled by the men in my life. It didn't feel right to manipulate Max, even though I could. I took the scholarship to prove to myself, and to them that I can take care of myself.

"Get the fuck outta here, you good-for-nothing bastard," Sara screamed.

"It's raining cats and dogs out there. I'm not going out in that rain," Dylan yelled.

"Get your ass outta here before I slit your gotdamn throat!"

7

Somebody's feet hit the floor, and made fast tap, tap, taps. Something broke! I jumped and picked up the phone. The bright green numbers on my phone, and the numbers on my clock radio provided the only light in my unfamiliar room at 2:45 a.m.

The sounds of leaves and twigs crunching outside, and the pouring rain made me feel like I was in the twilight zone. Dylan tapped on Sara's window. "I'm sorry, baby. Open the door. Please. It's bad out here."

Sara didn't answer. I heard twigs snapping, and leaves crunching again. A minute or so later mixed in with heavy rain beating against my wall and windows were light taps on my windowpane.

Dylan whispered, "Gabby? Gabby? Can you open the door? I need to get my pants and my keys."

I gripped the phone. He must be crazy if he thinks I'm going to put myself in the middle of their lover's squabble. Thank God, the female voice in my ear was an operator saying, "Please hang-up and try your call again," and not me answering Dylan's pleas. Before I could press the button, to call for help, I heard the lock disengaging, and the door creaking open. A calmer sounding Sara said, "I should let your pathetic behind stay out there."

Dylan said, "I'm sorry, baby, I'll find a way to keep my promise." Five minutes later their bed was squeaking out another love song.

I was as horny as a convict, but I was too scared to play with myself until I could go back to sleep. The rain continued to pound on the windows, and Sara and Dylan continued to pounce on each other. All I could do was wish and pray that I could have my dental degree and my man back. My mother always says, God gives the hardest jobs, and the leaves the hardest decisions to us women. I had made my bed, now I had to live with the consequences.

⚏

The next morning the musical sounds of spoons, forks and knives clanging together jolted me awake. I reached for Max. I miss waking up with him spooned against my back poking me with his morning heat. I got up and headed for the shower. While I was soaping myself, a huge cockroach fell from the ceiling and crawled down my back. Talk about the heebie-jeebies; I cracked the shower door trying to get away from that damn roach!

The layout of the apartment and the hardwood floors are nice, but that was the third roach I had seen, and I wasn't even counting Dylan. I gave my clothes the shakedown before I put them on; the feel of that roach slipping and sliding and crawling up and down my back will forever be embedded in my brain. Cockroaches are survivors, every time I knocked the SOB off, it found another place to hold on, and in the end that son-of-a-gun got away.

Breakfast smelled delicious, but that roach had ruined my appetite. Max always made breakfast. Dinner was my job. My nose led me straight to the kitchen. Sara confirmed that she was wearing Dylan's plaid shirt and nothing else when she bent to drain grease from the bacon and gave me yet another reminder that this wasn't my home. Then I noticed Dylan letting it all hang out of his pinstripe boxers while he thumbed through the milk crate containing my CDs. I can't say what was more upsetting; looking at his nuts or the invasion of my privacy.

"Good morning, Gabby," Sara said as if last night had never happened. She had a Looney Tunes smile on her face, like the ones I have in the nude pictures Max takes of me, when the sex is so good it makes me feel disorientated.

"Would you like some bacon, eggs and toast?"

"Good morning. No thanks. I have to run out and get some roach spray," I said as I glanced at Dylan standing in the doorway now. "You forgot to tell me about all these big ass roaches around here, girl."

Dylan sang *Stay in My Corner* along with The Dells on my Classic Soul Greatest Hits CD while it played in my CD player. He smiled at me as though he had wanted me to see his balls when he said, "Don't act like you've never seen a roach. Just because you got tan skin and hair down to your ass and shit don't try to come up in here and act white. You're still a sister; you better act like one in here even if you ain't down." He paused for a reaction, but I've heard that stupid mess so many times it doesn't bother me anymore. I continued to smile and count in my mind like Max had shown me. Dylan wrapped his arm around Sara's shoulder and they both stared at me. "I saw those Beatles, Elton John, Sting and the Police, Bruce Springsteen, U2, and David Bowie, CDs in that box. I'm gonna tell you right now…" He paused again and looked at Sara. "We don't listen to that crap up in here."

Instead of saying that after last night, I was thinking that I probably should move my stereo to my room so I can drown out their fights and whatnot I said, "I'm gonna go get some spray for these big ass roaches who don't pay any rent, but think they are running shit around here." I looked directly at Dylan, and then I walked out.

🐲

Dylan was still in his underwear when I came back three hours later. He was sitting on the sofa in the living room grooving to Sting singing *Every Breath You Take* from my CD on my stereo. He was drinking a beer and smoking marijuana. He offered me a hit. I haven't smoked since Max's twentieth birthday. Max still smokes occasionally, and the loving is good on those occasions, so I don't complain. One time when he was high he shared his fantasies about doing me and my girlfriends. I told him my roommate, Gina, and I had kissed and messed around just to see what it would be like. He didn't believe me. I told him I would never speak to him again if he let Gretchen, my other best friend from college, get within ten millimeters of my stuff. I always sensed something weird between them. The loving was good that night. I fell asleep, and the next afternoon Daddy beat my butt, called me Max's whore, and made me doubt if I should ever marry Max, or any man for that matter. Anyway, that was the last time I smoked.

I eased into the living room and sat on the arm of the sofa. "Where is Sara?" I asked as I took in a lung full of smoke. It smelt like burning grass. It was probably home grown, too green, too wet, and not worth taking a hit.

"She took her behind to work," Dylan said.

"So, do you have a job or is this it?"

My basic nature is to be blunt. I'm working on becoming more tactful. Max says that my directness makes me appear to be less so-phisticated to his mother. I doubt if anything short of leaving Max would please her, but in the name of love, I try. She wants him to marry a debutante with a background more like hers. That's one of the other reasons I decided that I want to become a dentist.

"I work my ass off," Dylan said in a defensive tone. He looked me in the eyes. His bug-eyes were glazed and bloodshot.

"Boss sent everybody home." Dylan coughed and blew smoke out the side of his mouth and nose. "The foundation we were pouring was filled with water. I pay the rent around here, so don't look at me like one of the cockroaches, Miss Gabby."

"That was some kinda rain last night, huh?" I said more than asked. Dylan grunted and took another long pull on his weed. I took my tired behind to my room and finished unpacking.

Most nights living with Sara and Dylan were spent listening to them making love one minute and fighting like animals the next. The twelfth night was especially bad. Dylan called Sara a crazy bitch, and a minute later I heard something break, keys rattling, doors slam-ming and Sara yelling, "If you bring your sorry ass back, I swear be-fore God, I will kill you!"

"You better watch your back, I might get you first!" Dylan shouted.

It's a good thing, I didn't sign a lease. I need to get the hell away from my new roommates. Dylan's truck started up. His tires spit out gravel and loose rocks as he sped away. I need Max now more than ever. I need him to reassure me that everything is going to work out for us just as he did when Daddy beat me and put me out, and when his mother called me a gold digger, and all the times when other women threw their pussy in his face and made him weak, and all the times he just loved my blues away. Forget the scholarship. I shouldn't have left Max like a bad date. I want my man and my degree. Sleep eluded me. I got dressed around midnight. My car tires spit out rocks and gravel and burnt rubber all the way back to Nashville. I wanted to wrap myself around Max, and make him understand my reasons for leaving.

The next morning, I knocked on his door instead of using my key. A chocolate-blond answered the door wearing a satisfied-glow, and the red silk robe I had given his fine behind for Christmas. That's when I went ballistic.

2

Max's red Corvette was sitting in the driveway. His parents were storing their boat in the four-car garage. Either way, it was too early in the morning for a bitch to be at my man's house for a casual visit. I grabbed that hussy around the neck, and snatched at my man's robe. She was on the wrong end of a long-awaited-ass-whipping I had for her, and all the other hussies before her, for messing with my man. In the middle of the catfight, I noticed the life-size portrait of me hanging over the fireplace. It had taken Max all summer to find the perfect frame. It was in the frame shop when I left. This was my first time seeing it in its rightful place.

My hands slid from around Blondie's neck. Maybe Max understood my note, and my reasons for leaving him. Perhaps the situation isn't as bad as it looks. I smiled at Blondie as though I hadn't tried to scratch her eyeballs out.

She slapped me and yelled, "You're a psychopath, Gabriella Oliver! Don't look surprised. I know all about your sorry ass."

Our eyes meet as her chilling words sank in. The gloating smirk on her face made me reach for her throat again. Max's sweet-musk was all over her rotund frame. Maybe it was the robe? No. I know that satisfied look all too well. Max has quite a reputation. He has enough pictures of me wearing nothing but a smile to prove it. I looked at my larger than life portrait grinning down on me from the mantel, and wished I had let him frame some of the nude photographs he had taken of me.

"I'm surprised it took Maxi this long to see through your bullshit," Blondie yelled as she pried my hands from her throat. She gave me a good shove, and slammed the door before I could go for her jugular again.

"I have a key," I screamed. I beat on the door like a lovesick banshee. Rare tears flooded my eyes and forced me to concede to defeat. The five steps of the contemporary-style home I had decorated, and shared with Max all summer, felt like ten as I climbed down them. My inability to make a commitment to please my man, and forget my own needs, has cost me another fiancé.

Max is in his second year of medical school, and I'm going to start dental school soon whether he likes it or not. I wiped tears from my eyes and leaned on the red Firebird I had bought from Anthony, my first ex-fiancé. The car was my only support when I saw Max jogging up the street.

There wasn't a cloud in the sky. I was sure Max had seen me when he slowed down. He gave me time to plaster a smile on my face. Beads of sweat glistened on his dark muscular biceps and legs when he stopped in front of me. I was angry but I wanted more than anything to help him understand why I decided to go to dental school in Mississippi instead of staying in Tennessee with him. My kisses were supposed to make him know I will always come back. I needed him to be okay with me pursuing my own dreams. I needed him to understand how pursuing my dreams now would make our relationship better in the long run. Our loving is supposed to keep our hearts in the right place no matter where we are.

Max smiled at me salaciously and wiped the sweat from his brow. "Why did you leave me like that, Gabriella?" I love it when he calls me Gabriella, but I also know it usually indicates that he is pissed off.

"Shut up and give me some sugar. I'm back to make things right."

He flashed one of those sexy smiles that under normal circumstances would have made my panties wet, but this time it pissed me the hell off, because instead of his eyes searching mine with desire, they drifted toward his front door.

"You changed your mind?" he asked. His smile got sexier. "Tell me you came back to stay."

"I miss you, and your sweet sugar."

He flashed that smile again. "I'm kinda sweaty, and aahhh…" His eyes wandered toward the house again, but I wrapped my arms around his neck and pressed my lips to his. He pushed his tongue in my mouth and swept it around as though the scrooge hadn't already stolen our Christmases. I slipped my hand inside his jogging shorts and petted our puppy. He rose to the occasion and deepened the kiss.

"Let's go inside," I murmured as I choked the big dog's neck.

Max grabbed my hand. "What's wrong with you? That hurts!"

"All the mess you've pulled over the years with other women is what hurts! Why do you think I had to leave you like I did?"

"I don't know what you're talking about. You keep breaking your promises. You left me in the middle of the night as if I was some kinda moron, Gabby!"

"Who is she this time, Max? Were you screwing her last year while I was away at school rubbing my thighs together waiting on your conjugal visits? Let's go inside so I can finish snatching my robe off her ass!" I headed for the door, but Max grabbed my arm and yanked me back.

"No, Gabby, don't go in there!"

I reared back and slapped him hard enough to make him, and his mother, feel all the times they had made me feel inadequate. Maryanne was the other reason I had to leave. Doubting me is not something I can handle sitting down.

"It's over, Max," I said, but that wasn't what I wanted at all.

Rare tears probably gave me away again when he said, "Suit yourself. I love you, but I can't wait for you forever. I'm a man. I have needs. You promised to marry me. Why can't you go to school here? What am I supposed to do while you're in Mississippi pursuing your own dreams? Dreams that don't include me."

"You're supposed to concentrate on medical school, and when you need some loving, hop your fine ass in your Corvette, and come to see me. I would have been eagerly waiting."

"If you loved me, we would be married, and you would be here. That woman in my house, and the others understand how to treat a man like me, and they're a lot less trouble."

I slapped him again, and then I pounded each of my words into his chest. "I left you because I love you too much not to give you my best, Max. If you loved me, you wouldn't throw other women in my face. If you loved me, your heart would be aching as badly as mine!"

Blondie opened the door. "Maxi, your mother is on the phone."

"Tell her I'll call her back."

"Don't bother. I'm leaving!"

I hopped in my car and sped away. I was in no condition to drive all the way back to Jackson. I made it as far as Gretchen's apartment before my tears came again.

Gina and I had nursed Gretchen back to health after she nearly killed herself trying to abort her baby. She is back physically, but she is probably still dealing with it psychologically. That is not something a girl can get over easily. She opened her door. I fell into her opened arms. I had been strong for her last spring. Her situation had brought back my own suicidal thoughts about what I had done to Anthony. It made me come to terms with the possibility that I too may not be able to conceive again. I had talked Gretchen into applying to Meharry Dental School. I wanted to be close to her as well.

"What's going on with you and Max, Gabby? I stopped by his house to see you last week when I moved in. He said you had moved out. What happened?"

"I decided to take the scholarship Ole Miss offered me." Gretchen couldn't hide her disappointment behind her beautiful hazel eyes. "All Meharry offered me was a bunch of loans, and one of those government grants that you have to repay by working in medically underserved areas."

"Why didn't you tell me and Max that you had changed your mind?"

"I'm sorry, Gretchen. Do you want me to leave too?"

"No, Gabby, I just don't know if I can do it without your help, is all. Come in, you look terrible."

"I need to get some sleep before I head back to Jackson."

"Max wouldn't let you in?"

I started boohooing again. "He had company!"

"Get in here, girl, Alma's boxes are everywhere, but my bedroom is clean. Follow me."

We hugged when we reached her meticulously decorated yellow and burgundy bedroom. "It's going to be all right. I'm sure Max is just angry because you left him. You don't want to know the number of times men have used me, and left me with nothing, but my dirty sheets and a pillow to hug and cry on. They can't stand it when we pull that mess on them."

Gretchen's sparkling green eyes pooled with tears and specks of red dusted her light brown cheeks. Gina used to call us the three G's because of our names and our light skin tones. Gretchen and I hugged again and rubbed circles on each other's backs.

"Don't get sentimental on me—that's behind us now. You and I both know this is not the first time Max has gotten caught doing his thing, but this time it's not about me forgiving him, it's about him understanding what I'm trying to do for us."

"Max loves you, Gabby. Everybody at Tougaloo knew he sometimes did his thing on the side, but those hussies knew they didn't mean anything to him. He wants to marry you—that's what matters."

"Why does life have to be so hard, Gretchen?"

She laughed. "I know you're not asking me, the queen of drama and bad circumstances, that question."

"Men have put you through some stuff, but at least you're on the laughing side of it now."

"Yeah, with you and Gina's help, and the grace of God! Thank you, Jesus."

"Amen," we both said as we sat on her bed.

"I've decided that no man is worth losing your life and your sanity over. My father and I are taking it one day at a time, and I'm cool with him passing for white with his family now. And I just know the next time I fall in love, it will be with the right person, thanks to you and Gina. If I didn't learn anything else from you and Gina, I learned that it isn't love if you can't respect yourself in it. I'm going to spike you some tea with the Jamaican rum I got when I was over there with my father. It will help you sleep, and when you wake up, you can decide what you want to do about Max."

"Women flock to Max in droves. I'm not the first or the last woman to get turned out by him," I said. Gretchen blushed in a familiar way that made me wonder again if she had been with him. "Well, I'm sure as hell not going to give him up without a fight after all I've been through."

"Gabby, you know Gina and I have your back in whatever you decide to do about Max and school. I'm going to make your tea so you can get some rest. I need to go to Nana's to get the money Daddy sent to pay my tuition. Thank God for rich white fathers who desert you, reappear and have lots of guilt money."

"I thought your father was half black?"

"He's all black technically, but you and I both know how tricky genes can get when you mix them all up. Anyway, he looks white and he's lived as a white man most of my life, I ain't mad at him anymore. We're trying, that's what counts. Make yourself comfortable and chill here or wherever until I get back on Sunday. I'll leave Alma a note, but she said she won't be back until classes start."

Gretchen made us breakfast and tea. We caught up on how we spent our summers. I love her as much as my own sisters. It was dark outside when I woke up. Gretchen was long gone so I went to the store to get basic vendetta supplies.

Max's car was in his driveway when I returned. The house was dark. I slashed his tires, all of them. Then I smashed a dozen raw eggs on his hood--one for each child he wanted me to have. If he wanted some loving, he could have driven his ass to Mississippi. I stuffed a yam in his tailpipe and burnt my fingers, and when I yelled, "Ouch," his porch light popped on.

He stepped outside. It was a good thing I had parked around the corner. I hid behind his neighbor's hedges and woke-up their dog. It was a good thing I had fed her all summer.

"Gabby? Are you out here? You know I love you. I didn't mean what I said this afternoon. I want you to come home."

My heart pumped faster as Max walked down the steps toward me still talking that "baby, I love you, please come back home sweet talk."

"Gabby, if you're out here, please come out. I miss you, baby."

He looked as edible as chocolate covered cherries in his red robe under the late August moon. I couldn't fake the funk. I wanted to come home, and I damn sure wanted some of his good loving. I would have run into his arms and slurped up all his chocolate cherry juice if the neighbor's antsy Doberman pinscher hadn't been between us. She hates Max. She was growling as if she could already taste his bones as well.

"Darn, you, Gabby! You're driving me crazy, girl. Maybe Mom is right--I should just let you be!"

He stopped a few feet short of the dog and me. "Shut up, you freaking lesbo mutt! You're not a real Doberman anyway. You probably ran Gabby away. I know she was out here."

Sheba growled and leaped around the hedges before I could stop her. She chased after Max as if she knew he was bad mouthing her. Max took three or four giant steps, hopped over his steps and ran into his house. The door slammed. The light faded to black. Sheba barked and scratched at Max's closed door and reminded me of my actions earlier.

"Maryanne should just let us be," I said as I packed up my vendetta gear. I had planned to pour sugar in his gas tank, but what's the point? He has already replaced my sugar. I put a letter in his mailbox that blamed him and his mother for turning me into a woman whose love is so deep it makes me do the good, the bad, and the ugly, to him, and for him no matter how badly they treat me.

"No, Max, I can't just let you be. I can't be with you like this, but I won't be without you either," I whispered, and then I headed back to my car.

3

I cried like a baby after I was safe inside my Firebird. The little voices in my head made me think I was as crazy as Blondie had said. I reached all the way back to my breakup with Anthony. That had been my fault as well. Poor Anthony still wanted to marry me. He wanted me to have his babies so I could stop blaming him for losing my first, which isn't what happened, but it's easier than owning the truth.

Daddy ruled with an iron fist in those days. Marriage and children at seventeen scared me as much as it would have provided an escape. Daddy had threatened to throw Anthony in jail if he even thought about compromising me. When that didn't work, he promised to kill him. It had been way too late for that when I let Lorna talk me into doing what we thought was the only logical solution to my problems.

Daddy didn't want Anthony pressuring me into doing anything I would regret later, but it was his totalitarian behavior that had driven me into Anthony's arms and bed in the first place. We were secretly engaged and I was already pregnant when he mustered up the nerve to ask Daddy to let me marry him. Daddy wasn't having it. He started sitting in the living room with us, and bragging about how good a marksman he is. I used to believe Anthony was my underground railroad to freedom. Then I would foresee myself trapped in a house full of babies with a man that I loved, but not that way, and I would wonder if women are ever free.

Lora ran away from home around the same time. After she left, Daddy wouldn't let me go anywhere except church, school, and to play basketball. Sneaking around with Anthony had been my way of rebelling until we started having sex, and playing basketball was my only relief until the night I met Max.

My pride overruled my better senses, and my talent that night as well. I tried to kill the girl who tripped me. She yanked on my hair, and I choked her until her eyes bulged. She sounded like a chicken squawking as she begged for mercy. I was a raging maniac until a linebacker-looking guy with a baby-smooth face and soft hands grabbed me. Max's hands covered my breasts. I jerked when he squeezed. He pressed into my wiggling butt, gripped me like a football and snatched me away from the girl. I elbowed him in his chest and stomped his foot until he let me go. He had a docile grin on his face when I slapped him. The girl coughed and made the sign of the cross. I pulled my shirt down, and wiped my snotty face. I tried to explain, but the referees threw me out the game.

Most of Hot Springs had traveled fifty miles to St. Agnes to see that championship game. They didn't take being cheated sitting down any better than I had. They chanted, "One, two, three, kill the referee!" Hot Springs is a basketball town; it's a sweet relief from the farms and the paper-mill factories during our short winters. I was the center and the captain. I had led my team to three championships, but that night the rest of my life won over good thoughts and good deeds.

It was a chilly March evening with a full moon. Instead of going to the locker room, I went outside to cool off. Max followed me. My scalp hurt where the girl had pulled my hair, my breasts tingled where he had squeezed them, and I was mad as hell at myself for losing my cool. I ran my fingers through my hair and let it hang down to my tailbone. My eyes rolled and the steamy vapors from my nostrils frosted the cool moonlit air like an angry bull when Max approached me.

"Now what!" I'd snapped.

"I wanted to make sure you were okay, feisty," he said, and then he put his St. Agnes letter jacket around my shoulders, and adjusted my hair.

I looked him dead in his eyes when I said, "My fiancé is the only man I let call me feisty." Max flashed that sexy smile of his, and I retorted to my best I'm-taken look. He didn't fool me one bit with his concern routine after he had squeezed my breasts and pulled me to his reaction. Anthony and I had fought, mostly about nothing earlier that evening. I wasn't surprised when he gave me a lame excuse about not coming to my game. I wouldn't have blamed him if he had hated me--what I had done and the way I had blamed him was unforgivable.

How was I supposed to tell my twenty-one-year-old lover, I loved him, but I didn't want to have sex with him ever again? How was I supposed to tell Anthony, Lorna had helped me get rid of our baby? How was I supposed to tell him I was just as afraid to commit myself to him as I was of Daddy killing him when he found out? That was not something a seventeen-year-old girl with an overprotective father like mine was equipped to do. I hated having sex with Anthony, and he was all I knew, at that time. What did that say about me? I didn't think love and security were enough for me to make a commitment for life to a man who didn't please me between the sheets? I didn't know much about sex back then, but I had enough sense to know I couldn't promise Anthony a lifetime.

Max smiled and wrapped one of my curls around his finger. He is tall, dark, and amazingly cute for a man his size. I still can't believe the softening effects his smile has on me. He reminds me of my father, but his hands, his touch, are soft, gentle, soothing. When he smiles at me his eyes light up like an innocent child.

"My girl calls me, Maxi, but it sounds too much like those sanitary napkins you all use," Max said that night.

"Maxi? That has to be her?" I said out loud as I sat in my dark car. "That was Tammy? Max's high school sweetheart--his first! I'll be damned. I know I'm not going to let that hussy get you back, Max," I said out loud for my own edification.

I had noted that Max had a girlfriend when we met even though he flirted with his eyes and his smile. He closed the distance between us and stroked my cheeks. My stomach filled with flutters that I couldn't name until months later when we made love for the first time.

"I'm not into redbones, but I like your spunk," Max said. Then he tipped my head up and held my gaze. Instead of getting angry my mouth watered and my mind wondered how it would feel to be with him? No, lie--we had just met and I wanted to get busy with him. Before I could recover from my naughty thoughts he stared into my eyes again and played with my hair like he had known me, and loved me for years. People are always touching or pulling my hair without my permission, which is why I usually wear it up. Max seemed like a gentleman even though I wasn't acting or thinking ladylike. I didn't mind when he wrapped my curls around his finger. He made my anger dissipate as he tangled my hair around his fingers and smiled at me knowingly.

"She tripped me. She thought it was funny. I bet it wasn't funny when I was choking her silly behind," I said with too much of a pout— I'm not a pouter.

"Tammy has a way of provoking people," Max said and he continued to stare into my eyes as if he were reading my thoughts.

He was wearing a T-shirt with the logo of one of the colleges I was in the process of considering. After I had gotten rid of Anthony's baby, I decided that it would be best if I gave him his ring back. I wasn't wearing it anyway.

"I was running full speed. I could have broken my neck. The referee pretended not to see her."

Daddy considers any public displays by any of his children to be a direct reflection of him. I was picturing him scolding me when I said, "I may look cute, Max, but I don't take any mess." After I had spoken my mind, it sunk in how foolish I had been about that game, Anthony, Daddy, and life in general. Now here I am sitting in my car crying and feeling stupid again. I didn't know any better at sixteen and seventeen, and I obviously still have a lot to learn at twenty.

Daddy says that Black people living in America, must fight for every bit of respect we get. It doesn't matter how pretty I am, or how long my hair is, or even how light my skin is. We live in Mississippi and even though things are changing--we are nowhere near free, and anyway, most things in life are nowhere near fair. Daddy says half the victory is learning to pick battles worth fighting. He always reminds us that he fought in what he calls the white man's war. He said when he got back to Mississippi, white people were so afraid of black men in uniform they would string them up in a tree before they would give them a job. It is no wonder Daddy is so angry.

"I wish you hadn't let her get to you," Max had said. He lifted my chin and our eyes met again. "I came to see you play." He flashed another one of his sexy smiles, "Hell, half the men here came to see the pretty girl who plays basketball better than half the boys. I think you are beautiful, and a thrill to watch. Your team is nothing without you."

"I blew it—that's why I'm out here."

I wiped at my tears and reminded myself that I'm still young. I fell for Max right from the start. All he had to do was smile, and I was weak in the knees, and my brain turned to mush. He had noticed me on the court. Anthony thought basketball was a waste of time. He couldn't understand how it boosted my confidence, my self-esteem, and the power within me to compete in the bigger world. He didn't need or want me to be any of those things to be his wife.

"I'm usually stronger, but lately everything has been going wrong," I added.

Anthony would have done anything to make me happy, but sex with him--all the time, and children, and convincing daddy--I knew it would never work out. I knew then, and I know now, I need to be happy with myself first. Boyfriends and husbands can make me happier, but they can't make me happy if I'm not already happy with myself.

My parents have always wanted things for me that they never dreamed were possible for themselves. Anthony had been my way out for so long, I didn't know how to tell him I had been offered seven full scholarships to go to college, and new dreams and possibilities that suited me a whole lot more than marriage and babies at seventeen. Now my dreams are having another head-on collision with my love life. Things are different with Max. I love him with all my heart and soul, and everything crazy in me. I'm a slave to his loving, but I don't trust going into a marriage with him until I can find a way to be his equal in the bedroom and otherwise. I smiled between my tears. I had been thinking about my problems with Anthony the first-time Max looked deep into my eyes and smiled. I looked deep into his and beyond. He pulled me into his arms and kissed me. To my surprise, I pressed my body into his and reciprocated. Anthony's kisses never made me loosen up like Max's. He never called me feisty when we had sex. He didn't call me anything. He did it quick while I gritted my teeth, and when it was over, he always pissed me off by saying, "That was good, if we did it more often you would learn to relax and maybe even start to enjoy it."

How was I supposed to enjoy it with my lies and Daddy's threats controlling my body and my mind? How am I supposed to commit to Max knowing that he can replace me with the snap of his finger, and that his mother thinks I'm a gold digging lowlife?

From the moment, Max ran his hands over my butt that night, I loved the way his soft hands warmed and cooled my flesh at the same time. He sucked my tongue into his warm mint fresh mouth and squeezed my breasts again. I pulled away. He smiled at me innocently and played with my hair. I was more speechless from the unfamiliar tingling in my nipples and beyond than his unexpected kiss. I was Anthony's fiancée, at that time, but after Max's first kiss, my heart, body and soul has only wanted Maxwell Johnson. I backed away. Max let go of my hair but he held my stare with his smile. My hair made ribbons in the wind. His kiss and his smile made ripples in my soul that night, and this afternoon when he reached for me and I ran away.

"No, Max, it ain't over. It can't be. We've only just begun," I said to myself. I started my car and drove around the corner to his house with seduction on my mind. Hell, sometimes a girl must do, what a girl needs to do, to survive. I am a survivor if nothing else.

4

I glanced at Max flirtingly that night, gave him his jacket, shook the strange feelings off like a dog does fleas and ran inside. My team lost, and to add insult to injury, I was stuck on a yellow school bus filled with crying girls who had blown a twenty-point lead. Max kissed Tammy the same way he had kissed me, and they left in a shiny Mercedes Benz. My lips were still tingling from his kiss when they disappeared into the frosty night. My heart is still confused by my reaction to him. I wiped at my tears and pulled into his driveway this time. The house was dark. All was quiet so I dug through my purse and found my key.

A part of me wanted to crawl back into Max's bed. I stopped taking the pill two months ago, and if God had given me another chance at having children during that time, I wouldn't have left. Dr. Morgan tells all his patients not to panic. It can sometime take six to eight months to get pregnant after you stop taking the pill. Max wants a house full of kids. I'm not giving up, but I need to do this just in case.

Tammy flashed through my mind and spoiled my positive attitude. What if that heifer tricks Max into getting her pregnant first like Evelyn did with Anthony? She had better stay the hell away from my man. I shook those negative thoughts off as I tiptoed up Max's steps. My hand trembled while I struggled to fit my key in the lock, and as soon as I stuck it in, I heard a woman's voice.

Max probably fell asleep with the TV on I thought. Then I recognized the voice as Mommy's. She reminded me about how she had fallen head over heels in love with Daddy when she was only thirteen, like I had done with Anthony. She told me how her grandfather had tried to keep her away from Daddy. She told me that she was pregnant with my sister Renee by the time she was sixteen and Daddy had gone off to the war. She told me about their shotgun wedding, their shotgun shack, and how the babies just kept coming. She loves all her children and Daddy, but she always wondered how her life would have turned out, if she had listened, and finished school first. Having us was oftentimes the only thing she and Daddy controlled about their lives. That's why she didn't stop Daddy from beating me that day. She wanted me to learn from her mistakes.

I dismissed Mommy when I finally got the lock to disengage. Then Lorna's warnings popped into my head. She reminded me how hard it is for her to make it on her own with just her high school education. People said she was the epitome of true Black beauty, and she could sing her ass off. She wished she had gone to college and studied music. She could have given Whitney and Mariah a run for their money. She still has lots of men chasing her, but she learned the hard way that love, marriage, and children can stop an ambitious woman dead in her tracks.

All my life, I worked hard so I wouldn't end up like Mommy. Lorna helped me abort Anthony's baby because she didn't want me to end up like Mommy even though we never want her to think badly of us or herself. Lorna says that my Bachelor of Science degree in Chemistry won't do me much good if Max cheats on me, and things fall apart ten years, and ten kids from now?

Daddy's voice invaded my better senses next to put his two cents in. I opened Max's door when Daddy said my sisters and I are supposed to be perfect daughters. I'm nowhere near perfect, I whispered. Hope and I have tan skin, hair that flows down to our butts, big chests and cover girl smiles, like Mommy's, but what do those things make us perfect for? I cracked the door to make sure none of the voices were coming from inside. Max was snoring. I slid inside and hung close to the door for a while listening for changes in his sleeping rhythms. As I approached the bedroom, Mommy's voice came in loud and clear again. Dream dreams that were not possible for black women in my day. Strive for things beyond your beauty. Good looks don't mean anything if you're not living life how you want to live it. My babies were my good life--my most important contribution to the world. Is that the life you want? I didn't answer, but that is the one thing I know for sure--I want to be free to live my life on my own terms, which is why I shouldn't have committed to Anthony at seventeen, and I can't commit myself to Max fully right now.

Max likes to leave the bedroom door open. I tiptoed as I approached it. My heart melted when I saw him in bed alone hugging my pillow the same way I had left him two weeks ago. My feet seemed as if they were glued to the carpet as I stood in the doorway watching and wishing. The negative voice in my head said--if marriage means giving your life to Max, and sealing your bond with children, Gabby, you are nowhere near ready. I still haven't figured out how to distinguish the elusive feelings that separate, like from love, and love from lust, and I at least need to know that before I marry you Max. There is something freeing yet holding about your kiss, but marriage to you still scares the hell out of me.

I had wanted to feel free yet committed like that to Anthony before I married him, but I couldn't be that honest with myself and love him on a lie. I wanted to be able to kiss him and walk away knowing that I would always want to return.

"I have always felt that way about you, Max," I lip-synched as I backed away.

I left him another note, a love letter. I explained the life my parents had given me, and why it is important for me to do what I must do. I got back in my car, and said a prayer. When I started the engine, I whispered, "I'll be back, Max, my heart is aching, but I have to do

STAY IN MY CORNER

this for me. Tell Tammy to stay away from you before I have to beat her ass for real." This time I headed for the highway.

❧

Lorna's words were ringing in my head again as I guided my car down the highway. "You'll be in love with the first dick you ever had for the rest of your life, Gabby, if you don't hate his ass when it's over." She was referring to Anthony. I do love Ant in my own way, but his dick doesn't have anything to do with it. I can't lie and say the same for Max, and I sure as hell can't let it end this way. "Not if it wasn't good," I had said about Anthony. Max is as good as it gets.

My mind was set on going to college when I left Anthony. I thought love could wait even though I didn't know how to tell him, just as I don't know how to tell Max. If I hadn't listened to Lorna I wouldn't have been in that predicament with Anthony in the first place or this one with Max.

"Correction," Lorna had said, "If you had wrapped your skinny legs around Anthony and worked your flat ass you wouldn't be in this predicament!"

"Well, I certainly wrapped my legs around Max." I chuckled when I realized I was talking to myself. I told Lorna to shut up, but I'll never forget the smirk on her face when she said, "All I'm saying is if you want some control of the situation with men, you have to learn how to pitch as well as catch."

I wiped tears from my cheeks again. That's not a problem with Max either. His kiss had been the only thing that had kept me from breaking down when Anthony told me he had gotten a girl from his college pregnant. Ant claimed that he still loved me. He said that he always will, but if that was the case, why did he turn to someone else? Why does Max turn to other women? I had prayed for another lover because Anthony had told me numerous times that he didn't believe in divorce or abortions, and I can't tell Max my fears because he doesn't either. I pulled my car over and wiped my eyes. Damn, it took me all this time to figure out that Lorna was talking about more than sex when she said that thing about catching and pitching? Control, games, men! Shit, I'm never going to get it right. I can't let history repeat itself with Max. We've come too far to turn around. I steered the car down the dark highway and prayed that our last kiss meant as much to him as it did to me.

5

Max was the first person I saw when I arrived at Tougaloo College four years ago. Mommy parked our rusty bucket next to his shiny red sticker-still-in-the-window Corvette Stingray. I hid behind my hair and sneaked peeps at him when a giggling girl with ruby-red Billie Holiday lips, blue eye-shadow and a tight expensive-looking red halter dress got into his car. We made eye contact while I was getting my mismatched suitcases from the trunk of Mommy's Impala. The giggling girl's red lips were moving nonstop when Max drove away, but his eyes and his smile were dead on me, just as they had been today.

Belinda and I lugged my suitcases filled with my sisters' and the white woman Mommy worked for hand-me-downs to my dormitory room. Gina Mays was my roommate. She had checked in hours before me. She was a talkative thing, but I liked her the minute she gave me the scoop on Maxwell Johnson. He is the only child of a prominent doctor. His father bought him the car when he announced that he wanted to be the fourth-generation Johnson man, to graduate from Tougaloo, become a doctor and pledge Kappa. Max is right on target with his goals, so why should I forget mine just because I want to be his wife?

Max smiled and winked at me another day while another girl slid into his car. It seemed as if every time I saw him a different girl was getting in or out of what I called his hot seat. He continued to stare and smile at me from a distance, but he didn't ask me out. After I gave up hope, he dropped a young lady off while I was on my way to the library with Gina, and Gretchen. Max pointed at me and winked. I shouldn't have been happy, but I was.

"What's up, feisty? You wanna go for a ride?" he asked.

I headed toward his car, but Gina snatched my high-yellow ass (her words not mine) back so fast my arm felt as though she had jerked it from its socket.

"What in the hell are you doing, Gabriella? You're not like the others--he likes you. Don't act like a damn groupie," Gina said.

I smiled over my shoulder and headed to the library.

"I'm sure tons of men like him have approached you," Gina said. "Don't you know when you have a dude's nose open?" I didn't. Anthony had chosen me when I was twelve and I had gone with the flow. I was leery about Max even though I had been dreaming about him since our first kiss.

"He only wants one thing. Trust me, the brother is trifling," Gretchen added as if she was speaking from personal experience. She used to obsess over how she looked in those days. She was forever comparing herself to Gina and me. I didn't know if her comments were scornful, or envious.

"Don't listen to her, you guys are perfect for each other," Gina said. "You're the sweetest and prettiest girl I've ever met, and he's a big-time player, but when he looks at you I see a sensitive loving brother. Trust me; I've dealt with more than my share of players like him. You all would balance each other out perfectly."

Gina has a way of knowing and understanding things about other people without being told; my great grandmother is the same way. They knew and I knew Max made me feel weird inside long before we were lovers. But the mistakes I made with Anthony could still last the rest of my life if I can't get pregnant again.

The guys at Tougaloo used to call Gina, Gretchen and myself pretty, but we all have features that make even their attitudes toward us feel pretty-ugly. Our light skin tones are the most obvious thing, but it goes deeper than that. Gina has a Barbie doll figure and she could pass for white if her golden-brown hair wasn't so curly and wild. And Gretchen has green-eyes and a curvaceous butt that I would die to have, but she would rather have a pancake like mine. I can understand her frustrations because whenever guys obsess over my long hair and big breasts I tell them straight up that there is a lot more to me than titties and hair.

When we got to the library, I opened my Physics book and started studying to get my mind off Max. Someone pulled my hair and said, "Pretty and smart." I didn't have to turn around to know it was him, but I loved the fact that he called me smart.

"Smart enough not to get involved with you," I said without looking at him directly. Gretchen's words had spooked me, and after fooling around with Gina, and listening to her stories about heavy petting, I realized that Anthony had been as unskilled and as incompetent as I was.

Max and I flirted from a distance while Gina and Gretchen hooked up with other freshmen. Max figured out my library schedule and found all my hiding places. He helped me with a Physics equation a month or so later and I said, "Rich and smart." I laughed that time, he didn't. He finally asked me out, and I made sure he was asking for a real date before I said, "yes."

We went to the State Fair. Our second kiss took place at the top of the Ferris wheel. It made me feel higher in the sky than I already was so I vowed to stay focused. I still can't trust my feelings or Max. He spent a small fortune winning me a teddy bear, and we took pictures in one of those small booths. I got the bear and he kept the black and white pictures of us dressed in Western gear. He tried to convince me to go to his apartment. I made him wait because I wanted to go much more than I knew how to control. We weren't exactly a campus couple; I didn't want to rush because Max was still giving other girls occasional rides. The percentage of males to females on campus was eight to one, and with Max's reputation there was always a willing victim who would spend a few hours with him. I couldn't blame them--Max was handsome, rich and a smooth operator. My heart was wide open when it came to him. Besides, I was still communicating with Anthony--lunch, dinner, stolen kisses here and there--friendly but risky--he was married. He wouldn't let me make a clean break, and I didn't know how. It wasn't over in my heart--maybe Lorna was right.

Max poured on the charm, which was easy for him, and after another month of special treatment, a lot of sweet talk and gifts galore, I agreed to go home with him.

Nothing was on the dark highway at four in the morning, but me, a few trucks, and my memories. I was somewhere between Memphis and Jackson. I wiped my wet face and kept driving.

It didn't take long for me to see that Max was as right for me as he was wrong. If I want to be his wife and to be happy, I know I will have to stay focused. That's all I was trying to do when I left him. My kisses were supposed to tell him I will always come back. I shouldn't have to choose between my career and my man again. Max is the man I want to be with, after I get myself together. There must be a way for me to make him see that I'm doing this for us.

We shared an apartment my sophomore and junior year. Neither of our parents approved of us living together. Daddy's overreaction to me staying out all night, made us more determined to make our love work. When I was eighteen I promised to marry Max on my twenty-first birthday. We even invited our parents over for a dinner party so we could help them understand. Max called me the love of his life that night. He kissed me right in front of our parents, and for a while, I didn't care what they thought.

I continued to drive and reminisce my way straight down I-55. Day was starting to break; maybe there was a way for Max and me to make it over this hurdle as well. Max had given me a quickie to calm my nerves right before our parents arrived. Every time Maryanne grunted or flashed a look of disapproval, I repeated the sweet words he had whispered when we had climaxed minutes before she arrived.

"No matter what happens tonight, Gabby, I will love you like this forever," he had promised. I'd used his words to keep me strong. I repeated his words again and again as I drove down the long lonesome highway.

"I'm against this shacking-up mess, but from the looks of this place ya'll ain't hurting for nothing so we might as well give ya'll our blessings," Daddy said after I'd promised him that I was going to finish school before starting a family. Big Curtis paused and told Maryanne she needed to do something about the phlegm in her throat because she was starting to get on everybody's nerves with all that coughing and whatnot. Before she could protest Daddy said, "Gabby and Max had all summer to think about this after I beat Gabby's ass so ain't nothing we can do but accept it. Face it, Miz Maryanne, you done already lost your boy to my Gabby. I ain't no more thrilled about it than you are, so you might as well stop all that grunting. Your boy could do a lot worse than my Gabby, and as pretty as Gabby is, she could do a lot better than your son."

"Humph!" Maryanne said, and Julius touched her hand.

Daddy hugged me. Then he shook Max's hand. "You better take care of my baby. You ain't marrying her official, but as far as I'm concerned, she's your wife. Don't even think about breaking her heart 'cause what I did to her ain't nothing compared to what I'm capable of doing to you."

"Yes, sir," Max said. He gave Daddy his promise, and we sealed it with a kiss.

Maryanne's mouth opened wide, no words came out, but it didn't take her long to announce that she wasn't feeling well. They left, and Max, my parents and I played cards and drank beer late into the night.

We were happy even though the good, the bad, and the ugly came to the surface after I decided to live as what Daddy called Max's common-law wife. Maryanne continued to treat me like a gold-digger. And Max was a perfectionist, a clean freak and a great lover, but he needed it morning noon and night. I enjoy sex with him, but believe it or not, I can hang, but sex isn't the center of my world. Max became a homebody. I still loved and wanted to go out to dinner, movies, concerts, hang out with friends, and go to dance clubs. I love to dance, and I'm good at it.

Max let me move back to campus while I was pledging the same sorority as Maryanne. It was spring and I wasn't into the sorority girl scene, but I thought his mother would be more accepting of me if we were sorority sisters. After the first day on line, I knew that was a bad reason to make that type of a commitment.

Max was sneaking around and the girls couldn't wait to tell me. I was on line with Gina and Gretchen. I threatened to quit many times, but Gina said, "We are only as strong as our weakest link. This is our chance to prove to them that girls like us are strong. That we are not selfish and self-serving. That we are true sisters just like them."

"If you break the chain it's over for all of us, Gabby. So, what are you gonna do?" Gretchen had added.

They stared at me and waited for my answer. We were all being hazed about the things we hated most about ourselves, and that was hardest on Gina. Our boyfriends were also being berated, and that was hardest on me because it was probably true. According to our big sisters Max was a whore, Paul was a faggot, and Gina's beloved Charles (that's how she used to refer to him) was a nerd who couldn't keep it up.

Gina told the big sister who made the accusation that she was sure it was true because Charles was under her spell, and he would only be able to get it up for her until she let him, and that wasn't ever going to happen. Our big sisters laughed it off, but Gretchen and I knew Gina was dead serious. When Gina told me not to worry about Max--I didn't. Gretchen reminded me that Gina had a way about her that we didn't necessary have. We promised to look out for each other. I already had an inseparable bond with Gina, and by the time we went-over I had one with Gretchen as well. Those sisterly bonds made pledging worthwhile.

After we went-over, Max came to my room and swore that the rumors weren't true. He begged me to come home. I didn't waver until he got on his knees, and gave me a six-carat diamond ring. Max's parents had money, and Max's grandfather had also left him a small fortune when he died.

Instead of saying "yes," I called Belinda and Big Curtis to tell them I was a sorority girl, and Max's fiancée. They didn't give a hoot about the sorority stuff. Belinda gave Daddy the phone. I repeated my news for him. I had to explain what a sorority was, and I couldn't help but chuckle when he asked, "What in the hell does a girl with five big sisters need a damn sorority for? Put Max on the phone. I want to tell him personally that it's about time he did right by you."

I was so excited when Max finished talking to Daddy, I ran through the dormitory shouting to the top of my lungs, "Max and I are getting married so stay the hell away from my man!" I packed my stuff quickly. We were six weeks past ready for some good loving. On our way to our apartment Max decided to tell his parents.

It was eight o'clock on a Saturday night. Julius and Maryanne were in their den having cocktails when we arrived. I smiled from ear to ear while Max did the honors, but Maryanne cleared her throat and flashed Julius a look of disapproval. Then she looked me dead in the eyes and said an apathetic, "Congratulations, Gabby. You finally pulled the shades completely over my baby's eyes." My smile turned into a frown.

"I wasn't surprised by the way you used your body to lure him to bed, but, honey—" She turned to Max. "How many times did your father tell you, you don't have to buy the store when the candy is free?"

"Mom!"

"Son, you know your mother can't handle her liquor," Julius had said. "You all are young, just because they're engaged, Honey, it doesn't mean they're gonna get married."

Max pulled my stiff body closer to his. I had learned to block his mother out by imagining him whispering sweet nothings in my ears.

"Isn't it great that we are sorority sisters?" I asked as an afterthought.

"Humph!" was all Maryanne said.

But I couldn't stop myself. "In a few years I'll be your daughter-in-law, and after I finish dental school, Max and I are gonna have twelve kids. I know you all can't wait since he is your only child, and you all treat him like a—"

Max cut me off when I began to sound sarcastic. "What Gabby is trying to say is—we're excited and we hope you all will get excited for us."

"Humph!" Maryanne said again, and I can't remember wanting to slap anyone as much as I wanted to slap her ornery ass that night.

"We just stopped by to spread some cheer before we start our private celebration. Let's go home, Gabby."

Max tried to pretend that his bubble hadn't been busted. My parents were finally happy with us, and he couldn't deny any longer what I had known all along.

Our love making got better that night. We proved to each other that we were doing the right thing. Then we took our first nude pictures and caught the essence of our night forever. I thought we had finally realized that our love is about us, and not about them.

We continued to live together until Max graduated and moved to Nashville to attend Meharry Medical School. I moved back to campus to finish my senior year, which crept by without him. Anthony finally sold me his old Firebird, and I started working as a nurse assistant for Max's godfather--Dr. Morgan. I got closer to Gina and Gretchen. Gina and Charles were living proof that true love existed, but Gretchen and Paul's relationship went from bad to worse.

Gretchen got pregnant in hopes of holding on to Paul. He wanted the baby, but he didn't want her. She tried to abort the baby herself. I found her in the shower barely holding on to life! Gina and I rushed her to the hospital, gave her our blood, prayed for her, kept her secret and nursed her back to health. She damn near killed herself, and may have ruined her chances of ever having children.

While Gretchen was recovering, she told me a tear jerking story about her abusive boyfriend in high school, another painful abortion, the circumstances around her twin brother's suicide and why she was too frightened to talk to her father whom she had thought was dead most of her life. She was still suicidal. Gina and I were afraid that we were going to lose her. She desperately wanted children and after Dr. Morgan told her there was a good possibility that she could be sterile we were her only support. I spent all my free time with her and before we graduated we all promised to continue to love and support each other forever.

Gina and Charles eloped right after graduation and moved to Connecticut. Gretchen and I had decided to go to Meharry in Nashville. Ole Miss offered me a full scholarship shortly after I made that promise.

Max had put pressure on me to elope when he took me to New Orleans to celebrate my graduation. I lied and said I wanted to have a wedding instead of putting my cards on his table. I continued to work for Dr. Morgan. I pretended to be saving for our wedding, but I couldn't stand sleeping on Lorna's couch dodging broken springs and missing Max. I moved to Nashville to be close to him, and to save my back. At least that was what I told myself. As soon as I got there, Max started talking about marriage and babies, and dental school was pushed to the backburner since Meharry didn't offer me any real money. I didn't take any chances on not graduating from college, but if I had stopped taking the pill six months ago, I would either be pregnant by now or sure that it was never going to happen.

6

Women need their own degrees and their own shit these days. I drifted down memory lane all the way from Nashville back to Jackson. Sara was sitting in the kitchen feeding a stray cat a can of my sardines when I let myself into the apartment. After listening to her and Dylan go at it and fight for two weeks, it is no wonder I wanted to rush back into Max's arms. Sara looked up when I walked in.

"Where you been hiding? I was beginning to think you had run off with Dylan."

"I went to Nashville to see Max."

"Girl, I don't know how you do it. Dylan has been gone a couple of days and I'm climbing the walls. If he was in another state I would be fucking somebody else in a Mississippi minute."

My mouth fell open, but no words came out. Sara had a sneaky grin on her face when she added, "I went on a prowl last night. Girl, I hooked up with this white boy from my class—I'm sure I don't have to tell you how they get down." She smiled and said, "I wanted to kick myself for not letting him hit it before he got married."

I was speechless, angry, and maybe even envious. I don't care who she sleeps with, but I don't welcome the thought of having a bunch of strange men in and out of the apartment with her flip-flop temperament. If Max had been in Nashville waiting for me with opened arms, it would have been easy for him to convince me to stay.

"Don't look at me like I'm crazy. I don't have a cushy scholarship like you. Somebody has to help pay the rent."

"Is that why you guys fight all the time?"

"We don't fight that much. We've been on and off since high school. Dylan promised to pay for me to go to medical school, but now he claims he is short on cash because his baby's mama put a hit on his check for child support."

I felt sorry for Sara. "Can't you get a loan or something?"

Sara frowned. "So, was Max's loving good?"

"His loving is as good as it gets," I said from my heart.

"So why did you come back before Labor Day?"

"I need to rest before school starts on Tuesday. I didn't get any sleep in Nashville, if you know what I mean." I half smiled. I didn't feel close enough to her to discuss my relationship with Max. Lorna warned me long ago about telling my friends too many details about my man. "Well, I'm gonna call it a day."

I went to my room, locked the door, and called my mother to tell her about Max. "Stop that crying," Belinda said. "You and Max shoulda married way back when y'all decided to shack-up, so don't cry to me about him not wanting to marry you because you want to go to school here. Y'all wanted to do thangs your way so your daddy and I stepped aside. You got pills to keep you from getting pregnant, and you have an opportunity to live out your dreams. Now if Max is still a part of those dreams you'd best find a way to make him see it. Doors are opening for us women, but when it comes to getting married, men are in the driver seat now, and they always will be."

I frowned. "What makes you say that?"

"Max wants to marry you, Gabby, but he wants to marry you on his terms. Now I was there when you promised to marry him when you turned twenty-one. You promised me that you would delay having babies until you got your college degree. That was y'all's plan. Now correct me if I'm wrong."

"You're right, but Max wants to start a family now."

"And you want to run away so you can get another degree. I've watched you and Max over the years. I've been here for you through all y'all breakups and make-ups. Through it all the only thing I'm sure about is that you love Max and that boy loves you to death."

"But, Mommy, he's always fooling around."

"Gabby, do you realize how many times Max has asked you to marry him and you're turned him down. Both of y'all have been loving like that old blues song on a two-way street."

"I had my reasons, Mommy."

"Just remember what I said about him being in the driver's seat. If you were a man of means and your car kept breaking down you would test drive as many new cars as you need to until you find one that starts up when you want it to, takes you as fast you want to go, and has all the fancy gadgets that your heart desires."

"That is so sexist, Mommy!"

"Call it whatever you want, and while you're at it, tell me which part doesn't describe Max."

"He's not that bad. The first time he asked me I was barely eighteen."

"Y'all were young, but you were living like grown folks. That's why your daddy and I and Maryanne and them were all up in your business. I believe Max was trying to do right by you because he loves you. If you don't love him enough to marry him, you need to ask yourself why, because that is what Max is asking himself every time you turn him down."

"I do love him, but I was scared, and anyway, his mother doesn't think I'm good enough for him. That's why I want to become a dentist. I want to prove to her that I'm not a gold digger."

"Gabby, you don't have to prove anything to that woman. Putting up with her should prove to Max that you love him. When a man is ready to make a commitment, the only thing that is going to prove to him that you love him, is you saying, I do. So, get off this phone with me and figure out if you love Max enough to marry him, and if you do then you need to figure out how you're going to go to dental school, and start having those babies he wants."

"Why is life so hard, Mommy?"

"It just is, but you're a smart girl, you'll figure it out."

I stayed locked up in my room until Monday morning trying to figure it out. Dylan didn't come back, but I overheard Sara calling him everything but a child of God for not having the money for her tuition.

I got up early on Labor Day and went to the NorthPark Mall to check out the sales. My brother's annual Labor Day cookout started at noon. I overdid it with the beer and food when all I wanted was for Max to hold me, and tell me everything is going to be all right. I sneaked back into the apartment around eleven. My head was splitting from overeating and drinking at Lil' Curtis's house. I locked my door and fell across my bed ready-to-roll.

Someone came into the apartment around midnight. I woke up when my door knob turned. Sara's car was in the parking lot when I came in. She must have gone out with her classmate again. My door knob turned again. I always lock it.

I took my shorts off and crawled under the covers. My head was still hurting and I certainly wasn't in the mood to hear about Sara's date. The door to her bedroom creaked when it opened and a few minutes later the apartment was filled with screams and the familiar rhythm of her bed squeaking.

Sara's screams were making my blood curl when I reached for Max. I had drunk at least six beers, but damn! She's a screamer, but it sounded like they were acting out a sick rape fantasy. Sara wasn't swearing and talking shit like she usually does. Maybe Dylan was making good on his promise. Max and I can get freaky, but damn! Sara's violent love making had gotten on my last nerve when I pulled the covers over my pounding head and put my fingers in my ears. I needed to go back to sleep. I wanted to get off to a good start tomorrow. I must be crazy for leaving my sweetie, and a fabulous home in Nashville, to live with a bunch of cockroaches, and a sadomasochist.

Someone left the apartment around one o'clock. I woke up again. It didn't sound like Dylan's truck, but everything was quiet after that. I wrapped my legs around my pillow and pretended it was Max until I drifted back to sleep. My first day of dental school and the rest of my new life starts tomorrow, and I've never been so afraid of failing.

PART TWO

"Love makes me endure foolish things."

Gabriella Oliver

7

It wasn't just the first day of dental school--it was my opportunity to make my dreams come true. My stomach churned, and I would be lying if I said I wasn't scared. My first class was at eight. I had to stop by registration to take a photo ID before it started. I had a hangover, but I hopped out the bed and into the shower. The apartment was quiet. I pulled on a pair of jeans and a T-shirt with New Orleans scribbled on the front. Forget first impressions. Big Curtis used to tell me to impress people with my knowledge and my skills; you don't have to have either to dress well and to look pretty.

The bowl of corn flakes filled with sugar and the glass of juice I wolfed down made my stomach bubble even more. Sara still hadn't gotten up. My Firebird started without a ten-minute warm-up and I was off. My scholarship provided an extra twenty-five-thousand poverty dollars to cover food, rent, and books. Books were setting me back close to two-hundred dollars per class. It was a good thing Belinda had stocked me up with corn flakes, sugar, tuna, sardines, chicken and rice. If push comes to a shove, I won't pay my rent.

I wished I had paid more attention to how I looked after I took the photo ID. It's important to get off to a good start. I was determined not to let it get me down.

Dr. Wagner had started orientation before I walked in. The big clock on the wall had two minutes after eight on it! Dr. Wagner stopped mid-sentence and said, "There you are, Miss Oliver, just so you know--we operate on central-standard-time here at UMMC."

I lowered my head and wished for Max. The room looked like a sandy beach filled with pale bodies on the first good tanning day of the season.

"Miss Oliver, your reserved seat is over there."

My eyes followed Dr. Wagner's eye-nod to an empty chair across the room. He waited until I sat down. Then he applauded. The lecture room had five rows of long bench type desks that formed an oval. My seat was dead center of the classroom.

"Look at the person on your right. Shake their hand and introduce yourself," Dr. Wagner said.

I turned to my right and made eye contact with the bluest eyes I had ever seen up close and personal. He had a smile like Max's. He shook my hand firmly and flashed his sexy smile. I wondered if that smile was genuine or if he was simply being cordial when he squeezed my hand, and said his name was Bradley Pruter.

Bradley's tan perfectly sculptured face, blond hair, and the light blue well starched button-down shirt with a polo player embroidered on the breast pocket, brought out his undeniable movie star good looks. He had on navy blue pants and his tie and belt had matching duck decoys on them. His penny loafers didn't have any pennies, but I was willing to bet that he had plenty in the bank.

"It's nice to meet you," I said as I flashed my best fake smile.

"Don't let him get to you. He's a jerk," Bradley whispered.

"Now, turn to your left," Dr. Wagner said.

I extended my hand and looked deep into the face of a pretty woman wearing a flaming-red dress with lipstick to match. She shook my hand limply and said her name was Rachel Newberry. Rachel's strawberry-blonde hair, her alligator cowboy boots, and the diamond earrings in her ears made her look like Hollywood money as well. But her Southern drawl wasn't just Mississippi. I've lived in Mississippi all my life except for the weekend I spent with Max in New Orleans, and the few months we spent in Nashville. The smile on my face wasn't for Rachel it was for her drawl and the split in her dress, which would have been up to her panty line if she had been wearing a pair.

Rachel twisted in her seat when I searched her blue contact lens eyes again. I managed to say hello without sounding stupid. My decision to leave Max was starting to feel more and more like a bad dream. I hated the way Rachel squinted and the way Bradley smiled with interest.

"There are fifty of you here today. We have four years to transform you into dentists. It will take five years for some of you, and twenty-percent of you won't make it through this year," Dr. Wagner said, and the look he directed toward me, jumpstarted my survival skills. There is no way in hell I can tell Max, Big Curtis, and Belinda I got spooked by a white guy shorter than me, and as much as I would like to forget about school and marry Max, he is obviously not ready. I looked around the room again. There were forty-five white males, four white females and me. This is my chance. I will make it work for me. I'm sick and tired of being sick and tired. Black women have had greater challenges and survived, and I'm not going to let them down.

"Those of you who will succeed will live fine upscale professional lives as dentists, but remember there are no free lunches. You all have a lot of hard work ahead of you and if you make it, I suggest that you invest your money well."

I daydreamed about Max through the rest of orientation. Dr. Wagner announced a fifteen-minute break. I watched while everyone left the room. Then I sank deeper into my seat toward depression. I had never seen so many well-dressed white people in all my life. I was the only one wearing jeans! Three of the other women had on nice pastel spring-like dresses, and Rachel had on that sleazy red thing. Ninety-percent of the guys were dressed like replicas of Bradley, the best dressed and the best-looking male in class. After everyone left, I went to the bathroom and splashed water on my bare face. It was not a good time to have a hangover. I fumbled through my purse until

I found a tube of tomato-red lipstick—Max's favorite color. I did my lips and rubbed a dot on each cheek and blended it in. Then I let my hair fall over my shoulders and back.

"That looks better, but..." Rachel's and my reflections in the mirror startled me when I looked up. "Don't get any ideas about Pruter," she said. Then she walked out.

Bradley followed me back to the lecture room early. He had a cup of coffee in each hand. "I thought you might need one to help you stay awake." he said. He sat a cup in front of me and flashed another wide suggestive smile.

"Thanks, that's mighty sweet of you." His smile got broader, and I couldn't help myself when I smiled because I almost said that's mighty white of you--Big Curtis always says that when he is telling stories about how he sees white people.

"I needed a cup to get through Wagner's lecture. I heard he doesn't like women."

"And I thought it was just me," I said with an air of sarcasm.

"Don't let him get to you. He's a military man--just let me know if you need help with him or anything. Okay?"

"Thanks, Bradley."

"Brad. You know you're really cute when you smile. So, what does your fiancé do?"

I toyed with my ring. "Ex-fiancé."

"Well, from what I can see it's his loss."

Dr. Wagner went over our schedules for the first semester. We had Biochemistry, Pathology and clinical rotations in the mornings and Dental Anatomy, Dental Materials and Oral Pathology classes in the afternoons. Classes began at eight and ended at five every day. I survived the first day. No one talked to me except Brad and Rachel, and I couldn't tell if Brad was flirting, or if he was a white boy who was secure about his good looks and obviously rich enough not to care what other people think.

I didn't see Sara at school or at the apartment. I studied at the library until it closed, and I managed to avoid her completely, which was fine with me. I had decided not to share cooking with her when Dylan was around. I ate breakfast at the apartment, skipped lunch and had dinner in the cafeteria at the hospital. The food was bland but cheap.

When I got home from the library late on Thursday night it was raining and the air conditioning was freezing my ass off. I didn't feel like making waves so I didn't touch it. The utility bill was going to be a bear, and I hadn't even factored it in.

My ache for Max had turned to self-punishment by Friday. Dylan hadn't returned and I had managed to avoid Sara all week. I was ready to spend some time with my baby when I stepped out the shower. Max and I always rewarded each other with sex on Friday nights, and three stressful weeks had made me beyond ready. Sometimes we would go out to dinner or dancing, but we always made love before and afterwards. He hadn't called me since I jacked-up his car. I had picked up the phone several times to beg for forgiveness. I hung up when he answered. He is such a brat. I expected him to call and beg me to take him back, or curse me out, or at least ask for his ring. I threw the ring in my jewelry box. Maybe I should pawn it. My sister, Hope, hocked three before she finally got married. Two down, and one to go.

Max acts tough on the outside, but he is more sensitive than I am on the inside. He wouldn't have hung my picture over his fireplace if he wasn't still in love with me. His words were harsh, but his eyes were begging me to stay. He cheats when he can't control me. We wouldn't have made it this far if our love wasn't real. I put on his favorite tomato-red cotton dress, and a pair of high-heels. Then I painted my face, and let my hair down.

The guys whistled when I walked into the lecture room. Rachel and I are the only single women in our class. I strutted my stuff to my seat, and when I sat down, I slung my hair over my shoulders and crossed my legs high like Rachel. She rolled her eyes. Brad smiled. I readied my pen for taking notes.

The office of Minority Student Affairs is having a mixer after class. All the minority students are supposed to be there. I avoided Rachel's eyes; Brad had been the number one whistler.

"So, did you make up with your fiancé?" Brad whispered.

"Can't a girl look presentable without being hassled?"

"Jeez, Gabby, I'm trying to be your friend. You wanna help me out here?"

"Sorry. I get testy about my private life sometimes."

Brad flashed his million-dollar-smile. "So, we're friends, right?"

"We're cool. I'm feeling better today, okay."

"So, would you like to catch a movie with me after Dr. Brown's party?"

Brad seems to know everything and everybody. "Sure. You just might turn out to be my ace, Bradley Pruter," I said. I looked him over the way boys do girls when they are interested in one thing and one thing only. Then borrowing Maryanne's tone and words I said, "A girl like me could do a lot worse." And just as I was mimicking the last word Rachel tossed her hot coffee, cup and all at me! I narrowly escaped messing up my best dress. Brad helped her clean up the mess. She swore that it was an accident. I stewed through the first hour of Dr. Olynick's Biochemistry lecture while Rachel gloated over cleaning up a doggone coffee spill until I remembered I had made a date with Brad that I now intended to keep.

$$\mathcal{Q}$$

The party was at Dr. Brown's house in North Jackson near the Ross Barnett Reservoir. He lived in a large brick home with an outdoor pool. Dr. Brown was one of two black doctors on staff at UMMC. I had met him several years ago at Max's parents' house.

There were nine black medical students, one East Indian, and one student from Hong Kong. Seven were male, two were married.

There was a single black male in his third year of dental school, but I haven't met him yet. Word had it that he doesn't do minority events. The single males all had the prince of medical school syndrome. I figured if I had to deal with that attitude, I might as well deal with Max.

Dr. Brown joined me when he saw me sitting outside by the pool alone. "Didn't you move in with Sara James? Dr. Brown asked.

"Yep."

"Do you have any idea why she registered, but didn't show up for class all week?"

"She said something about her boyfriend helping her out. They had a fight--she put him out."

"Tell her to call me. So, I hear Bradley Pruter is your lab partner."

"You and Brad seem to know an awful lot about me."

"Brad lives next door. He got his house dirt cheap." Dr. Brown chuckled. "I brought the prices down in the neighborhood, and he went straight to the bank."

"It's almost a new decade do you think people in Mississippi will ever change?"

"I don't know, Gabriella, but it's up to young people like you, and Brad at this point. He's fond of you. He wanted to know if I could get Dr. Wagner fired for the way he treated you. He even asked his father about it. If anyone has clout in Mississippi, Trenton Pruter does."

I loved the way Dr. Brown said my name with a Spanish Southern twang. "Do you think Brad likes me because he wants to do what's right, or if he is interested in me as a woman?"

"Most men are going to be interested in you as a woman. I think Brad cares about you as a person though."

"You do?"

"Yes, but be careful. You can make a man's temperature rise just by smiling at him. How is Max doing, anyway?

"Don't know. He was pissed when I decided to take the scholarship. I was hoping that he would understand, but he has gone on with his life, so I'm going on with mine."

"Keep your head up. You won't have a problem finding someone else, and I wouldn't be surprised to see Brad at the front of your line."

"My Daddy would have a heart attack if I brought a white boy home. As far as my father is concerned Max and I have been married for years. If I hadn't taken the scholarship, we would be official by now."

"I admire you for being brave enough to pursue your own profession. One never knows how relationships are going to turn out. If you get your dental degree, no one can take it away."

※

Brad was wearing a pink Polo shirt and khaki shorts that showed off his athletic legs, arms, and butt when he crashed the party. The movie was at nine o'clock. Brad ushered me across Dr. Brown's lawn, and the brown eyes at the party were just as piercing as the light eyes in class. I got into Brad's black Porsche. He tooted his horn as we drove away.

We saw Mission Impossible with Tom Cruise. The movie was about an agent under false suspicion of disloyalty. He had to discover and expose the real spy, without the help of his organization.

After the movie, Brad took me back to Dr. Brown's to get my car. I followed him to his house. A Corvette like Max's zoomed by right before I went inside Brad's house.

Everything about Brad's living room was picture perfect. Even the pillows in front of his fireplace looked as though they had been strategically placed. He hit a switch and soft music drifted from speakers hidden in the walls.

"Do you like Chopin?" he asked.

"Sure," I said even though I didn't have a fucking clue.

Brad hit another switch and the lights dimmed. "Would you like a glass of wine?"

"Sure. Are your parents home?"

"I don't know. They live in the Delta."

"You live in this big ass house alone? Where is your wife? Your girlfriend?"

Brad frowned. "She turned me down. She couldn't stand my parents, and she hated Mississippi."

"I can understand that, but in my case love makes me endure foolish things."

"My parents are good people. They were just ass backward when it came to Ingrid and me. Would you like to come to my wine cellar to pick the wine?"

"You can choose. My wine list doesn't include anything that requires a wine cellar. I'm more of a screw the top off, and pass the bottle girl."

Brad laughed and left the room. I was afraid to move. I should be in Nashville snatching off Max's clothes and giving and receiving love as if my life depends on it. It's too warm to make a fire, but the room, the music, and Friday nights always put me in a romantic mood. This is exactly how I had pictured spending my evenings with Max.

Brad gave me a long-stemmed fluted glass half filled with a deep red liquid. The glasses chimed like musical notes when we clicked them together. "To, Gabriella, the most beautiful girl in class." We clicked our glasses again. I loved the way they chimed and the way Brad's barely detectable Southern accent sang my name.

"To, Bradley, only the strong and truly committed will survive." I took a small sip. Our eyes met. He cleared his throat, kicked off his Top Siders and sat on a pillow so I did the same.

"We can do this together."

My heartbeat quickened. "Do what together?"

"School."

I clicked Brad's glass again. "To friends and lab partners." Our eyes met again. He smiled. My mind had headed toward the gutter. I took another sip of wine and sat the glass down.

"Have you heard from Max?"

I didn't remember telling Brad Max's name. "No, and get your nose out of my business. So, Brad, what's your story? Why is a single, good-looking, white boy being so nice to a single, broken hearted, sista like me?"

His face turned bright red. "Do you swim, Gabby?"

"Didn't your mother tell you not to answer a question with a question? Why am I here, Brad?"

"Because you're my friend and I like you," he said with an impish smile on his face.

"After our first week of dental school I suppose the company of a friend is nice, but I would rather be in the sack with Max. So, name your game."

"Do you swim?"

"Is this a metaphor, Brad, or do you want to know if I can swim?"

"Both."

"Then the answer is yes, but not tonight."

"I was on the swim team at Yale. Going east to college changed the way I see the world. I swim to relax. I'll teach you my technique if you like."

"You want to teach me how to swim and relax?"

"Yes," he said as he stared into my eyes and touched his lips to mine.

I leaned back so I could see his face. "Damn and they say white boys don't have a rap," I said sarcastically. "Look, at you making a smooth move on a sista, but check this out, my love life is already screwed up enough without adding you to the mix." I stood up and smoothed my dress down as I slipped my shoes back on. "Thanks for the wine and the movie. I'll see you bright and early Monday."

He apologized for kissing me without my permission when he walked me to my car. Then he kissed for my lips again without asking for permission. I turned and his kiss skidded off my cheek.

I got in my Firebird, and thanked God when it started. I liked Brad's gumption. "Tomorrow might be a better time to start that relaxation lesson. I already know how to swim." Brad's entire face smiled when I said that. I didn't bother to tell him Max had taught me how to swim years ago. "Have a goodnight. I'll see you soon, my friend." I said as I pulled away smiling. Headlights flicked on when I sped by Dr. Brown's house. The car kept its distance even though I slowed down and sped up to see if it would pass. My Firebird was resting on E, and the rain was suddenly coming down in sheets. It was midnight when I pulled into the parking lot at my apartment complex. A dark-colored Mercedes pulled in next to me. A tall man hopped out and tapped on my window.

8

I didn't mean to smile the lascivious way that I did, but damn, he looked good! Max had cut his hair and lost at least ten pounds since I left him in August.

"Why were you kissing Bradley Pruter?" he asked.

I smiled again despite myself. It was a good thing he had only seen that one-way kiss. I wished he could have seen the big ass smile on Brad's face when I took a rain-check on his offer.

Why didn't you call? I would have skipped the party."

Max smiled at that and said, "I had to cool off. That dried eggs shit fucked up the paint on my car. You know I love you, Gabby." He flashed another sexy smile. "We both need to beg for forgiveness."

"Tammy answered your door wearing the robe I bought your sorry ass for Christmas, Max. Even you can't explain that crap away."

"She's just a friend. I needed a shoulder to cry on. I was missing you." He leaned in for a kiss. I dodged his efforts. "Tammy and I go way back, she knows it didn't mean anything."

I got out of my car and slammed my door. Max pushed a bouquet of orange roses in my arms. I threw them to the rain. "You only buy me flowers when I'm upset with you." He picked up the roses and followed me to my door. "I'm tired. Go back to Blondie."

"Tammy and I are just friends. Nothing happened. I swear."

"If nothing happened why was she wearing your robe and nothing else?"

"She probably had just gotten out the shower."

"Tell me the truth Max or get the hell out of my face!"

"Okay, we were both hurting, and it just happened. But it doesn't count because you left me." He grabbed me and forced me to make eye contact. Don't tell me you're going to walk away after four years without a fight. This isn't like you, Gabby. I thought you loved me. You said you wanted to be my wife."

"If you loved me you wouldn't cheat, and you wouldn't have been so cold."

"What was I supposed to say? You cold busted my ass."

"You're selfish, Max. I've been hurting all week because of you."

"I'm sorry," he said, "but I hurt too."

I opened my door and stepped inside. He blocked the doorway with his foot and stopped me from closing it in his face. I looked at his big foot. Then I looked over his shoulders to keep from looking at his pleading eyes and his sexy as hell smile.

"Kiss me, Gabby. If you can say you don't love me, I'll leave." Our lips and tongues met and the sparks reminded me of fireworks on the fourth of July. One hand went around his neck the other caressed what I've been missing. He flinched at first, but he relaxed when I began to moan-kiss. He coupled my butt and pulled me to him. "Say it, Gabby."

"Go back to Nashville," I moaned.

He kissed me again. My kiss said stay. His kiss was filled with promises. He slipped inside and locked the door. Then he started tugging on my dress before I could decide if I could make it through the night if I made him leave. "Maxwell, please. Slow down!"

"You know I love you, Gabriella."

"You have a strange way of showing it."

"You're the only one that matters."

"I want to be the only one period."

"You will be after we're married."

"Now, or never, Max."

"Why were you kissing Bradley Pruter?"

"You know Brad?"

"Everybody knows the Pruters. They owned the largest plantation in Mississippi and thousands of acres of land back in the day."

"That was a long time ago," I said.

"Well, yeah, but they still have quite a legacy."

I thought most of the slave owners in Mississippi had lost their riches after the war and during reconstruction. Max said some did, but not the Pruters. They still live in the original plantation home. They owned half the Delta.

"Brad is the only friend I've made this week. We sit in alphabetical order. Can you believe that? I sit next to him all day, every day, and I don't have any other options."

"Be careful, Gabby, the Pruter men have a reputation for enjoying the company of black women, if you know what I mean."

"So, are you saying I would be trading a black dog for a white dog."

"You need to chill with that dog shit. The Pruters are one of the richest families in Mississippi, if not the. Hell, they are probably one of the richest families in America. They're powerful attorneys, politicians, and businessmen now, but back in the day, they were big time slave and land owners."

"And your family is fourth generation physicians. And mine is only the first generation to have indoor plumbing. I'm out of my league either way. At least Brad understands why I want to get my own degree."

Max pulled me into his arms. "I understand, but I miss my baby." He smiled as if he really meant it. "Don't you want to be with me?"

"I'm telling you the same thing I told Brad."

"What did you tell him? What did he want to do to you?"

"I told him yes, but not tonight." Even though it was innocent it was nice to see Max sweat.

"I bet I'll kick a white boy's ass."

I giggled and hit Max in his chest. "Brad wanted to know if I wanted to swim and relax."

"Gabby, please let me stay. Please, baby?"

"No, Max."

"Why? Are you falling for Brad?"

"We're friends. I'm still in love with you."

He smiled and kissed me again, and if I had a defense, I lost it to his sugar. I unlocked the door and asked him to leave.

He locked the door and kissed me again. "I need you tonight. Where is your roommate?"

"Don't know. I've been avoiding her all week. Her car is outside. She's probably sleeping."

"What's that smell?"

"Roach spray. This place is infested. You know I hate sleeping with the air on. Sara froze my ass all week. I sprayed and turned the AC off on my way out this morning. I'm surprised she didn't turn it back on."

"Where is your bathroom? I have to take a leak."

"Down the hall to the right."

I went to the living room and put Chaka Khan's *I'm Every Woman* CD in the player. The toilet flushed. Max stuck his head into the living room a minute later and said, "Baby, it stinks in here. I'm gonna open your window."

"I can turn the AC on."

"You need some fresh air in this joint. Come home with me. This place is beneath you."

"It's all I can afford. Besides, I only sleep and shower here."

I was singing along with Chaka, and watering my Boston fern when I heard Max yell, "Holy Shit! Call the police, Gabby!"

I ran in the hall to see what was wrong. Max had opened Sara's door instead of mine. The stench was so bad I felt like throwing up. "Phew! What in the hell is that smell, Max?"

He was in a trance so I pushed by him. By the time he grabbed my arm, it was too late!

Sara was lying in her bed in a pool of dried blood. Her eyes were bucked. Her lips were crusty and both wrists were slit. Cockroaches were crawling all over her. She smelled like a combination of rotten eggs, dead fish and spoiled hamburger. I freaked completely the fuck out! I had heard her screams. Something had told me her car hadn't moved the last few days, but I hadn't cared. Something told me something was wrong--I didn't want to know--I was trying to deal with my own problems. My screams filled the air as Max pulled me from the doorway.

"I think she has been there a few days," I said.

After Max got me to calm down, he called the police.

I went to my room to lie down until the cops arrived. When I flicked on the light, a nude picture of me with a penis drawn on it was taped to my mirror. A note next to the picture was written on the mirror with my tomato-red lipstick. It said: You're next! I screamed again. The room faded to black.

9

Two cops and a reporter were standing over me when I saw light again. I was in the living room. Max held my hand while I cautiously answered questions about Sara James. We shared an apartment for three weeks, but I didn't know her at all, and what I did know was a bad reflection on both of us. They didn't ask me any questions about the threat, and I wasn't volunteering dilly-squat. Max took me to his parents' house after the interrogation, which were mostly questions about why I thought Sara had killed herself?

Julius gave me a sedative, and Maryanne made me chamomile tea at three o'clock in the morning. Maryanne can be sweet sometimes, superficial all the time, and this was no different. Her mahogany skin, overly styled hair and clothes were perfect even in the middle of the night. She hasn't worked a day in her life. Her father was a high profile civil rights attorney. She married Julius shortly after college. She was happy being Julius's wife even though she has a degree from Tougaloo as well. She was all for me getting my degree from college. A man with Max's social standing needed a well-educated woman, she said, but she didn't see any point in me going to dental school, and that was where her niceness ended at three in the morning.

𑀤

I woke up around noon the next day wrapped in Max's arms. He smiled when I opened my eyes. "You gave me quite a scare," he said.

"What am I gonna do, Max? I can't live in that apartment."

"Stay with my parents--I don't want my fiancée living in that dump anyway."

"I can't intrude on your parents." The thought of living with Maryanne was just as frightening as seeing Sara like that.

"Stay here or come back to Nashville with me. I think that note was probably a scare tactic, but I would feel better if you were with me."

"I wish I was there with you, but I don't have any money to go to Meharry." Finding Sara like that was all the scaring I needed. That note was not on my mirror when I left for class yesterday. The door was locked when we came in last night. Sara obviously had been dead for a few days. I don't believe for one minute that she killed herself. Did Dylan make good on his threat? As much as I disliked Maryann, there was no way I was going anywhere near that apartment anytime soon.

He flashed me a sexy smile. "You wish you were with me?"

"If I didn't love you, Max, do you think I would put up with your crap?"

He started nibbling on my ear, but I wiggled and avoided his advances. "I feel bad about Sara, but I can't picture her killing herself."

"Forget it, Gabby; we need to concentrate on our own problems."

"Maybe I should have told the cops about Sara and Dylan's fights and threats."

"People like that always get drunk and threaten to kill each other, it doesn't mean they will do it."

"I hate when you judge people you don't know, Max. Everyone didn't grow up with a circular driveway and a maid. Sara was no more a lowlife than me, and Dylan is very much like my brothers. Why do you think Daddy beat me that day? He was trying to stop me from letting a rich boy like you turn me into his little whore."

Max flinched. "You know it's not like that, baby. We would be married right now if you hadn't left me."

"I don't want to fight."

Max kissed my forehead. "Where is your ring?"

"I pawned it."

"My, God, Gabby, that wasn't a Cracker Jack's ring! Where is it? How much did they give you?" I bit my lip to keep from laughing. "Give me the money; they're supposed to hold it for thirty days. Boy, I really messed up this time, huh? You jacked my car up and now this." I took the fifth. Max fell back on the bed hard and stared at the ceiling.

"Dammit, Gabriella, you know I love you. Why are you messing everything up?"

"I need to be a whole person, Max. I have too much knowledge in me to be your shadow. I wasn't born with a silver spoon in my mouth like you. I've wanted to be more than a wife and mother all my life. I've dreamed of being a doctor just like you."

He stared at the ceiling and pouted. I did the same, but I couldn't get the last words I heard Dylan speak out of my head. If Dylan killed Sara a few days ago, why in the hell would he come back into the apartment and write that shit on my mirror!

"I'll get your ring before I leave. What was the name of that pawn shop again?"

"Max, I'm queasy. You feel like making your special pancakes?"

He pouted, kissed me on the cheek, and rolled out of bed. Twenty minutes later he brought me strawberries and pancakes, scrambled eggs and orange juice. He sat a tray set for two on the bed, looked at me strange and left the room. A couple of minutes later I heard him arguing with Brad outside the door.

"Stay away from Gabby!"

"She's my friend. I'll leave as soon as I know she is okay."

"Get outta my house, and stay the hell away from my woman!"

"I just want to make sure she is okay."

Max flung the door open. "Gabby, tell your friend you're okay so he can get the hell outta here!"

"Where are your manners, Max? Come in, Brad." Max's stare felt like daggers flying in my direction. "Max is taking good care of me. I'll fill you in on Monday."

"I take care of my lady," Max said. "She doesn't need your kind of help."

"You know where to find me if you need anything," Brad said. He winked. Max flinched and clutched his fist. He faced Max. "When are you leaving for Nashville?"

"Don't worry about that, and don't get any ideas about Gabby."

"I love you, Max; Brad is not a threat so why don't you use the good manners Maryanne taught you and walk him to the door." Max shot me a few more daggers before he left the room.

He came back a few minutes later. "Brad has a thing for you, and I don't like it."

"You can't pick my friends, Max. I'm not screwing him. I'm not you, okay."

"What in the hell is that supposed to mean!"

"I forgive you, Max, but I don't forget, and don't think you're gonna keep getting chances. If Brad treats me right, who knows, maybe I'll give him a chance. I'm tired of playing your I'm gonna do better games, Max. I'm tired of being your main squeeze. When we got engaged I thought that meant I was supposed to be your only squeeze. If we get married I don't want to hear any more of that, she didn't mean anything crap!"

Julius and Maryanne walked into the room in the middle of my tirade. "Good morning, Dr. and Mrs. Johnson," I said. Thank goodness, I was still wearing my red dress.

"I see you're back to your old feisty self, Gabby. Son, you need to give your woman something to smother that fire. I told you what you need to do." Julius chuckled and shook his head. Then he smiled at me like the perverted old men who used to offer me money to burst my cherry when I was a teenager. Max clutched his fist and pouted like a little boy. Julius needs to mind his own business. I'm never going to be like Maryanne.

"Dr. Johnson, I'm feeling much better thanks to Max's delicious pancakes and your hospitality." I flashed one of my sweet and innocent smiles, which are reserved for stubborn, old fashioned, stuck in their ways, afraid of change men like Julius. I hadn't missed the way he looked at Max when I said he made me breakfast. He probably told Max to go out and screw someone else the minute I left.

"Sweetheart, let Gabby rest. She's probably not in her right mind yet," Maryanne said. Max stared at me and I stared at Julius and Maryanne for interfering and treating Max like a child.

"Since Gabby is ready to resume her normal activities you better put out that fire so you can get back and study for your exam on Monday," Julius said. He winked at Max. "Come on, honey, let's go so these young people can work out their problems." Maryanne closed the door on their way out.

Max brushed his hair roughly and put on a Mets baseball cap. He banged his right fist into his left hand, then he said he was going out for a while. I wanted him to take me back to my apartment to get my books and clothes. Max said he would handle it. I couldn't get the horrified look in Sara's eyes and the rotten smells out of my mind. She looked surprised, and after I saw her corpse, I knew her screams, promises and pleas were not their usual sex games.

I had read the paper while Max was making breakfast. There was more in it about Max and his family than there had been about poor Sara. That's probably why Brad showed up.

"Max, aren't you worried about the threat?"

"Of course, that's why I want you to stay here." He kissed me, and got back into the bed. "I don't want you in the middle of a murder investigation, and you better not let Brad Pruter taste my sugar. The only reason I forgive you for cutting up my tires and smearing that egg shit all over my car is because, as sick as it is, I know you did it because you love me." He kissed me as though he belonged to me only.

"I'll know if you let Brad so much as smell the sugar on your breath. I'll be back in a few hours. Have my sugar ready."

I reached for him when he climbed out the bed. "Max, I'm scared."

"Baby, you're safe here. The cops don't need to know about the threats. Whoever did that, probably went through your things, found our pictures, and they just wanted to scare you."

"If Dylan killed Sara on Monday night he probably came back for me yesterday. I didn't see him do it, but I heard Sara's screams and pleas for help and I did nothing."

"The cops called it a suicide." Max kissed my nose. "You watch too many movies. Let the cops figure it out, that's what they get paid to do."

"How can they when I didn't tell them everything?"

"Sara probably didn't kill herself, but you should be happy those cops took the easy way out and didn't try to pen that shit on you. I saw how they were looking at you. Given a choice, they don't worry themselves over investigating the deaths of poor black people. Think about the questions they asked you. 'Were you the last person to see her alive? How can you explain not seeing your roommate for four days? Why were you avoiding her?' Don't you get it? I'm more worried about Dylan than those sorry ass cops. Did he come on to you? Did you say something to him to make him threaten you?"

"I sorta called him a cockroach." I said sheepishly.

Max chuckled and got out the bed again. "Stay away from that apartment. You're safe here. You'll be even safer in Nashville in my arms every night." He had a twinkle in his eyes. "Think about it." He kissed me again and left.

10

I roamed through Max's things until I found a pair of blue pajamas, and an old photo album. There were pictures of at least ten different girls with notes telling him the nature of their love. The pictures we took at the state fair were mixed in with the trash. I stuck our pictures in the corner of his mirror and put the other pictures back in the photo album. I was studying Max's senior prom picture when he walked in with a smile on his face. His arms were filled with my clothes. He threw my things in a chair, and then he unbuttoned my pajamas and kissed each spot as he exposed it. I shimmed out of the bottoms. His kisses ripened my body for him in delicious ways.

"I found your ring in your pawn jewelry box. As a matter of fact, I found two." He licked me from my navel to my lips. "Here you go." He slid the ring on my finger and stole another kiss. I made him get down on his knee and propose again.

"Marry me, Gabby. You know I don't love anybody but you."

I giggled. "You better get up before Julius comes back." I offered Max my hand and helped him up. My eyes must have had the look of love in them. He kissed me, and backed us to his bed. He tumbled on top of me. I opened my legs and said, "This is the last time I'm going to forgive you."

"Is my sugar ready?" He asked. He flashed a wicked smile that made me aware of the throbbing between my thighs, and in my heart.

He slid my top off, and licked, and nibbled until his sugar turned into syrup. He tugged on my responsive nipples with his teeth, and found my love bud with a thick finger, and milked it like a pimple. In less than a minute, I was bucking like a wild stallion. "Now, Max, I need you right now!"

He flashed a sinister smile and said, "Show me how much you missed me first." He continued to do sweet things with his hands, his teeth, his tongue and his sweet lips. We kissed until 'yes' meant like that, and no meant don't stop. I was still angry, so I let him tease me, and I took what he gave. This was a battle I didn't mind losing. My first orgasm hit me hard and fast. Amid coming apart, all I could see was Max's sexy infuriating smile.

"Yeah, baby, come for, daddy," he said. "You like that, don't you?"

Hell yes, I did. "I want… need… all of you now, Max!" I rode out the first waves by rocking on his fingers. A second wave was already building. "Now, Max, please?" I whimpered.

He went in fast, hard, and deep. I was so wet. Before I could meet his rhythm, he pulled all the way out. Our eyes met. He smiled smugly. "You are not the only one still angry, Gabby."

"Max, please, I need you." I held his stare. My pussy was throbbing like an abscess. I wanted him, cocky smile and all. I missed him. I didn't want to go on without him. "I love you, Max. No matter where you are, or how angry I am, my love for you stays the same." He plunged into me again. I wrapped my legs around his back and tried to ride hard with him. He pulled away again, and again, and again. And it felt incredibly delicious.

"I don't want to fuck you, Gabby. I want to make love to you. I want to show you how much I miss you. How much I want you to come home. How much I need you, baby." Our eyes locked again. He kissed me, and while our tongues tangled, and we breathed the other's air, our bodies became one totally in sync with the other. I gazed into his eyes as he made slow deliberate strokes. I met each thrust with my own determination. My body had a mind of its own. We flowed together stroke for stroke, thrust for thrust. It felt delightful.

We were in the smooth sailing zone when I heard his parents laughing and talking in the hallway. I hadn't heard them return. Max turned up the volume of the radio with his toes, and the volume of my love calls with his down strokes. I made a mental note to start taking the pill again. There was no way in hell I could give this, or him up without a fight. If he doesn't come to me, I will have to go to him. We will have to find a way to make our love last. Max must have noticed that my attention was elsewhere. He locked his fingers with mine and raised my arms over my head. He flashed that wicked smile again. We kissed. He worked his way to my plump nipples again. He licked both breasts with his tongue, nibbled on them with his teeth, and sucked them between his juicy lips while we slow grind until I came again. My hands were still pinned above my head. Our fingers were locked. My nails dug into his palms with each lick, stroke and kiss. I moved my body like I didn't have a spine. I tried to be quiet. I failed. We continued our voyage to the land of screaming big O's. When our carnal needs were totally satisfied, he called my name, and filled me with his seeds. Thousands of them. It only takes one. I called his name, and came hard a third wonderful time.

"Why were you holding back?" he asked still catching his breath.

Instead of answering I rolled out the bed and started dressing. I love to cuddle, but not with his parents around. "Didn't you hear your parents? I came three times, or was it four." I'm sure I had a silly grin on my face as I mimicked him. "What happened to, 'Baby, I got three base hits and a homerun. That's some baby making loving right there.' I couldn't hold back with you if I tried, Max." I playfully bent over and shook by butt at him. I couldn't believe he needed his ego stroked after he had made me come completely undone like that.

"Don't make me get up and hit it again doggie style."

I stuck my tongue out and wiggled my butt again. He laughed. I liked playful Max. He grabbed me around the waist and pulled me back into the bed. I straddled him and pent his hands over his head.

I had my way with his lips and his nipples this time. I couldn't believe how quick he recovered.

"This is for accusing me of holding back." I kissed him with all the passion I could muster. Then I held his chest down with one hand, and slapped his hips and thighs as hard as I could with my other hand. "And this is for fucking Blondie." I slapped his hip again. His cock seemed to get harder with each blow. "I wasn't holding back, I was trying to figure out what I need to do to keep you from straying." I wacked him again. "I see you like your little spanking. This is what you get for being a bad boy."

He raised up and flipped me over on my belly. I yelped when he grabbed my hips and pulled my ass in the air. He slapped me on the ass and hammered into me as he whispered. "All you need to do is marry me and stop playing with my feelings. You are not the only one with feelings." He slapped my ass again.

The sting made me even wetter. "Yes, baby." I whimpered.

He slapped my ass again and said, "Come home."

"Yes, baby." The sting felt delectable as he slammed his body into mine over, and over again.

"Have my babies."

"God, I love you Max. We have to find a way to make this work." I felt my whole body tighten again. I had no control of the sounds, or the words, coming from my mouth, or the way my body undulated with his. He stifled my screams of joy with one big hand over my mouth. He caressed my nipples with the other, and pounded into my core until we came together. I tasted blood when I bit into his palm.

He collapsed with me pinned under him. He panted, "I love you Gabriella. Forever and ever. Always. I will never get you out of my system, and don't think I haven't tried." I felt his sweat or tears dripping on my back. He continued to kiss my shoulders, my ears and my neck. When he finally rolled over, I got up again and dressed quickly in the jeans and t-shirt I had worn to school on the first day. Max and I can, and have spent whole days in bed making love.

Max gazed at me lovingly while I brushed my hair. He loves my hair. All the girls in his pictures were nice and brown with short hair styles except me. I twisted my hair to put it in a bun.

"Who in the hell is Blondie?" I smiled knowing that he had heard that. I ran my eyes over his dark handsome body. He looked round three gorgeous wrapped in his sky-blue satin sheets.

"That Tammy bitch in most of your pictures."

"Leave your hair down."

"It's too hot."

"You had it down for Brad."

"Don't switch the subject to Brad." Max got up and put on the pajama bottoms he had taken off me. He stood behind me and rubbed his cock on my booty while he sucked on my neck. I leaned into him, when I said, "Stop—as good as that feels, I hate when you leave your mark."

He continued to dry grind into me when he said, "She was letting me cry on her shoulders. It wouldn't have happened if you hadn't left me."

"Do you think I'm pretty?" I said to change the subject.

"In your own way."

"What in the hell does that mean?"

"You have a pretty face, beautiful hair and a nice body, but you could use a little sun and some more booty."

"Is that why you cheat?"

He picked up the picture of us I had stuck in his mirror. "I have to step out for some chocolate truffles occasionally," Max said teasingly, but that shit still hurt so close to our good loving.

My eyes got misty. "So, why did you ask me out?"

"I saw you, Gina, and Gretchen walking across campus looking like white girls and thinking you all were better."

"How in the hell could you see what we were thinking?"

"I know how redbones think. Anyway, I got a rise just watching you all. I wanted to fuck all three of you. I wanted to break your hearts before you could break mine."

I wiggled away from him. "That's sick, Max. You didn't know shit about any of us." Tears rolled down my cheeks. I threw my engagement ring at him. "Sometimes you are so insensitive. I'm outta here."

"Where you gonna go? Brad? He's no different from me. Why do you think you all look like you do?"

"Screw you, Max!"

He flashed that sexy infuriating smile again. "You just did, and I must say it was damn good. I busted a nut, and if you weren't on the pill, my sperms would be getting you pregnant right now. Instead of worrying about Tammy, worry about us!"

"I wasn't holding back. I was trying to figure out how to make our love work until I finish school!"

Max hugged me and kissed and sucked on my neck again. "I'm sorry, baby. I was joking. You know I can't get enough of your sugar. You push my buttons. You're supposed to be with me in Nashville. Don't cry. I didn't mean it. I swear."

I lied and said, "Lorna said I could stay with her."

His back straightened. "You can't stay there! You don't need to be around those kinda people."

"I may look like a Barbie doll but I'm not stupid. So, here's the deal, Mr. Chocoholic, I'm gonna get my degree from UMMC, and if I must live with my sister in the hood--so be it. If I need to get help from Brad--so be it. If I lose you because you're not man enough to say, 'Gabby, I love you, and I understand why you have to do this' then--so be it! Because, baby, in this world and in this relationship, I have learned that I won't survive unless I stick to my convictions."

I put my hair up in a bun and walked out the room before Max could lift his bottom lip to close his mouth or drag me back to his bed again. The Firebird started and I made good on my threat. I had tried to call Lorna while Max was out. She sings at the nightclub down the street from her apartment on Friday and Saturday nights, and she works as a secretary at Jackson State during the week, which amazes me because she can't type, she has no patience, and she has no tact.

Men are drawn to Lorna like flies to watermelons. Max thinks she is gorgeous, but they can't stand each other otherwise. Lorna got her heart broken when she was fifteen. Now she uses what she has, to get what she wants. She doesn't bother with falling in love anymore. She wants to be famous, and any man who can't help her get there will only slow her down.

Lorna was born a diva. When we were kids, her favorite pastime was singing into a hairbrush in front of the mirror, and her favorite stage was Daddy's rowboat. Big Curtis stored the boat upside-down on three saw horses. Lorna would climb up on the boat and give me a show as though she were performing for ten thousand people. She sang into her brush and pranced from one end to the other shaking her booty, bobbing her head and waving her arms. Lorna thought she was Diana Ross and the Supremes, Tina Turner and Ike, and Gladys Knight and the Pips. I named the song and Lorna sang it. I spent many a spring and summer day enjoying her concerts.

Lorna has a strong alto voice with the range of Leontyne Price. She never had a traditional Southern drawl, not Lorna; men go crazy over her deep sensuous voice. She was voted the most beautiful girl at Hot Springs High four years in a row. She's tall and voluptuous with long flowing curly black hair and curly eyelashes. People say her flawless mocha skin, high cheekbones, and large slanted almond-shaped eyes make her look exotic. But there is one thing about Lorna that even I can't understand: babies and young children flock to her. Lorna hates children, and it's a good thing because she can manipulate them into doing almost anything.

I pulled my car into the gravel parking lot next to her rundown apartment building. I locked my doors and windows before I got out. It was early September, but it still felt like the dog days of August. The smell of stale beer and urine hanging in the thick humid air almost knocked me out. A wino stumbled in my path before I could make a run for Lorna's stairs.

"Hey, pretty mama," he said.

I ignored him and tried to sprint to the stairs.

"You one of them high yelluh thank you too good to speak to a brother a little down on his luck gals?" he asked when he grabbed for my arm.

I dodged him and made a frantic dash for the stairs.

"Can you spare a quarter?"

Feeling bold, I tossed him two and I said, "If you call me yellow the next time--you get nothing."

I could hear heavy breathing and panting coming from Lorna's apartment long before I reached her door. Lorna moaned, "Who's the best, baby?" Her friend shouted, "Lorna Elena Oliver." I didn't bother to knock. Lorna and Gina are the only sisters I know who can flip that "who's the best crap" on a brother and get their full name as a response.

The wino staggered across the street and went into the package store. Lora screamed satisfaction, her friend grunted gratification, and I ran to my car. Turning on the AC was risky, but I needed to cool off in more ways than one. I sat in the cool air and plotted my next move while my head cleared of the stench outside and my eavesdropping. I closed my eyes and took a deep breath of cool fresh air while I did a few Kegel exercises. I was drifting toward bliss when someone tapped on my window. I started the engine and put the car in gear before I checked to see who it was.

"Follow me," Max said.

"I'm headed to the mall. I need an appropriate dental school wardrobe."

"I have to go soon. Come help me understand why you won't come with me."

"I have to do this for me, but I still love you, Max. I thought you loved me enough to understand.

Maryanne and Julius had gone out again when we arrived. Max started kissing and undressing me before we closed and locked the door.

"You're the only woman who can make me do this without doing anything." He swirled a lock of my hair around his fingers.

"I want to be more than a sexy body, Max. Belinda used to tell me, "Pretty will get you a house full of kids and a husband with a broken back trying to feed them. Times are changing--I don't want to be like either of our mothers."

"I'm not saying I want to keep you barefoot and pregnant. I'm trying to tell you that I love you."

"No, Max, you have to say that with your heart not your hard-on."

He pulled me into his arms. "Why do you have to be so difficult? I'm trying to tell you how I feel and you're twisting it around."

"Then stop talking from your groin and let your love speak as your action verb." I caressed his cheek. "I know you love me your way, Max, but you're blocking the connection between your dick, your ticker and your brain." I tapped his forehead with my index finger, and then I kissed him. "If all three were in sync, you would understand that because my heart belongs to you, it is important to me for you to understand, and support, my dreams like I do yours. That's what people in love do."

"You promised to go to school in Nashville. You broke the connection, Gabby."

"No, you break the connection every time you say you love me and you screw someone else!" Max flinched. "When you love someone, it doesn't matter where they are. If you love them, you love them, and there isn't a damn thing you can do to stop loving them. I wanted to hate you when Blondie, I mean Tammy, opened your door." Max flinched again. "But deep down inside I still loved you. I was tired, and all I wanted and needed was to be in your arms so I wouldn't be afraid when I started school." Max didn't say anything, but his sexy infuriating smile was long gone. He pulled me close and squeezed me to his chest. "I needed to know we were still okay, Max. It won't be easy, but I love you enough to try. We can hold on and support each other as we pursue our dreams, or we need to let it go. Please don't let me sit here loving you while you're in Nashville loving someone else.

If you love me at all, please be a man and say, Gabby, I can't." Max held me tighter. "You can't have it both ways; not anymore."

"I can't believe you still have doubts about my love." He kissed my forehead. "I've asked you to marry me at least three times. I'm trying to become a gynecologist for us. I bought the house for us. You and me, and our children. Everything I do is for us. It's hard for me to stay focused with you here and me there, but even when I mess up it doesn't mean I stopped loving you either." He nibbled on my ear and whispered. "Now there is this real possibility that you could end up dead like Sara. That's why I don't want to go back to Nashville without you."

"Don't say that. You're scaring me, Max."

He slid his hand in mine and led me to his room again.

11

Max turned the radio on just in case his parents came home. *Stay in My Corner* by the Dells was playing. We held each other while the song played. He twisted a lock of my hair and our eyes did the talking after the song ended. I didn't resist, yet I didn't encourage him.

"Only if you can love me right," I said.

"I always love you right." A cocksure smile washed over his face again. "I burst a nut every time I love you, girl."

"It's time to grow up, Max. Real men learn to control their desires. Yes, you sex me right, and Tammy, and all your other bitches. To love me right, you need to understand and support my physical, mental, spiritual and emotional wants, needs and dreams as I do yours."

Max's smile was replaced by an un-sexy umbrage stare. "We're both hurting, okay." He slid his hands under my T-shirt and unhooked my bra as he kissed me. "I have to go. Please don't send me away needing you like this."

I gave in to his kisses, but I didn't let him take me this time. We connected with our hearts, and our spirits. We couldn't go back to the days when making love was our top priority, and everything else including studying just fell into place, but we made love. Our loving used to open our minds to learning. We aren't good--we are great together. We loved as though Tammy never happened, and afterwards

Max opened his Pharmacology book and started studying. I opened my Biochemistry book. We studied and sneaked peeps at each other like old times. The two years we lived together were the happiest of my life. Max stole a kiss and smiled.

"What are you thinking about, and don't say biochemistry. I know that look."

"I was thinking about the good old days when we first met."

"I took one look at you and all the dots connected," he said. "My feelings for you were so strong I didn't understand them at first. I was afraid to ask you out. Then I was afraid to make love to you. Remember the first time we did it in this room?"

I giggled and pulled the covers up. Max was eyeing me again.

"I was ready to marry you on the spot. Do you still have that stretchy top, and that blue pleated skirt?"

"Time for a study break," I said. I took the high road. It was quick and sweet. I honestly started studying after that, but Max got up.

"Gabby, I've been begging you to marry me since your father beat you and challenged me to prove my love for you."

"We were too young then, and you were screwing around on the regular."

"I never screw around when things are going good with us. I just get so angry when you refuse me. I start to question myself, and us, and that's when I mess up. The first time I asked you to marry me you locked yourself in the bathroom and cried all night. I didn't want any more trouble from Big Curtis. My intentions were always good. I had the ring and everything, but I didn't know what to think."

"But you didn't give me the ring until almost a year later."

"I know, but I always promised to marry you. Dad kept telling me we were too young. He begged me to wait after you reacted like that. That's when Mom started saying you probably didn't love me. Dad threatened to cut me off financially if we got married before I finished college. That's why I said I would wait until you graduated from Tougaloo when I asked you again. Every time I screwed around I was reacting to all of the confusion in my head."

I slammed my book shut. I couldn't believe he was blaming his cheating on me.

"Let's get married Christmas," Max said.

"Let's wait until June so we can spend the summer together." I pretended to study to avoid looking at the disappointment in his eyes.

Max threw his book at me. I jumped. The book slammed into the headboard.

"Dammit, Gabby! Why are you doing this to us?"

Julius knocked on the door before I could explain. I hadn't heard them return. Max pulled his jeans on. He threw me my shirt and panties before he opened the door. He went into the hallway to talk to his father.

Max was calm when he returned to the room. He had to go but he made me promise to stay with his parents. He wanted to know I was safe. His parents would agree to do whatever they thought would make Max happy. I told him I loved him; he said he knew. He wanted me to understand the pressure I was putting on him, but he promised to come back in a couple of weeks for some loving. He got his books and threw his clothes in a duffel bag.

"Call me every night at eleven, Gabby. If you don't call, I'm gonna come get you and lock you in our bedroom in Nashville. I'll turn you into my sex slave, and you'll never get your degree."

I giggled and told him to stay away from those sleazy stray cats up in Grand Ole Opryland, and his kitty would be purring when he got home. School was doing what our parents had failed to do. I put on my jeans and walked him to his car. We kissed and he played with my hair. When he drove away, the sad unresolved look in his eyes ripped through my soul like his first kiss. My mind, body and spirit missed Max before he was out his parents' circular driveway. But I wasn't about to be held hostage by his parents, while he did whatever with whomever in that big lonely house in Nashville. I had an open date with Mr. Bradley Trenton Pruter!

12

A promise is a promise, and a friend is a friend. I had promised Brad that I would take a dip with him in his pool. It was getting late so I decided to call Lorna first. She picked up on the fifth ring and yawned hello.

"I stopped by your apartment earlier. You were putting a whipping on some poor boy."

She laughed. "A girl has to do what a girl has to do. Why were you trying to track me down?"

"I think my roommate's boyfriend killed her. They're calling it a suicide, but they asked me a shitload of questions that I couldn't answer. It's all over the news. Lorna, there was a nasty note telling me that I'm next."

"Oh, my God, Gabby! When did all of this happen?"

"Last night, Max was with me. I'm staying with his parents for now. I don't want to worry Mommy and Daddy until I get some more details."

"You know I move fast, and you know Max don't want you hanging with me."

"This is between sisters. Max doesn't have a say."

"You can stay, but I don't know where you're gonna sleep?"

"I have a little money; we can get a bigger place."

"I don't live high on the hog like you, Gabby, and I don't want Belinda and Big Curtis saying I'm corrupting you. Besides, this is the worst place to be if somebody is looking to kill you. Do you know how many unsolved murders there are on this side of town?"

I figured she was making excuses to keep from hurting my feelings. Lorna will do whatever she needs to do to be a star. She isn't going to let me or anyone else get in her way. I like that about her--she always has a plan.

"Hey, I'm singing at Mr. P's later. Can you come? I need my biggest fan at my reserved table."

It was a good excuse to get out the house. I showered and put on my blue pleated skirt and a knit blouse with a high neck to hide the cannibalistic kisses Max had put on my neck. I put on my dancing shoes and tried to sneak out, but I ran into Julius nursing a Tanqueray and tonic.

"Shouldn't you be studying?" He asked. I told him where I was going and why. Then I invited him and Mrs. Johnson.

"Maryanne wouldn't be caught dead in a place like that," he said.

"The only reason I'm going is to hear my sister sing. Do you think I can get a key? I don't want to disturb you guys when I get back."

I don't think you should be hanging out in sleazy bars in that outfit." He looked at my blue skirt and raised a brow.

Max tells his father almost everything. I had a feeling Julius knew about the quickie I gave Max the first time he brought me here to meet them. I hid my anger behind a smile.

Julius gave me his key. I said, "Gee thanks," and left.

Brad turned into his driveway when I approached his house. Julius had already popped my elastic and woke up vindictive Gabby. I braked and backed into Brad's driveway. He smiled when I stopped next to him in his driveway.

"You feel like hanging out with a friend? I'm going to Mr. P's to hear my sister sing."

Big Curtis used to say--white folks can come and go as they please. I figured Brad was richer than most and could do as he pleased.

"Do I need to change?"

"No, you look fine."

Big Curtis also says white folks don't have to do anything they don't want to do.

"Hop in."

"You want me to drive?"

"No, it will be best if I drive if you like your cute little car." Big Curtis also used to say if white folks were as smart as they think they are, they wouldn't be surprised when they go to the hood and find themselves walking home.

Mr. P's was so dark the regulars probably thought Brad and I were two white people who loved the blues, and weren't afraid to cross the tracks to enjoy some real music. We sat at Lorna's reserved table in the front. Brad ordered wine for us. He was disappointed because they didn't have a wine list.

"We have red or white. What's it gonna be?" Our waitress asked as she popped her gum and adjusted her blonde wig.

"Red," I said quickly.

Our waitress smiled broadly and showed off her gold tooth with a star in its face. "You got you a pretty white boy. Is that yo real hair?" She felt my hair and adjusted hers again. "This here is a wig."

I smiled. She smiled again and strutted away. She came back twenty minutes later with two plastic cups filled with warm wine. I smiled at the surprised look on Brad's face. I picked up my cup and said, "To friends." Brad tapped his cup to mine, but when he took the first sip, I had to move quick to avoid his spit-out.

Lorna opened with her theme song *Respect* by none other than Aretha Franklin. Brad was as smitten by Lorna's beauty as he was by her voice. She was doing *I Wanna be Free* by the Ohio Players when Dylan pulled up a chair and sat at our table!

Lorna loves to take songs written by men and put a female spin on them. My mind had drifted to Max the minute Lorna sang about not having to listen to any more lies. I hadn't seen Dylan coming even though he was wearing a pair of pea-green polyester pants, and a matching flowered shirt.

"So, this is your man? Well, I can't say I'm surprised," Dylan said.

I stared at him, but before I could say anything he continued. "How is your crazy ass roommate doing? She hasn't called me this week. I guess she's trying to make me jealous. Y'all women are always tripping on a brother."

I held my tongue. He was either tripping or a good damn liar himself even though there was something about his eyes and his tone of voice that showed true love and concern for Sara.

"I know you're glad I'm gone, but tell your roommate, I love her."

I couldn't hold back any longer. I looked him dead in the eyes and said, "According to the police, I'm looking at my roommate. Your name is on the lease, and I want my brother's money back."

I don't know anything about your money. Sara said she could no longer count on me. She put me out of my own place so you could move in."

"Well, Sara is dead... your name is on the damn lease, I owe my brother five bills, and I don't have anywhere to live, because I'm certainly not going back to that shithole."

"What in the hell are you talking about? What happened to Sara?" He straightened his back and his speech seemed a little less slurred.

"She's dead! Don't you read the F-ing paper and watch the damn news?"

I stared at Dylan again and watched as tears flooded his eyes. Brad put his hand on my knee to calm me down.

"Yeah, I read the paper, but not on Saturdays. What happened to Sara?"

"You tell me."

"This is the first I'm..." His lip trembled, and he was crying like a pussy. "What happened to her?"

"They say suicide, I didn't mention you to the cops, but they're looking for you."

Dylan wiped his tears and his snotty nose. "I told her everything would be okay. Damn, damn, damn!" He slapped both his hands against the table and pushed his chair back. I jumped. He was sobbing like a wet cat, but worse, he was stealing Lorna's show. She was telling me with her eyes to shut his ass up. His legs wobbled when he tried to walk away. He sat back down and continued to whine a broken man's song. I studied his gestures. The tears and the shock seemed to be authentic.

"I just got back from Chi-town," he said after he got himself somewhat under control.

His father had died and left him some money. He was planning to pay Sara's tuition with it, but his mother said she hadn't called while he was away. He called the apartment when he got back today. No one answered so he stopped by, but he couldn't get in because Sara had taken his key.

Lorna ended her set with, *Only the Strong Survive* by Jerry Butler. She sung it from a female point of view and dedicated it to me and all the sisters in the audience who were trying to get it together.

Dylan sniffled and his voice sounded humble when he said, "Make this white boy pay for his rights. If he was a brother, your high yelluh behind wouldn't be giving away freebies. Hell, if he was a brother you would make him work two jobs and you still wouldn't be satisfied." He sniffled again and wiped his face. "I tried to make Sara happy." Tears ran down his cheeks again. "I loved her, Gabby. She was smart and pretty, but she was always on my ass about money. I'm taking computer classes at night at State. I would have made a good husband for her. She was always so damn impatient."

He pushed his chair back again. "I don't have your money. Between Sara and my son's mama my bank account is empty." He wiped his face again and wobbled away. I was more confused than ever.

Lorna finished her set and joined Brad and me at the table. I introduced them. They hit it off like lovers. He seemed disappointed when she said she wasn't going to do a second set. She had to sing early the next morning at church with the Jackson Harmony Choir. Malaco Records is recording a live album of the group. I promised Lorna that I would come. She tells everybody that I'm her good luck charm.

A Hercules looking guy walked up to Lorna and grabbed her butt. She giggled when he pressed himself against her back and whispered something in her ear. She turned around and deep kissed him. Two months ago, she was madly in love with a cute guitar player named Chance Foxx. After the kiss, Lorna introduced Brad and me to Richard. Then they left.

The DJ played *Brick House,* and I pulled Brad to the dance floor. The only thing that saved me from being called a white girl by my friends was my dancing skills. I can dance my tail off. It's one of my favorite things to do. I had Brad in the middle of the dance floor and he was dancing like he was constipated.

"Let your ass move," I shouted over the music.

"What?"

"Loosen your butt. Let it catch the rhythm of the drum beat. You're dancing like a white boy."

He laughed and said, "I am a white boy, I'm surprised you didn't notice."

"You better loosen up and stop embarrassing me on this dance floor before somebody takes a notion to put some fire to your stiff behind." Brad chuckled, but he started to shake his rump after I said that. "Follow my lead and remember to shake your booty." He was still off beat but at least he had Saturday Night Fever moves.

$$\mathcal{Q}$$

I dropped Brad off and tried to sneak into the Johnson's house a few minutes after midnight. Julius and Maryanne were waiting up for me. Maryanne fanned her hands in front of her nose when I walked in. "Whew." Her face was twisted like a cork screw. "You reek, and I'm sure Max wouldn't approve."

GLORIA F. PERRY

Max had taken me to Mr. P's lots of times. He was fascinated by our social differences. Maryanne wasn't surprised. She already had me pegged as a bar hoochie.

"I doubt if Max would approve of you taking Brad Pruter with you," Julius added before I could put Maryanne in her place.

"I appreciate you all letting me stay here until I can find an affordable apartment, but my parents and Max don't have any problems with me giving my sister some moral support. Considering what happened to Sara, I was happy to have the company, and the safety of a friend like Brad," I said then I went to Max's room and slammed the door.

I said a prayer and asked God for strength before I went to bed. The next morning, I got up bright and early and washed the smoky smell from my hair and studied Biochemistry while it dried. Then I got dressed for church. The simple black cotton dress I had on cost me seven dollars at Kmart, but after I dressed it up with fake pearls, a gold belt, and a pair of two-inch sling back pumps I looked just as sophisticated as Maryanne. Gretchen, the fashion queen of our crew, used to say I could make a dish rag look good. That was a high compliment coming from her.

Julius and Maryanne were in the kitchen smooching when I walked in. I had found an unused pack of birth control pills mixed in with the things Max had retrieved from my apartment. I was planning to take a double dose, but I didn't want Max's parents asking any questions.

Maryanne offered to make me breakfast, but I had to hurry if I wanted to get a parking space at Lynch Street Baptist Church, named after the man not the deed. I sure didn't want to take a chance on having to walk a mile in the heat in my best clothes and my worst walking shoes.

Max had brought my cereal and Tang. I rambled around the kitchen trying to find it. Julius eyes followed every movement I made. He raised a brow when I poured sugar on my corn flakes. I prefer Frosted Flakes but they went too fast in our house with all of us kids. Belinda

90

used to say sugar and corn flakes equaled three times as many Frosted Flakes for half the money. She said our stomachs wouldn't know if we were putting a tiger in our tanks or a poor man's replacement.

Belinda is an amazing mother. I didn't realize how poor we were until I met Max. Belinda taught us how to take care of ourselves and how to love from within. I'm not so sure if Max got that from his parents. Now that I'm trying to make it on my own, I feel bad about calling her meek all these years.

I was in my car before I realized I had forgotten to take my birth control pills again.

⚘

Lorna sang like a pro. She had one chance and one verse to be noticed. She sang hallelujah, waved her hands and hair, and stomped her feet. I was with her all the way. It wasn't just Lorna singing on Big Curtis's boat anymore. She was on her way to reaching her dreams. She wanted me to be with her every step of the way. I wanted Max to be with me, but I need to do what is best for me in the long run.

Lorna introduced me to The Harmony Choir. The group's agent was Harold Bolton, a middle-aged brother with a Jeri-Kurl mistake for a hairdo and three gold teeth. One had an H cut in its face; another had an A and a L. He was kicking fifty, but he had dreamy eyes for my twenty-six-year-old sister. Harold smiled and I didn't know whether to gag or to laugh, but I was sure I had a frown on my face. Belinda says that frown is going to get me killed one day. I still haven't figured out how Dylan killed Sara, if he was in Chicago and Sara took his key, and I sure as hell haven't forgotten about the note on my mirror and picture.

Harold was nice so I could understand how Lorna could deal with him. He had been in the music business for twenty-five years. This was business for Lorna. Harold insisted upon taking us to lunch. We piled into his new supped-up black Cadillac Eldorado with gold rims and a gold vinyl top. Thomas, Hal's look-a-like brother, slid on the back seat next to me. He had Tom spelled out in his gold teeth. I was glad I had put Max's ring back on. I hoped Tom didn't think I was acting uppity when I slid over and hugged the door nearest me.

Lorna bragged about me being in dental school. They probably thought I was going to get my degree tomorrow after hearing Lorna talk about me. She was my number one cheerleader as well. Hal and Tom wanted to know how much I charged to make gold teeth. Every time they get a gold record they get another gold tooth. Harold said when he gets Lorna hooked up he is going to let me fill his mouth with gold because Lorna is going to be a big-time star.

We beat the Sunday crowd to Morrison's Cafeteria. Harold couldn't believe how much food I could put away. Max used to tease me about it all going to my hair and my titties.

Harold rolled off five one-hundred dollar bills, and gave them to Lorna. He whispered something in her ear and squeezed her behind after he took us back to get my car. She kissed him then she ran her finger over his lips and rubbed off the lipstick. She waved goodbye and got in my car.

I started my engine. I love to drive fast when I'm trying to fig-ure stuff out. I hopped on I-55 instead of going straight to Lorna's apartment.

"So, what do you think about my friends, Gabby?"

"They're nice. So, you're seeing Harold and Richard?"

"Harold isn't young and rich and fine like Max, but he treats me right," she said. "And Richard is just a dick thing. I'm not like you, Gabby. I'm not looking for a husband."

"What about Chance Foxx?"

"Chance was everything I used to dream about in a lover, but he wanted my independence--I will never give that much power to a man again. I don't have time for a bunch of babies and being a housewife is not my idea of success. That's all too damn boring for me. Richard, and Harold, and I have an understanding. We are playing the other side of the game," she joked.

"I caught Max cheating again."

"You oughta stop putting up with that shit, Gabby. Good dick is one thing, but life goes on. Trust me there are a lot of cocks out there who would love a taste of you, so don't lose sight of your dreams over one."

I stepped on the gas. "Fasten your seat belt."

"Brad seemed nice," Lorna said. "And I can tell that he likes you."

"I know, but in case you didn't notice—" I whispered, "He's white."

"So, what. You're damn near white yourself."

"Don't start that, Lorna. You know I don't roll that way, and I'm not trying to get with a white boy."

"They're always trying to get with you."

"That's their business. They can do whatever they want—they're white men," I whispered again. She gave me a high five. "Lorna, we need to cut that light skin, dark skin, good hair, bad hair stuff out."

"I'm joking with you when I say stuff like that."

"I know, but it still hurts."

"I catch hell too because of my hair. Black women are always saying I think I'm better because of it. But I'm just a poor black woman out there trying to get a nut like the rest of my sisters."

I gave her another high-five. "Amen to that because I have the double whammy. Sisters go after my man as if I don't exist, because to them I'm not a real sister anyway. I went to see Max last weekend and this heifer was there wearing the robe I brought him. Max has a big ass, larger than life picture of me hanging over the fireplace. But does she care?"

"No," Lorna said.

"You wanna know why? Because to her I don't count. I might as well be a white girl. She feels as though she is reclaiming a brother who has lost his way."

"That's true, but Max opened his door and let the tramp in."

"He's angry because I promised to marry him and go to school at Meharry."

"Tell him to pay your tuition and you'll be there tomorrow. Otherwise a girl gotta do what a girl gotta do. I'm scared too, but I don't want to end up like Belinda."

I pushed the pedal to the metal and we were cruising at 100mph when a blue light special pulled out of nowhere and pulled me over.

"You ladies rushing to or from a fire this afternoon," the officer said as he took off his hat.

"No sir. My old man dumped me, and my roommate upped and killed herself. I was just blowing off a little stream. I didn't realize how fast I was going. I'm sorry, sir."

"License and registration, please."

I smiled as I handed everything over. "Did I mention that I'm a student at Ole Miss?"

"Are you that gal whose roommate killed herself the other night?"

"That would be me."

"Why would a pretty girl like that kill herself?"

I didn't know, but I sure as hell wanted to know. The officer clocked me at 110mph, but since I was having a string of bad breaks he said, "Here's what I'm gonna do—I'm gonna say you were going ninety. This here is a nice car, but it ain't a jet. Slow down before you end up like your roomy."

I forced my cutest smile and said, "Thanks," as I took the ticket.

He smiled and said, "That boyfriend of yours must be some kinda crazy." He peeped in the car at Lorna. "Hey, you that gal that sangs at Mr. P's on Friday and Saturday nights?"

"Yes, sir," Lorna said.

He gave Lorna a blank ticket and asked her to sign it. "You're gonna be famous one day. You sang just like that Tina Turner lady. You pretty as her too." He tipped his hat. "Y'all ladies have a good day."

I kept it under 70mph all the way to Lorna's. The ticket was like pouring hot sauce in an opened wound. Lorna and I joked about the way we had swallowed our pride, but if it had been Max or one of my brothers the officer would have made them get out of the car while they searched it and them as well. And if they were to make one wrong move there is no telling what would have happened.

Lorna's lease is going to be up on her dump of an apartment in a few months. Harold has connections in California. Her next move is going to be Hollywood. I was happy for her. I guess I'm going to be stuck with Max's parents until I can find a place I can afford.

"Pray on it, Gabby. You can't go wrong if you follow your dreams." I hugged her. "Promise me that you won't give up and give in to Max. It's not gonna me easy, but you can do it. I'm proud of you, and I never thought I would say this, but I agree with Mommy and Daddy on this." I pushed back tears. "I gotta go."

I was happy things were coming together for her. "I'm gonna miss you. I must go. Max's mother wants me home for dinner."

"Well, don't let the cows fall asleep before you get there," Lorna said mimicking Big Curtis's voice and mannerisms. She chuckled and ran upstairs.

Brad was in his driveway washing his car when I drove by. I blew my horn. He waved for me to stop. I backed up.

13

My lollipop red Firebird with the gray screaming chicken decal stands out more than I do. Anthony used to joke about buying the car because it reminded him of me. We don't talk about our escapades since sex ruined it for us, but we're still good friends. I checked for peeping Toms before I got out the car.

"You look great," Brad said. He was so busy gawking at me I don't think he realized he was spraying me with water.

"Bradley Pruter!" I snatched the hose from him and sprayed him until his pink nipples puckered and the brunette hairs on his chest ran slick against his tanned skin. My dress was clinging to me like a wet T-shirt.

"I'm gonna kill you, Brad--I can't go to Max's parents' house wet!"

He took off like my Firebird on a good day. I dropped the hose and chased him to his back yard. The hose snaked around and wet me even more. Brad was swimming laps in his pool by the time I reached his backyard in my Sunday-go-to-meetings shoes.

"Come in, Gabby. The water feels great."

"Go to hell, Brad. Where is your laundry room?" Instead of answering he got out the pool and dropped his wet shorts without a warning. I turned away, but not fast enough. He wrapped his nakedness with a towel and led the way to his bedroom. I backed away. He gave me a white bath robe and told me to give him my dress and underwear so he could put them in the dryer. There was no way in hell I was going to let him touch my wet clothes on or off. After I changed and put my things in the dryer Brad offered me a glass of wine. I rolled my eyes. I wasn't going to drink his wine after he had dropped his pants like that. I may be naive, but I'm not crazy. He said he was sorry, but his smile was sinister.

"I just finished belittling myself and I still got a ticket. I'm not in the mood for your stupid jokes today, okay."

"Give me the ticket. I'll take care of it."

"I can pay my own tickets."

"I'm not going to pay it. I'll have someone from Dad's firm fix it. You don't want a speeding ticket on your record."

I ironed my dress and slipped it back on while Brad watched. I suppose I was feeling a bit risqué when I let him zip me up. I brushed my hair and put on lipstick. I felt guilty as I don't know what so I ruffled my hair, and wiped the lipstick off.

Julius raised a brow when I walked in. "There you are. I saw your car at Brad's house."

Oh crap! I thought.

"Dinner is getting cold," Maryanne said. "Max called. You'll have to call him later." I didn't trust the sneaky grin on her face when she said, "Come help me set the table," but I dropped my purse on the sofa next to Julius. I would have headed straight for the kitchen, but my keys, lipstick, and my unused pack of birth control pills spilled out. I scooped everything up, before I gladly followed Maryanne.

"What's going on with you and that Pruter boy?" she asked as soon as the door closed.

I rolled my eyes to the ceiling and "Oh boy," slipped out.

"That boy's family is way out of your class. A rich white man like that only wants a girl like you for one thing." I wanted to scream, but my mouth opened and nothing came out. "You should be happy you were able to use your looks to snag someone as well to do as my Max. I warned my darling son about girls like you. You'll do anything to climb the social ladder, want you?"

I may be poor but I have a hundred times more class than Maryanne. "Mrs. Johnson, I don't mean to disrespect you in your home, but Max and I would be a lot happier if you would just let us be."

"Poor Max is blinded by your good looks. The way you use sex with him is scandalous."

I couldn't burn any bridges with Maryann and expect to marry Max, and be happy. I swallowed my response, and settled with giving her a good tongue lashing in my mind.

Julius walked into the kitchen. "Gabby, Maryanne and I want what is best for our son. He is under an enormous amount of pressure at school with you walking out on him the way that you did. This is a critical time in his life."

"This is a critical time in my life as well. I miss Max just as much as he misses me, probably more, but I'm not the one sleeping around. Brad is my friend, period, end of discussion."

Julius and Maryanne looked at each other. "Max loves you. We can't understand why you left him, unless you have your sights set higher," Maryanne said.

"I left to pursue a higher degree. It was one of the hardest decisions I've ever had to make. I love Max. I want to marry him. I wanted to go to Meharry, but they didn't offer me enough money. I've never given a hoot about being in a social class that you don't need a brain to get into." I looked at Maryanne and smiled like an innocent child. "Max didn't fall in love with me because I'm pretty. He fell in love with me because I'm smart and determined. He was in love with me before we had sex." I bit my lip and fought back tears. Julius looked at me the way Max did right before he threw his pharmacology book at me. I flinched.

"We won't let you compromise our son. If you loved him you wouldn't have left him like you did," Julius said.

"Max is the one screwing someone else every chance he gets. I've forgiven him so many times I'm too embarrassed to tell."

I ran out the kitchen, up the stairs, and down the hall to Max's room. The door slammed hard enough to make his football trophies fall over. Belinda would have been disappointed in me.

"Dear Lord, please give me strength. I love Max too much to hate his parents," I said as I leaned against the door. I went to Max's private bathroom and splashed water on my face and practiced my smile in front of the mirror. The coast was clear when I cracked the door open. I tiptoed back downstairs. Their house is too big for three people. It is no wonder why Max used to get lost in it when he was a small child.

I walked into their huge formal dining room and stood in the doorway. I said I was sorry, but I probably wasn't any more convincing than Brad had been. I do appreciate their concerns for Max and me so I thanked them for taking me in under the circumstances.

Maryanne grunted and Julius said, "If you would control your firecracker temper, and support Max, he wouldn't have to sleep with other women."

My mother raised her six daughters with the notion that we should go to school and learn a trade or a profession so we could be helpmates to the men we married. I tried to explain that to them. Max loves my firecracker temper. I was sizzling again, and ready to pop. I flashed Julius a sweet smile and bit the inside of my lip.

"Max needs a woman who will support what he is doing. You're too busy trying to be equal to him to take care of your duties," Julius said.

"When Max and I are together we can't keep our hands off each other. Max cheats, but my desires are only for him!"

"He cheats because you're not there for him, Gabby."

"Am I allowed to cheat because he doesn't support my dreams?"

"He didn't walk out on you." Julius shot back.

"Julius, Gabby, stop it! Sit down, Gabby, and eat your dinner." I pouted and sat down. I'm not a pouter.

Maryanne and Julius act as if the Civil Rights Movements and the Women's Rights Movements were fashion statements which are as passé now as Dylan's lime-green polyester pants and his flowered shirt. This is only one of many reasons why Americans are losing their edge. Everybody knows Mississippians are afraid of change, but I always thought black people had better things to worry about than social classes. I've been putting up with Max for four years maybe it's time for me to make a change.

I closed my eyes, bowed my head, and pressed my palms together. "Thank you, Lord, for this food which has been prepared for the nourishment of our bodies. Thank you for giving me Max and the love we share when he lets his heart connect with his wonderful mind. Thank you, Lord, for giving me strength in tough times like these. Forgive me, father, for being a poor house guest. But, Lord, I know you didn't let black folks make it this far to start acting like we're too good for our own people, Amen." I opened my eyes and Maryanne and Julius were staring at me with their mouths wide open.

Maryanne's food didn't taste anything like Belinda's. I picked over it for a while, before I pushed back my chair and asked to be excused. I gathered up my books, my keys, and a change of clothes and headed to Brad's house. Then I thought about how tense we had been earlier. I zoomed by his house so fast it looked like the yellow brick road instead of his yellow brick house.

I jumped on I-55 and headed south. I didn't give a damn if I got another ticket. If Brad's father could fix one, he could fix two. I blew my horn when I pulled up to my parents' car porch. Their four-bedroom brick ranch is one fourth the size of Max's parents' house. Daddy is well known for building custom cabinets. He used to have more work than he could handle, but now most cabinets are factory built. He has built custom cabinets, libraries, and bars for some of the richest people in Mississippi, but he is not as busy as he used to be. My brothers are carpenters, bricklayers, electricians and plumbers. Daddy and my brothers built a mansion that was featured in *Southern Living* magazine. I should take the magazine and show it to Maryanne. I'm proud of my family. I would rather have a loving family than a classy one any day. Belinda came outside to see who was leaning on the horn. She opened my car door. I fell into her arms and cried like Dylan.

She tightened her arms around me and led me to the kitchen. "Hush, baby girl, Mommy will make it better. Sit down. Let me fix you a plate."

Food and castor oil are Mommy's remedies for everything that ails one of her children. None of us ever got more than a cold, and I had the mumps for two weeks. Every year on the first day of school she used to give us a teaspoon of castor oil and a lemon, and I can still hear her saying, an apple a day will keep the doctor away, and feed a cold starve a fever, but my favorite is, eat your vegetables if you want the rest of your dinner.

She sat a full plate in front of me and said, "Ain't too much left. If I had known you was coming I would have saved you something on the side. All your brothers and their youngins done been here today."

I took a sip of iced tea. Belinda refilled my glass. She is so used to serving others she can't stop even though she has retired.

"What's wrong with Mommy's baby girl? You upset about your roommate? Lord, I feel for that child's mother. God don't like other folks doing His work. Ain't that many problems in the world for a young baby like that to take her own life."

I shook my head. "I don't think she did it, but I've been too caught up in my own problems to cry for Sara."

"Tell me what's wrong."

"Max and his parents are upset about me going to UMMC. I spoke my mind to his parents, and now I don't have anywhere to live." Belinda rubbed my back while I told her everything.

"Sometimes people with a little money in they pockets forget where they come from. They think they're better, but what they need is a reality check. Today was your day to write the check," Mommy said. "Don't worry they'll get over it. When you finish your dinner,

I want you to call Maryanne and Julius. They're probably worrying themselves silly about you about now."

I laughed. Belinda may not be educated but I can only pray to have as much wisdom as her and Big Momma when I get old.

"Don't worry--you didn't say anything they didn't need to hear. Max's parents have him believing he can do all that foolishness. He's not used to dealing with real people, but he'll come around. That boy loves you. I know it, and they know it, that's why I know they're worried."

I smiled. I should have come home on Friday. I drunk the rest of my sweet tea and ate Belinda's heavenly mixed greens, cornbread, and rice pudding before I called Maryanne. Then I went to the den to say hello to Daddy.

He was flipping back and forth between the New York Yankees and the Cincinnati Reds baseball game and the Pittsburgh Steelers and the Dallas Cowboys football game. When I was a little girl, Daddy used to call me from my room to come change the channels. We didn't want Belinda changing channels for Daddy after we all left home so we got together and bought a TV with a remote control. It was the first time my brothers didn't make excuses about helping out.

"Where is your husband with my money," Daddy asked when I kissed him on the cheek. Lil' Curtis had borrowed the money I borrowed from him from Daddy.

"Max had to go back to Nashville. I'll give you your money next week." Daddy and I watched TV until Mommy called me and said Max was on the telephone. I went to my old room to take his call.

14

Maryanne must have called Max the minute I left and told him I had flown the coop. She even sent Julius out to find me. Then, she had to call Max again to tell him I was at my parents' house. She pretends to be indifferent about me, but the woman keeps more tabs on me than the FBI.

Belinda told me to tell Max, she was going to spank him if he didn't straighten up and fly right. He chuckled and said he would rather have me spank him. He scolded me for not telling his parents where I was going before I left. According to him Maryanne was worried sick about me. He begged me to be careful just in case there is a killer on the loose.

"Max, you're scaring me."

"Gabby, please let my parents help you since you won't come home with me."

"I want to be with you forever that's why I'm here."

"I don't understand."

"I want you to marry well. I care what your parents think, and right now they don't think I'm good enough for their baby. I think your mother hates me."

"Mom wants me to be happy; she knows how crazy I get when you're not around."

"I want you and your family to understand why I have to get my degree."

"It's not that I don't want you to go to school--I'm afraid we will drift apart and you won't have any time for me when we're married."

That's the thing that I like best about dentistry--it's more of a nine to five job. I'll have plenty of time for you and all those babies we're going to make after I finish."

"But, baby, I miss you. I want us to be together now."

"I want to be with you, but I have to do this. I don't want to wake up fat twenty years from now with a house full of kids and wish I had done this when I had a chance."

"Dad told me what you said."

"Did he tell you what he said?"

"Baby, I love your spunk. Dad just wanted to get you going because he loves it too."

"He could have fooled me."

"Dad said, Max, you better hang on to that hot-tempered Gabby--a woman as pretty and lively as that could send a man to his grave pretty damn happy. Baby, you're my philter."

"So, what's the problem?"

"I was going through withdrawal. I'm addicted to you, and when I can't have my drug of choice I seek anything to satisfy my needs. Baby, it's hard for a man like me to accept the hold you have on me."

"Max, you have the same hold on me. I wouldn't keep forgiving you if you didn't."

Belinda knocked on my door. "Gabby, you have a visitor."

I covered the phone and said, "I'll be right out."

Belinda closed the door.

"Max, I have to go. If you love me, now more than ever, I need you to prove it. I don't want any more excuses."

I wished I could afford a new car. If I didn't know better, I would swear Anthony had rigged my car with a pager to let him know when I'm home. He is more at home at my parents' house now than he ever was when we were dating. In many ways, he is more charming than Max. His business is doing well and he has built a nice house next door to his grandmother's. He still knows how to charm me, and he still has a good heart. If I hadn't done what I did, and if I had enjoyed sex with him, and if he hadn't messed up, we would more than likely be married. He would probably support my dreams as much as I supported his.

Anthony has been preoccupied with cars since I can remember. His grandmother was disappointed when we didn't get married, but at least he completed his dreams of owning his own auto-body shop and used car dealership. I never doubted his abilities, which is the main reason we have maintained our friendship. I admire the fact that Anthony and Max weren't just big dreamers like most of the boys I grew up with. They both worked very hard to make their dreams their reality. Anthony looked up from the plate Belinda had fixed him when I walked in. He flashed the same impish smile he used to have when we were lovers.

"Hey, smarty pants."

He gave me that nickname because Belinda used to make me wear tight girdles to keep him at bay. He wasn't allowed to touch anything below my belt until I turned sixteen. My parents thought he called me smarty pants because of my good grades.

"Are you taking good care of my car?"

"It's my car now."

"It was always your car. Anyway, how is it going? Is slick treating my sweetheart right?"

"Max is doing fine."

"That's not what I asked. I don't give a damn about him. I know it's not my business, but I want you to be happy."

"I'm happy. We just have some things to work out."

"Well, if he's smart he'll get his ass off his high horse and work it out. Pride ain't worth jack when your woman is with someone else. If you need me to kick his ass or jack up his car you know where to find me."

I laughed and said, "I'm good, I have the jacking up the car part covered, but can I ask you something?"

"Sure, anything."

"Do you love Evelyn?"

"Sure, I do, but it's not like it was with you and me."

I laughed. "Ant, we didn't have a clue."

"Speak for yourself. Our love was sweet, innocent and pure. We loved each other from the inside out. You never demanded anything from me, and you always encouraged me and supported me in whatever I wanted to do. You gave what you were and everything was perfect until I demanded something you weren't ready to give."

I gazed into space. Maybe Max isn't ready for my kind of love either. Maybe I'm demanding something from him that he's not ready to give up.

"Do you remember the few times we did it? I used to feel like I was floating on a cloud when I touched you like that. That's why I was always so quick."

I didn't mean to laugh out loud. How in the world could he have been in ecstasy with me just lying there wishing he would hurry up?

Belinda walked into the kitchen. "What's so funny," she asked.

"Nothing," I said.

"Just an empty wagon making a lot of noise I guess." She looked at Anthony. "Gabby, Big Momma was asking about you earlier. Take her some more rice pudding, and make sure she took her medicine."

"You should move her here with you and Daddy. She's over a hundred years old, and you do everything for her anyway."

"Big Momma ain't leaving that house without a fight. So, get yourself up. Anthony has to go home to his family anyway." Belinda emphasized his and family. "Big Momma had a dream about you last night. I pray it's ain't what I think."

Belinda and I made eye contact. Big Momma is known for her psychic abilities and her special teas and ointments. I didn't want to think about why she wanted to see me; I just hoped it didn't have anything to do with my love life.

Big Momma lives in a shotgun house across the street from what used to be the Colored elementary school my older sisters and brothers attended. Belinda calls Lorna and me her menopause babies or her second chance babies. The school's parking lot is the meeting place for Hot Springs's Firebird Club every Sunday. When I parked in Big Momma's driveway, one of the members from my class yelled and made a motion for me to join them. I told him I had to visit my great grandmother, but I promised to join them another time. Hot Springs is a town where everybody knows everyone, and everyone knows everybody's business. It pays to be nice in a town like this, and it doesn't hurt to have the hoodoo lady in the family. There are tales about the strange things that happened to people who dared to cross Big Momma. She may not believe she has that type of power, but I've seen enough of what she and Gina call strange coincidences to take them both seriously.

The drivers revved up their engines one after the other. Each car purred until the last engine had started and warmed up, then they took off one at a time; white, yellow, blue, black, and then the red one. The screaming chickens on their hoods flashed by like eagles going to meet their maker. I couldn't believe I was excited by the show. I went inside after the last car zoomed by. Big Momma's door is never locked. Everybody knows that she keeps her money in her mattress, but here again, nobody is foolish enough to steal from her. I gave her the pudding and kissed her on the cheek.

"Where is your sweater, Gabby? You shouldn't be in the night air in your condition dressed like that."

I'm used to her fussing over me. I usually agree with her and move on. "My sweater is in the car. What condition, Big Momma? Do I need a sweater for a broken heart?"

"Put your sweater on before you catch pneumonia and lose that boy you're carrying." Panic rushed through my body like a bolt of lightning. Big Momma knew when Hope got pregnant, and Belinda said she knew when she got pregnant with Renee.

"I'm not pregnant," I said not knowing whether to be happy or sad if she was right.

"You've been heavy on my mind all summer, and when it came to me clear in a dream yesdiddy, I knew I had to let you know before you upped and did something crazy again." I should have known that she knew what Lorna and I had done.

Belinda didn't ask any questions when I got home. She held her arms open. I walked in. "What am I going to do about school?"

"Baby, this is your chance to make something outta yo'self. I had all y'all, and I worked for Ms. Beggins right up to the day y'all was born. If I can do that, you can go to that dental school and learn to be a dentist. You were born breech and purple. The doctor even told me you were dead, but after a minute or so you started kicking and hollering. You came into this world walking and proving people wrong, baby girl, don't you dare stop now."

Belinda made the tea Big Momma had put together for me and put me to bed. "Don't worry, baby, this may slow you down, but it ain't gonna stop you as long as Big Momma and I are breathing."

I was still staying at Maxi's parents' house a month after Sara killed herself if that was what she did. Julius and I were cordial, but I could only imagine what he told Max about me studying with Brad. And

Maryanne was so nice it was disgusting. She took advantage of the opportunity to try to turn me into an acceptable daughter-in-law. Her efforts were superficial, and they made her like me even less.

I called Max every night at eleven, but I hadn't seen him in four weeks. We talked about how we missed each other and about what we were learning in school. I never mentioned my visit to Big Momma's. He promised that he was behaving himself. Our conversations about missing each other soon advanced to--I need some satisfaction or I won't be responsible for my actions. I told Max I would drive up, but he promised to come down instead. I wanted to spend as much time enjoying him as possible. I studied before he arrived, and I stocked up on condoms since I was afraid to take the pill.

Maryanne and Julius had gone to their beach home in Biloxi for the weekend. I'm not sure if they didn't want to be around when Max and I got together or if Max knew we would have the house to our-selves. He arrived around midnight. I was wearing a black silk teddy he had given me. I haven't gotten a period since I feed him, sexed him and left him in August.

15

Max kissed me and removed my clothes faster than it took me to put them on. I tugged his Kappa T-shirt off. He kissed sensitive places while I fumbled with his belt and jeans. I was as nervous as I was excited. He dropped his pants, and sat me on the kitchen counter. I wrapped my legs around him. He forgot all about foreplay and tried to go directly for gold. I grabbed his hand, snapped my legs together, hurt Max, and completely killed the mood. He grabbed himself and yelled. "Please don't tell me you're on your period, because as much as I've been missing you, I'll have to swim in the red sea tonight."

"I got off the pill."

Max frowned. "Why did you do that?"

I kissed his face and shoulders as I said, "I figured it was a good time to give my body a break since we rarely see each other."

"Why in the hell didn't you tell me? I don't have any condoms." I tried to kiss him. He dodged my kiss and picked up his underwear. He pulled them back on, and then he threw me my teddy.

"You use condoms when you mess around, don't you?"

"What in the hell is that supposed to mean, Gabriella?" He turned away and pouted. I slipped my arms around his waist and kissed him. He grabbed my hand. "Don't start with me, Gabby."

I traced his back muscles with kisses and told him I had bought condoms.

"I'm tired. I didn't drive all the way here for you to mess with my head. I haven't been with anyone else--so drop it. Okay?"

"Come on, Max, I miss you. I'm sorry." I caressed and kissed him until he grabbed my hand and led us upstairs. I tried to rekindle the flame, but Maxwell Johnson got limp every time he tried to put on a condom. I had been anticipating this moment all week. I was willing to try anything. My white girlfriends in high school used to brag about oral sex so I went there. Max accused me of doing it with Brad. By the time, I got the condom on, I was on the verge of tears. Max was on me before I could stop him.

"Tell me you love me."

"I love you, Max," I said even though he was hurting me.

"Say it like you mean it"

"I mean it."

"Have you been giving my loving to Brad?"

"No! I love you."

"Mom says that you practically live at his house. Say it, Gabby, tell me you love me. Come home with me, baby. I need you."

"Max, you're hurting me," I said when I couldn't whole back the tears any longer.

"Gabby, you're killing me slowly. I love you." He pushed deeper.

"Max, stop! You're hurting me."

"I just want to love you. I want things to be like they used to be." He grunted and I didn't know if it was satisfaction or if he was hurting inside as badly as I was. I never thought I would see the day when I would see Max cry, or when I would have to grit and bear it with him. He said he was crying because he thought he was losing me. And I was crying because I was losing him. He fell asleep in my arms. As much as I want to have Max's babies one day, I lay awake and prayed that Big Momma was wrong.

Max rolled his tongue and wet kisses down my spine. I woke up, but I didn't move. Bright sunshine was peeking through the window. I prayed that the sunshine was a sign of better times ahead.

"I'm sorry," he said. I turned to face him. He twisted a lock of my hair around his finger. "I'm going crazy missing you all the time." I feared saying the wrong thing while he was pouring his heart out. I listened with my heart and communicated with my eyes. We kissed until we started a fire and then we loved each other until our flames erupted from yellow, to blue, to orange and then we doused them back to black. I cried when it was over. This was the Max I had fallen in love with. This was the Max I wanted to marry and have his babies.

"We're not doing so good with this separation thing, are we?" Max asked.

"No, but I love you too much to stop now."

Max wrapped my hair around his fingers. "I didn't mean to hurt you. I don't know what to do without you and that makes me crazy."

I cupped his face in my hands. "I love you no matter where I am. I'm not doing this to hurt us. This is what I have to do to keep from going crazy."

"When are you going to start on the pill again?"

"If, and when I get my period."

"If?"

"Big Momma thinks we're pregnant, and I'm late."

Max sat up in the bed and looked at me in the morning light. "Is that possible?"

"Maybe."

"How maybe?"

"More maybe with each day. I was going to double up on my pills after we made love when you were here in September, but Big Momma told me I was already pregnant."

"What are you gonna do if you are?"

"You mean what are we gonna do, don't you?"

He smiled broadly. "I'll marry you and drag you back to Nashville if I have to."

"This isn't the dark ages, Max. Women don't have to run and hide anymore because they are pregnant. My brain functions the same as it did before."

"Forget school. Come home with me." He pulled me close and started kissing and feeling my breasts, which were awfully sensitive.

"Stop, Max. I can't."

He kicked the covers away. "Dammit, Gabby, why are you doing this? If you were using your brain you wouldn't have gotten off the damn pill and forgot to tell me in the first place. Don't you think it is stupid to leave me and then decide to get pregnant?"

"Stupid?"

"You're messing everything up! Why are you trying to run a game on me now?"

Max put on the robe I had given him last Christmas, and stormed out the room. The door slammed. I jumped. The phone rang and I jumped again. He cracked the door open and caught me wiping away tears. The phone was for me. I was prepared to yell at Brad for calling. He knew Max was visiting.

It was Gina. I had been heavy on her mind as well. Charles was treating her great. Marriage was an adjustment but it was good. She was ready to come home because Connecticut was cold, the people were cliquish, and she didn't have any friends outside of school.

"Max didn't sound like himself, are you guys okay?" Gina asked.

"Things aren't going exactly according to our plans, and to make matters worse Big Momma thinks I'm pregnant."

"I knew it! Birth and death feelings are especially strong."

"You knew?"

"I knew something was going on. I'm not as good as your Big Momma. I just kept thinking you needed a friend about now."

"I could use a miracle at this point."

Gina promised me that everything would be okay before she rushed off. Her budget was so tight she said she probably wouldn't have a phone next month. She was calling everyone that she knew while she could. She had talked to Gretchen. She wants all of us to get together when they come home for Christmas.

Max peeped in the room after I hung up the phone. He sat a tray with breakfast for two on the bed. "Promise me that you will at least eat right," he said.

Maryanne makes breakfast every morning. I've already gained five pounds. I may be in denial, but Big Momma is rarely wrong. "You don't have to worry; I'm taking care of myself," I said.

"That's the problem--you don't need me anymore."

"That is so not true. I need you now more than ever. And I'm not stupid."

"If you're pregnant, I want to marry you. Say what you want about my family, but there are no bastards in it. Johnson men take pride in taking care of their women and children. You can either marry me or take care of it. I won't shame myself, and my family by looking like a hood-rat."

"Let's wait until we're sure. Big Momma is a hundred years old. Maybe she is confusing this negative energy between us for something else." Max sat on the bed next to me. I rubbed his face and kissed his soft lips. He played with my hair and looked dreamlike. "I'm tired of fighting. Let's try to enjoy the time we have together," I said.

We ate our cold pancakes and eggs. Then we made love, and studied, and napped in-between. Max wanted to skip the condoms, but I was still praying for a miracle. The idea of me being pregnant was a turn-on for him. The possibility of being pregnant after what I had done behind Anthony's back had me excited even though the timing was lousy. Max went back to Nashville late on Sunday night. I promised to call him the minute I was sure.

I made 100% on my Biochemistry exam. Max's good loving had helped me relax. Brad and I had studied all week just in case I didn't find time to study while Max was visiting.

Brad was the perfect study partner. He had a thing for me, but he seemed to be sincerely concerned about Max and me. I didn't mind discussing my problems with Brad since it let him know where my heart was at. Brad took dips in the pool when we took breaks. There were times when I wondered if he swam because a cold shower would have been too obvious. I guess I was in denial on that as well.

Maryanne and Julius didn't like me spending time with Brad, but they didn't dare say anything else directly. I continued to call Max every night at eleven. He didn't understand how Brad and I could spend hours together without becoming intimate. I told him I cry on my friends' shoulders occasionally, but I don't have any desire to sleep with them. He didn't say anything else about it for a while.

I didn't bite my tongue around Brad. I didn't care how many tickets he got fixed, my heart belonged to Max. Brad and I exposed ourselves to each other without any hidden agendas--it made for a nice friendship.

I believed Brad wanted Max and me to work our problems out, but of course I didn't tell Brad that I might be pregnant. One night while we were studying Brad surprised me.

"What's lower than a nigger in Mississippi, Gabby?"

I would have been shocked, but I'm used to white people slipping when they get comfortable with me. Most people who don't know my family think I'm mixed. But in Mississippi mixed means you're a Black person who looks half black, or one with white blood gone bad. Either way you were still a nigger.

"A Russian Jew," Brad said.

"That shit isn't funny, Bradley Pruter." I got up and started putting my books in my backpack.

"It's not a joke, Gabby. That's what my parents said about the love of my life."

I sat down because Brad was red in the face and his eyes were out in space somewhere.

"You wanna talk about it?" I asked.

Her name was Ingrid. She was a student at Yale. He said she was tall and beautiful, like me, but she had long curly blond hair, and eyes the color of algae. He brought her home to meet his family since she didn't have anywhere to go for the Christmas Holidays. His family rejected her because she wasn't an American, and she was Jewish.

"Wow," I said, but my mind didn't have any problem picturing Ingrid and Brad's pain. "We should at least be able to fall in love without having to deal with stupid people shit."

"It hurt, Gabby. Ingrid never recovered."

Brad's eyes got misty and his voice quivered. At first, he rebelled by switching his major from pre-law to pre-med. He didn't want anything to do with people or laws, which were supposed to represent justice, but were nothing more than expensive smoke screens that only a select few can hide behind. He didn't speak to or visit his parents for two years.

"If this is too painful you don't have to say anymore."

"It's okay. You reminded me of Ingrid when you walked into class the first day of school and Dr. Wagner picked on you. I wanted to be your friend. Ingrid helped me to open my mind up to new ways of thinking, new ways of being--you're a lot like her." He chuckled. "My parents accused her of turning me into a communist."

"Parents sometimes think they are protecting their children when actually they are protecting their own values. Most people are afraid of change. Afraid of things unknown, but if things don't change they don't stay the same, they become old, battered and worn out. The world continues to progress and you stay stuck in your clutter muck."

"I think you're ready to swim, Gabby."

"I think I'm already drowning, Brad."

"I will never let you drown."

He dropped his khakis and pulled his polo shirt over his head. He had on red Speedos. He has been prepared to take a swim since that first time. Brad hopped in the water and went back and forth several times like a racer. The water splashed and the sound echoed as his arms and legs beat against it. After five or six laps, he got out. I gave him a towel. He didn't use it. He wrapped it around himself and thanked me for understanding.

"It's the least I can do for a friend who would never let me drown."

"Ingrid and I were the same as you and Max--we were trying to find our way and we ran into a road block that we couldn't get around. You and Max can make it around that block. You have too."

⌘

I hated living under Max's parents' watchful eyes. It felt like I was walking on egg shells around them. I wanted to prove to Max that I could take care of myself. I inquired about an ad for a one bedroom apartment close to school. The landlord took one look at me, and said the apartment was no longer available. Then she had the nerve to ask me if I was "one of those Mexicans." I was livid when I told Brad what had happened.

He called his father. The next day the landlord called me and said she didn't have any one bedroom apartments available, but a two-bedroom apartment was available. The rent was only ten dollars more. I suspected Brad had something to do with it. I was too happy to have my own place, to worry about why he had gone out on a limb to help me out again.

I called Dylan's landlord to let him know I was coming to move my things, but he said someone had already cleaned out the apartment. He thought I had moved my stuff, which was why he hadn't bothered to call. Maryanne didn't want my roach infested things near her house. And my brothers didn't want to take my stuff to my parents' house, and then turn around and bring it back to Jackson. And since I had paid my rent and security deposits my stuff should have been safe for at least two months. Someone had stolen my TV, stereo, and the new bedroom set that I'm still paying for. Maryanne gave me Max's bedroom set, and Max gave me his old stereo and TV. Big Momma gave me a small dining room table and four chairs, and Belinda gave me the raggedy sofa from the den. My brothers moved everything. Max had promised to help until I mentioned that Brad had helped me get the apartment.

"Stop being naive," Max said. "He helped you get your own place so he can--I can't even say it. You need to stay away from him."

I refused to argue with Max; I didn't see him helping. I had looked forward to seeing him. I appreciated everything his family had done for me, but I was disappointed when he said he didn't want me to move.

"Did you forget about that shit that was written on your mirror?"

"No, Max! How can I forget something like that?"

"I'm just saying, you need to be careful. You can't trust every Joe Blow you meet, Gabby!" He yelled, and then he coughed and cleared his throat. "Did you get your period?" he asked all sweet and calm again.

"Not yet."

"Did you take the test?"

"Not yet."

"Well, let me know what you wanna do. You don't want to wait until you're too far along," he said and his tone was tight and strained again when he hung up.

16

Mommy suggested that inviting Brad to dinner would be an appropriate thank you gesture. I'm a good cook, but she reminded me that she is the expert at entertaining rich white people; she even volunteered to take care of everything. Everybody says Belinda is the best cook in Hot Springs. Max and Anthony love her cooking. Mommy said she didn't have a problem with anyone willing to help her baby girl succeed. "There are good white folks, and there are good black folks, and you're damn lucky if you cross paths with either," Belinda said.

"I guess that makes me lucky," I said.

"I think it's time for me to meet Mr. Bradley Pruter since Max is bent out of shape about him. Don't worry; you do the inviting, and I'll take care of dinner."

Belinda and Big Momma arrived two hours early with two boxes and a cooler filled to the brims. She brought her best linen and the Lenox china Mrs. Tiegs had given her after she divorced Mr. Biggers so she could marry an older richer man. She also brought her Waterford vase, and an arrangement of orange Asiatic lilies, pink Gerbera daisies, blue irises and lavender Chrysanthemums.

"You didn't have to go all out," I said.

"I'm just thanking the man properly," Belinda said.

Belinda had on a purple dress and matching shoes. And Big Momma had taken off her hairnet and taken out her pin curls, which she almost never does. A blue Sunday-go-to-meeting- hat was sitting lopsided on her head, and silver curls flowed down her back. She had on a green dress. She sat her silver walker in the corner while she helped Belinda set everything up. I tried to help, but they shooed me away. I went to my room and called Max.

We hadn't talked all week and I wasn't sure if he was avoiding me or if I was avoiding him. We made small talk for a few minutes about school and exams and missing each other, but eventually he got around to what was really on both our minds.

"How do you feel?" Max asked.

"The same." The only thing I was owning was my own denial. "I made the highest score on my Biochemistry exam again. I think I earned a little respect from my classmates." I said to change the subject.

"That's good, Gabby. You have a good head on your shoulders for the most part. When are you gonna take *the* test?"

"I haven't had time. I'm just stressed from missing you and moving. I have to go--I'm on a serious budget now."

"You need me to send you some money?"

"No, I'll be okay if I don't splurge."

"I'll send you something so you can go to a doctor. Don't go to Uncle Lester's office if you think you're gonna... you know. We need to know soon so you can decide what you're gonna do."

"Whatever, Max, I gotta go, Belinda is at the door. When are you gonna come down?"

"Maybe next week. I'll call you."

Belinda and Big Momma had transformed my kitchen and dining area into a perfect photograph for *House Beautiful* except for the Bama jelly caps, which supported the table legs.

Brad arrived exactly on time, as usual, with a bouquet of pink roses and a bottle of wine from his wine cellar. He was wearing his clinic day attire--blue pants, button down shirt, and his duck decoy tie and belt. His hair was still damp. We eyed each other for a tense moment before I invited him in. He was nervous about meeting my mother, but his bright blue eyes danced when I introduced him to Belinda and Big Momma. Brad referred to my mother as Mrs. Oliver, and he called my great grandmother Big Momma the same as any well-bred Southern gentleman would do.

We sat at my little table, which was idea for two, but was set for four. Big Momma did the grace and took all of three minutes, which was good for her. She had so much to be thankful for last Thanksgiving; she took ten minutes, all praises. Belinda piled succulent pot-roast and vegetables on our plates since the table was too small to fit the food.

Brad talked freely about our first day of school, and our budding friendship between bites. Then he said, "I can see where Gabby gets her beauty and charm," and that was the opening Big Momma had been waiting for.

"Exactly what are your intentions for our Gabby?" Big Momma asked.

Brad took a sip of wine and made eye contact with me. "I don't have any intentions, ma'am. We're just friends."

Our eyes locked and we spoke in the secret eye language we've come accustomed to using at school. Big Momma and Belinda had their own secret codes. You would have to get up in the middle of the night to fool Belinda, and fooling Big Momma is a hopeless feat that only a fool would attempt. Belinda raised a brow and Big Momma wiped her mouth with her napkin and folded it into a neat triangle.

"Tell me about your peoples," Big Momma said.

"Daddy is an attorney. He has ten firms spread over the state. Mother doesn't work."

"Do you plan to introduce Gabby to your peoples?"

Our eyes met again and so did Big Momma's and Belinda's.

"I've mentioned Gabby to them. They would love to meet her."

Brad gulped down the rest of his wine. I wanted to do the same, but I was starting to come to terms with the soreness in my breasts, and my body's screams for more sleep than usual.

"You're falling in love with Gabby, aren't you?" Big Momma asked. Brad's bowed head sprung up like a drowning man in search of fresh air. Our eyes met, and he couldn't conceal his feelings. I'm not psychic, but after spending so much time around Big Momma and Gina, I've gotten good at reading eyes. I wasn't shocked when Big Momma asked the question. She always told me if you want to know something it's just a matter of finding the right time, place and words to spit it out. I hadn't done to well at concealing my feelings either. Belinda wiped her mouth and placed her folded napkin in a neat triangle. I wondered if it was a secret code or another quirky habit that had been passed down. Belinda pushed her chair away from the table and looked Brad and me square in our eyes again.

Belinda asked Brad if he wanted coffee or tea with his dessert. He said coffee. She told me to clear the table and come help her. Big Momma changed the subject to Max when she thought I was out of hearing range. Belinda was busy placing butter pecan turtle squares and sweet potato tarts on a serving dish.

"That boy is in love with you. Y'all been spending so much time together you probably didn't see it coming. Did you tell him about Max and the baby?"

"He knows about Max," I whispered.

Belinda gave me a stack of Lenox saucers and a pot of hot coffee. "Humph, you're in as much denial about the baby as that boy out there is about you? Do I need to remind you about our family history with white men?"

"No ma'am." I knew the story about how Belinda's mother left home to go work for a wealthy family when she was sixteen. It was a live-in position. Her job was to help Mr. Chesterfield's wife take care of their newborn son. Mrs. Chesterfield had what they would call a severe case of post-partum depression today, but back then they just thought she was overwhelmed. My grandmother was pregnant by Mr.

Chesterfield by the time she was seventeen. He took her to the doctor when Belinda was born. His wife still hadn't shaken her blues so my grandmother raised Belinda with her older brother in the big house. It took a few years for my grandmother to realize that she had been fixed. Big Momma said sterilizing black women without their knowledge was a common practice in those days. Mrs. Chesterfield came out of her fog long enough to figure out what was going on with her husband and my grandmother. My grandmother had seen Mrs. Chesterfield comparing the children's eyes, ears, noses, lips, fingers, jawlines, toes and other genetic markers that are even more powerful giveaways than skin color. Mrs. Chesterfield didn't have any power in the marriage, and she still didn't have a clue about how to care for herself or her little son. My grandmother stayed on even though Mrs. Chesterfield hated her, and Mr. Chesterfield could have her anytime he pleased. My grandmother had long tired of trying to fight off Mr. Chesterfield by the time she realized she couldn't get pregnant again. The kids were tucked away in their separate, but unequal schools when my grandmother supposedly slipped down the stairs, and fatally broke her neck and back. Mr. Chesterfield wanted Belinda to stay with her brother. My grandmother had been a mother to them both, and even Mr. Chesterfield knew it would be too devastating for his son to lose both. Big Momma had to fight to gain custody of Belinda. But with the fact that Mr. Chesterfield would have had to fully own his fatherhood, and the possibility that his mentally unstable wife had caused my grandmother's death, and could just as easily do harm to Belinda, he relented. Big Momma told me the story when I was a twelve. She said, Mr. Chesterfield offered her the live-in job. She had Big Daddy and her other children to consider, but in truth, she didn't trust herself not to feed Mrs. Chesterfield something that would put her out of her misery for good. Mr. Chesterfield arranged secret playdates for the kids until the son developed romantic interests in Belinda when they were preteens. Big Momma ended the farce and told Belinda the truth. Mr. Chesterfield and his son continued to bogart their way into Big Momma and Belinda's lives with bits of money and small gifts, but they never fully acknowledged her until the old man died. Mr. Chesterfield willed Belinda a small portion of land, and enough money for the down-payment of the little house my parents live in now. He also left her some money to go to college if she ever got a chance. She spent the money helping to educate her girls, one is an army nurse, two are secretaries, one is a bookkeeper, one is a teacher, and I'm going to be a dentist. A few years after Mr. Chesterfield died, Mrs. Chesterfield jumped out her second story bedroom window screaming my grandmother's name. The Chesterfield mansion has been vacant for years. Everybody says it is haunted. The son went to college in New York and never returned.

"Baby, when a man like Brad sets his heart on having you, he is not going to give up until he gets what he feels should rightfully be his."

Belinda and Big Momma have worked for some of the richest white families in Mississippi. They probably know more about those families than the families themselves. Big Momma often joked about everything going on in the big house coming to light in the laundry or the kitchen. My parents may have lost their daughters to fast talking men, but they are proud of the fact that none of us had to do the only work readily available to Black women in Mississippi in their day.

Belinda and Big Momma played, *do you know Mr. Charlie,* cross reference with Brad while he picked over his dessert and avoided making eye contact with me. I washed the china. Belinda dried it and packed it back in the box. Big Momma told Brad everything she wanted him to know about Max and me. As far as my family is concerned, I became Max's wife the day I left my daddy's house and moved into Max's. Belinda was quiet and that made me nervous.

Brad wasn't his usual joking self so I wasn't surprised when he left shortly after he took everything to Belinda's car. He helped me restore the apartment back to normal then he said he needed to go home and take a swim. He kissed me on the cheek, thanked me for a wonderful dinner and said he would see me at school. Since I didn't know my neighbors, I waved goodbye from my doorway instead of walking him to his car. I prayed that I hadn't lost another admirer because he wanted something I couldn't give him.

I went to bed and stayed there until late the next day when Max's phone call woke me up. I had never lived alone and it felt good to be in my own place. I didn't have to get dressed. I didn't have to comb my hair. And best of all, I didn't have to lock the door when I went to the bathroom. It was two in the afternoon. Max didn't believe me when I told him I was sleeping.

"Were you hanging out at Mr. P's last night with Brad and Lorna?"

"No, I guess I was tired."

"Gabby, I think you should go ahead and take *the* test. You don't want to wait until you're too far along."

"I hope you're not suggesting an abortion?"

"All I'm saying is take *the* test so we can decide what to do. I'd like to get married, but if you wanna stay there. You're gonna have to choose."

"I feel fine--it's stress. And I never said I didn't want to marry you, Max."

"Gabby, being married and living apart doesn't work for me."

"Max, even if I'm pregnant, quitting school or an abortion is not an option!"

"Take *the* test, Gabby. I gotta go. Goodbye!"

Brad was back to his old joking self by Monday. We didn't discuss our feelings for each other, but we were free to talk about other people. I needed Brad to be my friend. I wanted to be his.

Most of our time was spent in medical classes that made me wonder why I needed to take them to be a dentist. We were also learning about oral diseases and teeth in the afternoons. We had to learn tooth anatomy and one of our first tasks as future dentists was to carve blocks of wax into wax teeth. Big Curtis and I used to dibble and dabble with wood carvings. Wax was easier and faster.

I carved my wax block into a molar in no time. Then I checked on Brad to see how he was doing. He asked to see the tooth I had carved. We exchanged teeth just as Dr. Wagner was making his rounds. Dr. Wagner took my tooth from Brad and examined it using his magnifying glasses. He patted Brad on the shoulder, gave him an A, and told him he was going to make a mighty fine dentist. By the time, he finished with Brad I had carved Brad's tooth. It looked as good as the first tooth, if not better, but Dr. Wagner gave me a C.

Brad was about to confess, but I told him with my eyes that a confession would only make matters worse. Rachel witnessed the exchange. She was about to tell until Brad put his index finger to his lips and signaled for her to keep quiet. Later in the bathroom she accused me of stooping low to get Brad's attention. She openly bats her eyes and flirts with her hair, and the splits in her dresses seem to be getting higher with each passing day. Her overt flirting doesn't stop with Brad; she flirts with the teachers as well. Brad said he was happy when I came on the first day and sat between him and Rachel. Brad says women like Rachel are attracted to him like flies to shit, which about sums up how he feels about them.

Another week had passed and I still hadn't gotten my period. I was sleeping more but I felt fine otherwise. Max and I were no longer calling every night and it was just as well. I had been eating better, and I had carvings for sardines, hot sauce and crackers, and peanut butter and strawberry jelly sandwiches.

Max was angry when he finally called because I hadn't taken the test. I was no longer in denial, but I was waiting to confirm because I didn't want to be tempted or pushed to do anything that would sever my connection with him completely. I've been afraid that I wouldn't be able to conceive again since I found Gretchen clinging to life that night and Dr. Morgan told her she might not be able to have children after what she had done. I've been given a second chance, and I'm not going to blow it, but of course I couldn't tell Max that.

"I need you with me when I take the test," I said.

"I want to be with you always, but you prefer messing with my head. You know I love you and babies."

"How am I messing with your head?"

"I don't think you're pregnant. I think you're trying to run a game on me, Gabby."

"F-you, Max. Who have you been talking to? Have you been crying on that bitch Tammy's shoulder again?" I slammed the phone down. It didn't ring again until four a.m., and then it was some pervert breathing heavily. He didn't say anything so I slammed the phone down and went back to sleep.

I didn't bother to call Max when I got the positive results the next day. I got up and went to bed the same as I had done before the confirmation. I continued my new life living in denial of that which I was not going to change under any circumstances.

I had gotten into the routine of dental school. We were into our seventh week and things were going well. I had made friends with some of my other classmates and I had learned everyone's names. Everyone already knew mine.

Christine was a cute petite red-head who was married to a medical student in his second year. She overheard me talking about Max and we formed a bond. She wanted the women in our class to stick together. She detected friction between Rachel and me. She didn't like the way Rachel flirted with the professors or the way she dressed. She said if we wanted to be taken seriously as future dentists we must prove it with our brains and our ability instead of our sex appeal. Rachel was smart and talented, but being a vamp was part of her nature.

Christine planned a dinner party for the women in our class and our husbands or significant others. It was on a Friday. Max wouldn't have made it in time even if I had asked him to come as I had promised Christine. Brad offered but that would have opened us up to too many questions.

I tried to think of an excuse to skip the party, but going was as much a part of my education as taking Biochemistry. I wanted to drive to Nashville to show Max the test results. Even though I was scared, I was happy to have a part of him with me. I had gotten several of those late-night calls with the heavy breathing. I figured Max was trying to scare me into coming back to Nashville.

I went to the mall during my lunch hour. I brought a pretty tomato-red sweater dress that I could wear for a while even though I'm pregnant. It felt like I was being watched while I shopped. It wasn't the usual "black person in a store we better keep an eye on her variety. I sensed that I was being followed. The store clerk said I looked radiant so I accepted the feeling as people noticing my pregnancy glow. It had poured rain all week. Friday was an especially dreary day. I've been smiling since I got the results; maybe the world was smiling back at me for a change. I was still smiling when I went into the classroom for my afternoon classes.

"You're the only person I know who looks radiant even when it is pouring outside," Brad said.

"My skin always glows when it rains," I said. I felt a happy flutter inside and wished it was Max complimenting me and noticing the changes my body was going through.

"Well, I hope it rains until Christmas."

"Are you trying to use flattery to inch your way into my heart, Mr. Pruter?"

"No, ma'am, Miss Gabby, I don't have any intentions for you." We laughed until Rachel walked in wearing a black dress, which had a split up to her yang. She was carrying a cup of coffee with steam coming from it. We held our snickers until she sat down, then we burst into laughter again.

"What's so funny?" she asked in her usual nasal twang.

"Inside joke," Brad said. We chuckled until Dr. Wagner walked in.

Later that evening I put on my red dress and went to the party my usual hour late. It was still pouring and I was still trying to talk myself out of going. Christine greeted me at the door.

"There you are, Gabby. I was about to call the police to see if there had been an accident. This weather is atrocious, I was starting to worry about you, girl."

"Sorry, I forgot we were on Central Standard Time." She chuckled. I didn't.

"You look great. Where is Max?"

"Girl, stop yapping and let me get out of this rain." A gust of wind blew my cheap umbrella inside out. Christine grabbed my arm and pulled me inside.

The party was different. There was no music, not even the kind Brad plays. There were lots of cold and hot hors d'oeuvres, but other than the pigs-in-a-blanket, I didn't recognize anything. Even the names sounded strange pate, sushi, and caviar.

Everyone sat around and talked about business deals, the stock market, President Clinton's failed healthcare reform initiative, his federal assault weapons ban, and the recovering economy while they guzzled down beer. The women finally grouped off and talked about dental school--the last thing I wanted to discuss on a rainy, Friday night. I wanted to be wrapped in Max's arms planning our future and making mad passionate love. It was hard to stay focused with Max and me having so much to work out, and knowing I could solve all our problems by dropping out of school.

Christine served a sit-down dinner after we had filled up on alien hors d'oeuvres. Rachel sat next to me; she was dateless as well. After dinner, we played Charades. Christine put numbers in a basket to decide who would be on each team. I was the only female on the team with the guys. I was glad to be away from Rachel although I wasn't thrilled to be stuck with a bunch of rowdy, beer drinking white boys. I was better at acting than guessing, but my team won. After the game was over, I chatted with Christine's husband. He confirmed that he missed Sara in class, and that he had stopped by for a few minutes on Labor Day to talk her out of dropping out of school. I didn't know if he was the classmate Sara had mentioned. I didn't have time to wonder if Christine's husband had killed Sara, or if he wrote that note on my mirror, or if Sara had threatened him like she had done Dylan. I knew he was a married man, and they had an affair or maybe just sex. If he stopped by the afternoon of Labor Day, that would make him the last person to see her alive, except for the fact that I heard her late-night screams. And I didn't do a damn thing but pat myself on the back for avoiding her. When the first couple called it a night, I jetted right behind them.

I need to set things right with Max. It was still raining cats and dogs. I decided to go home, get some sleep, and drive to Nashville at sunrise. I want to see Max's face when I tell him I'm going to have our baby, and I'm staying in school.

17

Max hopped out of his Corvette when I pulled into my parking lot. We kissed and kissed in the pouring rain. He got an overnight bag from his car. We hugged as we walked upstairs to my apartment. He dropped his bag when we got inside. He embraced me tightly and kissed me hard and deep again. Then he pulled away and flicked the light on. He smiled and played with my hair while he checked me out. Water dripped from my hair and dress. I must have looked a hot mess. But his smile let me know that our love is special. My analytical brain was busy trying to find a way to make this work. I don't care if we are separated by distance. His seed is the bond that will always make him a part of my life.

After a while he said, "Baby, you don't have any idea about how hard it is for me not to see you every day. I'm so in love with you, Gabby, I'm lost without you. I've hugged your pillow so many nights it doesn't smell like you anymore. It never did snore like you."

I giggled. "You snore after we make love, Max. I guess you don't get into your REM sleep zone when I'm not around."

We stared at each other. I was afraid to tell him. I wanted the moment to be perfect. I didn't know what else I wanted, but I wanted to do this right. I wanted to make up for my not knowing any better at seventeen. Max pulled me in his arms and squeezed me to him. I shivered and kicked off my shoes.

"God, Gabby, you're even more beautiful pregnant. Let's get you out of those wet clothes before you catch a cold."

"How did you know?"

He smiled, and looked dreamy eyed again. "Baby, I know your body better than the back of my hands."

"Yeah, right."

"I'm serious. Your smile and that happy scared look in your eyes gave you away."

"Are you okay with this, Max?"

He sat down. "I'm not thrilled that we're not married. When you wouldn't take the test, I didn't think you were pregnant. That's why I got crazy on you."

My wet dress slid to the floor. He smiled again. "Have you been skipping meals? You look skinnier except for your breasts."

"I've been good. I gave up the tang and the Frosted Flakes. Belinda has been sending me nutritious meals every week since I moved."

Max looked at the bowl of fruit on the table. Then he opened the refrigerator to check it out. The cabinet was filled with a six-month supply of sardines. I told Belinda about my craving. She went to the Food Warehouse and stocked up.

"What's with the sardines?"

"The baby likes them."

"Yuck! Are you sure I'm the father?"

"Shut up. He likes peanut butter too. Besides they're good with hot sauce and crackers."

"Well, at least they're more nutritious than all that sugar you used to eat."

"You never complained about my sugar before." I smiled when Max finally noticed me hovering over him in my panties and bra. "You need me to help you out of your wet clothes?" I whispered into his ear. Then I took off running. He chased me around the table and the sofa while he took his clothes off. When he was down to his briefs I rushed to the bedroom and closed the door. He had me in a body lock and kissed me like a starving man before I could get away.

"You miss me, Max?"

"Every second you're away." He relaxed and leaned against me and sighed. It was nice to feel safe in his arms.

"Have you been good?" I asked.

"Between school and worrying about you I couldn't get it up if I tried."

I giggled. "You don't have a problem now."

He wrestled me to the bed, slipped my panties off and put our hearts in the same place with one smooth movement. We loved with a savage sweetness. It didn't last long; it didn't have to--our hearts were free, but still in the same place.

He kissed me and played with my hair while we laid together still basking in our love. "Sorry I came quickly like that."

"A girl needs to know that her man missed her, and that she has a little power of her own," I added timidly.

"Gabby, let's not fight over power any more. Hell, if you want to know the truth, I lost that fight the day you loved me with that little blue pleated skirt on."

"You're not going to let me live that down are you"

"Never! That was the first time I felt it in my heart. I was serious when I asked you to marry me that day. So, when are you gonna say yes and mean it?"

"Do you want to get married because we still have love power or because we're having a baby? I'm not dropping out of school, and I don't want to marry you if you're not planning to honor our vows."

Max didn't answer, but he didn't argue. We connected our hearts again, but this time the pace was slow and guarded.

The phone rang in the middle of the night. I heard the heavy breathing and slammed it down. Then I felt Max move next to me. I panicked. If it wasn't him, who in the hell was it?

The next morning, I woke up with morning sickness. I hate throwing up more than anything in the world except prejudice, senseless murders, and low down dirty thieves.

Max knocked on the bathroom door. "Are you okay?" He opened the door when I moaned instead of answering. He helped me get back to the bed.

"I thought you said you hadn't been sick."

"This is the first time. I shouldn't have eaten those strange hors d'oeuvres at the party."

"Can't you get a deferment or something on your scholarship? Let's get married. Come back to Nashville. I don't want to leave you here alone."

"I'm okay. I would go crazy in Nashville with nothing to do. And if I didn't go crazy I would drive you crazy."

He chuckled. "I would rather have you driving me crazy like last night, than to go crazy with you here and me there."

"Hold me, Max. I'm going back to sleep." I curled up next to him and rested my head on his shoulder. "I want everything to be sweet like last night. My loving is best when I feel free."

Max played with my hair. "Are you saying you don't want to get married?"

"No, when I say 'free' I mean it in the full sense. Look it up. There are over twenty-five meanings."

"I know what free means."

"Max, sometimes I feel free with you, sometimes I don't. I've been told who, what, when, where, and how since I could breathe. My friends and family said you were no good for me, and your family said I wasn't good enough. I want to be a doctor, your wife, the mother of your children and the only lover you want and need now and forevermore--those are the things that will make me confident and content--those are the things that will make me feel free." I kissed his cheek. "You have my heart and my soul, and I'm going to have our baby. I've always given you the freedom to love me on your own terms, Max. You haven't always done what I wanted, but somehow your kisses made me stay. You should know by now that I give myself to you freely because I'm totally committed to you."

"We should be together, Gabby."

"Max, we are together. My heart is with you wherever you are. Accept my love the way you did that day when I sat on your lap. I had my doubts until you dropped your pants and I sat on you and loved you. I didn't care about anything but us. That was the first time I made love to you. That was the first time I felt free enough to just go with my feelings. You proposed, and I've been yours since."

He smiled and continued to play with my hair. "Baby, that wasn't the first time we made love."

"It was the first time I expressed my love freely. I was told that good girls didn't do it, and if they did they weren't supposed to enjoy it. I was beginning to think I was frigid. That was the first time I had an orgasm."

"You almost got us caught when you screamed. Wait a minute, you mean I don't make you every time?"

"Sorry, sugar. Only when I give myself to you freely." He tried to kiss me. I covered my mouth with my hand. "You don't want to do that."

"Stop lying. You want me to make breakfast?"

"Nope, can't keep anything down before noon. All women fake it occasionally."

"Not with me."

I moaned.

"I thought you said you were okay."

"I am. Ssshhh, I'm going back to sleep." He wrapped me in his warm arms and kissed me on my forehead. I closed my eyes and prayed that we could make it work this time.

❧

I felt better and a bit feisty when I woke up again around noon. I put on Max's robe. Then I went to the bathroom to pee, brush my teeth and rinse and goggle with Listerine. Max was sitting at my desk studying. I sat on his lap after I had freshened up.

"Time for a study break," I said as I kissed his face.

"You want breakfast now?"

"No--I want you, now." I kissed him hard and deep. He stood up and dropped his pants and untied my robe. We were in striking distance when the doorbell rang. Almost was not the place to be.

"Oh, shit! It's my mother. She's coming to get my laundry and her Tupperware."

Almost got closer. The bell rang again. Max froze. Almost slipped back, but the tickle got stronger. I kissed Max and rotated my hips in half circles.

"Come with me, Max. I gotta answer the door."

He smiled and locked my knees under his armpits. "Just making sure you're not faking it."

I leaned back and braced myself on the desk Big Curtis had built. I didn't know what Max was doing, I didn't care. My insides were laughing when I let out a classic squeal.

"Ssshhh. She's gonna hear you."

"Shut up, and hurry up." The chair moved like a rocker. Max took me to the edge and froze again. "Come on, Max. My mother probably heard me scream, she'll call the police if she thinks something is wrong."

He smiled—that sinister, I love you but I'm going to make you pay smile. He was teasing me. I moved my legs and planted my bare feet firmly on the floor. Then I leaned into Max and loved him until I soared like an eagle queen. I screamed satisfaction, hopped up, grabbed a towel, cleaned up, threw the towel to Max, closed the robe and tied a knot.

Max caught the towel. "I can't believe you make your mother do your laundry, and you call me spoiled."

"Shut up. You weren't complaining when I was washing your dirty drawers. My mother can't buy me houses and cars. It's her way of helping me out. I told her she didn't have to do it, but she told me not to look a gift horse in the mouth."

I ran to the door and opened it with a happy smile on my face. "Good morning, Mommy."

"Hey, what took you so long?" she asked.

I probably turned ten shades of red. "You woke me up."

"You didn't wake up that happy when you lived with me," she teased. She looked over my shoulder. "You can come out Max. Where are your manners?"

"How did you know?"

"Your smile, his robe, all that racket y'all was making, and his car parked next to yours."

Max had a mischievous smile on his face when he entered the kitchen where we were. He kissed Belinda on the cheeks and gave her a hug. "Good morning, Mommy."

"Morning, Max, if you and Gabby call one o'clock morning."

"Thanks for taking care of Gabby while I'm in Nashville. I'm trying to convince her to marry me and come home."

"The marriage part I agree with. Instead of shacking up, you should have married her four years ago when Curtis tried to kill her. Now our Gabby got that scholarship and ain't no baby or nothing else gonna stop her from becoming a doctor." Whenever Belinda has her hands on her hips, she means business. "You young folks do things different. But what's good for the goose is better for the gander."

"I told Gabby to check into deferring the scholarship until after the baby is born."

"That's left up to her. I had eleven babies and worked until the day they were born. Ain't no baby ever stopped a woman from doing what she gotta do. That's why God gives the real work to women. You done yo part so you can go on back to Me-harry and let my baby girl get hers."

"I want to do what's right, but Gabby doesn't want to get married." Max slid his arm around me and kissed me on the cheek. "I can take care of her and the baby."

"I'm sure you can, and I'm here to help too. Taking care of my babies is what I do best," Belinda said. I smiled. Max didn't have anything to say about that.

"Get your dirty clothes and my Tupperware ready," Belinda said and she tipped her head in a way that let me know she wanted to speak to Max alone. I left but I stayed within hearing and seeing distance.

"I gave Curtis eleven pretty babies, Max, and if you treat Gabby right, I'm sure she will give you a big family as well." He smiled, but he may not get this lucky again.

"My baby is pretty and all, but she is turning out to be a mighty fine woman. I'm gonna do whatever I can to help her make her dreams come true. You just make sure you're doing right by her while you're up in Nashville."

"Yes, ma'am. I'm straight. I just want my family with me."

"They're gonna be yo family whether they are here or there. Ain't nothing gonna change that. Both of y'all need your schooling, but ain't nothing keeping y'all from getting married but your spoiled ways and bunch of sorry excuses. Gabby, and yo mamma, and daddy done spoiled you. Y'all got a baby on the way now and we all need to get pass the mess and help y'all work this out. Curtis and I got Gabby's back until she gets out of school either way; it's up to y'all to work out the rest. Gabby, what's taking you so long back there?"

I put on my jeans and a T-shirt. Then I yanked the sheets off my bed, picked up the towel and stuffed everything into my large wicker hamper. I pushed the hamper into the bedroom and called Max. I felt a tinge of guilt. Seeing Belinda work her fingers to the bone for our family and other families has always been a motivating factor for me. She could have done a lot more with her wisdom if she hadn't gotten pregnant at sixteen. She didn't have birth control to forget to take. She had a good-looking husband who couldn't keep his hands off his pretty young wife. Daddy once told me that Mommy and his children helped him to forget about the ugly things in the world that he couldn't change. I want my parents to have something other than their children and grandchildren to brag about. Lorna is going to be a star soon, and I'm going to be a doctor. Mommy came with Max into my bedroom.

She gave Max the keys to her car. "Put that hamper in my trunk, and bring that bag of maternity dresses Hope sent for Gabby."

"Don't worry, I'm going to take care of Gabby and the baby even though she won't marry me. She doesn't need anybody's hand-me-downs."

"I never said I didn't want to marry you, Max."

"What did I tell you to do, Max?" Belinda asked.

He smiled and went to the car. He loves it when Mommy fusses over him like one of hers. After he left she got on my case, which was probably her plan all along.

"Put your brassiere on. You're sitting high and mighty now, but if you don't wear your brassiere while you're pregnant by the time you finish nursing those things will be down to your knees."

I sucked my teeth and rolled my eyes. Belinda threatened to sail me into next year for disrespecting her, and then she left. I popped open a can of sardines, put them on a plate, and soaked them in hot sauce. Max came back and sat a bag of clothes next to me. They smelled like mothballs and cedar.

"Gabby, those things stink."

"Not as bad as those clothes."

"Baby, I need to go see my parents."

"We can go after dinner? I need to study."

"It will be better if I'm alone when I tell them," he said and then he left.

18

L orna and Harold stopped by while Max was out. Harold had gotten rid of the gold teeth and the drippy-drip hair, and Lorna looked as if she had been in Belk and raided the place. She hugged me. We went to my bedroom to talk while Harold watched a Mississippi State vs. Arkansas game on TV. We let our feet dangle over the edge of the bed while we chatted like a couple of teenage girls.

"Are you all right with this baby thing," Lorna asked. "I'll hook you up if you can't hang."

"I'm hanging. I still regret letting you talk me into doing that the first time. I was starting to get excited about this baby until Max said it was best if he breaks the news to his parents alone."

"Max doesn't want you to have the baby?"

"He loves kids. He wants me to marry him, forget school, and move to Nashville."

"And if you don't?"

"He didn't say, but he's worried about how his parents are going to react."

"Do you think they will disown him?"

"No, but I'm sure they will be disappointed."

Lorna frowned. "Is he still messing around?"

"He says that he's not, but I can't worry about that now."

"What about the baby."

"It's still his baby. I love him. I just can't live with his terms right now. Belinda and Big Momma are behind me. It has to work out"

"I saw you teaching Brad how to dance. Did you give him some yet?"

I giggled despite myself. "No--we're just friends."

"Let me get this straight. You let Max do whatever the hell he wants to do while you sit in this big fine ass apartment and wait?" Lorna glanced around my bedroom. "Any plain fool can see that Brad has a thing for you. Girl, you can't be my sister." Lorna whispered, "When Harold is out of town, which thank God is often, I let Richard come over and tighten me up. Did I tell you he plays football for JSU?"

"You didn't have to—he's JSU's pride and joy." Lorna and I always had a thing for football players. "I'm so busy studying; I don't have time to think about sex. I wouldn't feel right doing it with someone else while I'm pregnant anyway."

"Why not?" Lorna chuckled. "You can't get pregnant."

"It's not right."

Lorna frowned like she could smell the sardines on my breath. "What's not right is men get to have their cake and eat it too. When you said, you were pregnant, I thought you were joking. You're not the type to accidentally get pregnant again, so what's the deal?"

"No deal. I was giving my body a break from the pill, then Max caught me at a time when I wasn't thinking straight. So, Lorna, how did you get Harold to get rid of his Jeri-Kurl and those gold teeth?"

"That was easy--I told him they had to go."

"You have that much power over him? Can you help your baby sister out?"

"I wouldn't kiss him, and he wasn't coming anywhere near my satin sheets with that greasy hair."

"You used sex to get what you wanted."

"Nope, he wanted sex. It doesn't take much to please him. Most of the time, all I have to do is get naked and lay on him. That shit does wonders for my ego. He will give me anything I want. I call Richard when I want to ride a bull. So, when was the last time you saw Mr. Rich, Fine, and sex you up, Max?"

"Right before you came." I blushed. "He should be back soon. He went to see Mommy Dearest."

"Why didn't you go?"

"I told you. Max didn't want me to get upset if his mother showed her ass. He said it is an embarrassment to him and his family that we are not married. His mother gave me all this stuff. She was glad to see me go."

"So, when are you getting married?"

"Before I start showing. I have to convince Max to let me stay here though."

"Well, I better go before he gets back."

"Why don't you like, Max?"

"It's not that I don't like him--I can't stand the way you let him treat you."

"I let him cheat occasionally because it makes it easier to do what I have to do. Those other women don't mean anything to him. I know I thought the same thing about Anthony, but he messed around because I hated sex with him. Max is whipped by my loving; he's a brat who acts up when he can't have his way."

Max can have almost any woman he wants, which is why he needs a woman who can take care of herself. I can't stop women from chasing him. I'm going to chase my own dreams in the meantime. Max would marry me today if I agreed to his terms. It would be nice to be married when our baby is born, but if I agree to his terms I will probably end up resenting him and the baby. The key to my future and my happiness is in my hands. I can't expect Max to make me happy if I'm not happy with myself.

Lorna agreed with me being happy with myself, but she disagreed about me letting Max cheat if I didn't plan to cheat as well. Harold was helping her with her music. He took her to California to meet some people in the business. She had to sing her ass off to impress his contacts. She is waiting to hear back from them. We hugged, and I wished her luck before she and Harold left.

Max came back in a sour mood long after Lorna and Harold had left. We went to Red Lobster to celebrate our pregnancy. We made plans to get married on my birthday, which just happens to fall on Thanksgiving Day this year. His mood didn't change much at dinner, or when we set our wedding date. He refused to talk about his visit with his parents. He swore up and down that it had nothing to do with me, or the baby since he didn't get a chance to tell them our news. He went back to Nashville after dinner so he could study for an exam. My instincts told me there may be something going on in Nashville that he doesn't want me to know about. I made a mental note to call Gretchen. She could check things out, and keep an eye on Max for me.

PART THREE

"Rich and powerful families make the rules, and everyone else has to follow them or suffer the consequences."

Gabriella Oliver.

19

I must have been crazy when I let Brad talk me into helping him host a Halloween party for our class. Everyone had to pay a dollar toward the keg, and everyone had to wear a costume. That was the price of admission. I made orange and black streamers, carved pumpkins into scary jack-o-lanterns, and hung fake spider webs and scary goblins all around his house. Brad called a caterer and ordered those unidentifiable hot and cold hors d'oeuvres. He rented Frankenstein and his bride costumes for us to wear. I wore the Frankenstein costume and Brad made such a cute bride he was almost scary. Rachel came as Elvira.

One guy came dressed as a prostitute with a black eye, hairy legs, heavy blue eye-shadow and a ripped red mini dress. His partner in crime was wearing a yellow pimp suit and platform shoes. He had on an Afro wig with a black power fist pick sticking out. His face was covered with brown makeup.

"Where's my money bitch?" the pimp asked.

"I didn't make any money tonight," the prostitute answered.

"I done told you to take yo ass to Mr. P's. Those niggers don't give a damn about how ugly you are as long as you're white, bitch."

I took my Frankenstein mask off. Brad and the two pranksters turned three shades of red. The pimp snatched his Afro wig off and started wiping the brown from his face. It was Christine's husband!

He ruined my party mood. Everybody else seemed to be having a good time. After the pimp and whore got a few more brews under their belts, they went back to their pranks.

Brad's moans woke me up the next morning. The last thing I remember, was drinking punch, and leaning over the toilet. Last night I thought it was just a pregnancy thing, but now I'm not so sure. I hopped out of Brad's bed. He was in his underwear. My legs had been tangled with his! Thank God, I was still in costume. Someone must have slipped something in the punch. I ran to the bathroom to check myself in the mirror. I rushed home to call Max even though I was sure Julius and Maryanne had already spotted my car. Max wanted the lowdown on the party. I told him the pimp and whore story.

"It didn't sound like too much fun, so why did you spend the night?" he asked.

"The smell of smoke and beer made me dizzy," I said quickly. "I intended to lie down in Brad's guest room until I felt better, but I didn't wake-up until morning." I emphasized guest room, and I didn't want to make matters worse by bringing up the possibility of being drugged.

"Baby, you should try to defer your scholarship."

"I'm okay--it was the strange food again. I miss you, Max. When are you coming to see me?"

"I don't know, but I need to get down there soon. Brad is getting too cozy with my babies."

I giggled. "I love it when you talk like that. I miss waking up with you."

"What would you do if you could wake up with me every day?"

I giggled again and said, "You know."

"I forgot--why don't you remind me."

I did--in details that shocked him, and me too.

Thank God it was Friday, my favorite day of the week. I'd had three exams and morning sickness every day, and I was as horny as a dog in heat after talking dirty to Max. I had fallen asleep early all week so we hadn't talked since Sunday. The phone rang in the middle of the night last night. Some pervert was breathing heavy in my ear. I slammed it down and tried to go back to sleep. I dreamed about Sara and that threatening note, and I was afraid to close my eyes. I've been avoiding Christine since Brad's party. Her husband wants to get together with Max and me. I don't want to be anywhere near her crazy ass husband. He could have killed Sara to keep her from telling Christine about their affair. After the pranks he pulled at Brad's, I don't put anything pass him.

I skipped happy hour at Friday's with my classmates. I wanted to rush home and call Max. I wanted to convince him to make a midnight run for some good loving. I needed to wake up in his arms, but when I dialed his number some bitch named Alma answered his phone like she lives there. I hung up and dialed his number again. She answered again. Alma had the nerve to tell me to stop calling her man's house. I threw a few things in my suitcase. I was going to drive to Nashville to kick some booty. The only Alma I knew was Gretchen's best friend from high school. I made another mental note to call Gretchen.

My classmates don't need to know I'm pregnant, but those Nashville hussies need to know to leave my Max alone. Pregnancy had turned my firecracker temper into cherry bombs, but I was a big bang with no follow-up. That song by the Dells that our baby was probably conceived to came on the radio. I curled up in the middle of my bed and cried like a newborn. I was in no condition to drive even though I was ready to kill Max when the phone rang again.

Brad asked me if I was okay; he had noticed that I hadn't been myself since he told me Christine's husband had slipped me Quaaludes at the party because he thought I was too uptight.

"So, is Max coming this weekend?" Brad asked.

I didn't want Brad to hear me cry, but I couldn't help it.

"I didn't mean to upset you."

"I'll be okay," I said. Then I hung up abruptly.

Twenty minutes later Brad was knocking on my door. He had a bottle of wine in his hands, love and concern in his eyes, and he gave me a tight hug that begged for more. I let him in. Maybe it was my hug that was doing the begging. He opened the wine and poured two glasses. I was tempted, but I didn't. I asked Brad if he thought I was crazy when I told him about Alma; he thought I was in love.

"Crazy in love," I said.

"You should let Max explain."

"I've already heard every excuse in the book. He will say she doesn't mean anything, and that he only loves me, but since I refused to marry him--," I started crying again.

Brad hugged me and offered me his handkerchief. "You want to hear one of my dirty jokes?" he asked after I calmed down again.

"Sure. Tell me a joke."

"Brad polished off his second glass of wine and said, "There was this medical student who was fond of pleasing women, but he wasn't particularly endowed, if you know what I mean. So, he prayed every night that his tally whacker would grow until it touched the floor. And sure enough, one morning he woke up and his soldier was at attention and when he got out of his bed, his legs fell off, and his tally whacker banged into the floor."

"Ha, ha, very funny. You should be more careful about what you pray for, Brad."

"It made you laugh, and you're not easy." His eyes moved from a "letting a friend cry on his shoulder look," to a hooded "let a friend share your bed look," and I could almost understand how Max got into trouble with Tammy. Almost.

"I have to go to my father's sixtieth birthday party tomorrow... Will you come with me?"

I couldn't think of a reason to say "no" so I made a lame excuse about not having a gift or anything to wear.

"I'll take care of it," he said.

"I want to be alone."

"That's the last thing you need."

"You should ask someone you care about."

"I care about you."

"We're just friends."

"I don't want to go alone--please come."

"Okay," I said. Brad touched his lips gently to mine. I didn't resist.

20

I called Max again at midnight to burst his bubble. No one answered. When I got up to pee at six a.m., I called again. No one answered. I was mad as a fighting rooster when Brad arrived with an expensive party dress and a pearl necklace with matching earrings for me to wear to the party. It was noon and I hadn't heard a word from Max. The dress was sky blue--the same color as Max's sheets. It was perfect. I grabbed my overnight bag and we left.

Two hours later Brad pulled into a long driveway lined with tall perfectly manicured hedges, and an arched wrought-iron gate with Edgewood Manor written on it. Brad had described his family's residence as an ordinary house sitting in the middle of a flat parcel of land surrounded by tall pine and magnolia trees. I was in awe of the huge white antebellum mansion until I reminded myself that we were in the heart of the Mississippi Delta on a plantation. It was a huge white mansion with green shutters and large windows that were all draped with frilly lace curtains. Massive columns ran from the front porch to the second-floor roof. It had double wide stained-glassed front doors. But it was the green grandma and grandpa rocking chairs that sat on one corner of the porch, and several smaller cottages, which sat back away from the big house that made me feel as if I had stepped one-hundred-years back into time.

"I'm not so sure about this, Brad," I said when strange flutters began to build up in my stomach. If his family had treated a green-eyed curly-head blond like crap what did they have in store for me? "You know how my temper is."

"Be yourself, Gabby. My parents will love you." He smiled at me lovingly.

I frowned. "You think so?"

"Don't worry. I'm not the same Brad who brought Ingrid home four years ago."

"Why do they call this place a manor, anyway?"

Brad stopped his car in front of the main house. A tall black man with snow white hair opened my door for me. He was wearing a black tuxedo and white gloves. Brad greeted him with a Southern twang that was completely different from the barely detectable Southern drawl I was used to hearing.

"Cecil this is my guest, Gabriella Oliver. Make sure she is comfortable while she is here. Her things are in the back."

"Sir, should I put Miss Oliver's things in the guest house or the main house."

"The guest house."

I looked away when Cecil's smile turned to disdain.

"And you sir? Should I put your things in the pool--?"

"The main house," Brad said, and Cecil didn't try to hide the relief in his smile.

Brad had his hand on the center of my back as he ushered me up the six steps leading to the porch. Cecil opened the large double doors. We entered the house and I got a peek at yet another world. The foyer flanked a high ceiling, marble floors, and a table with a huge arrangement of purple, pink, and yellow irises, lilies, and roses. There was a large crystal chandelier which provided perfectly dim light, and when I looked up, the domed ceiling was painted with angels. The house was even more grandiose than Max's parents' house and the mansions Belinda used to work in.

My stomach churned. It was too early for the baby to be kicking, but something was going on. They don't tell us about this part of Mississippi history in school. No one questions why rebel flags still wave at the Capitol. Nobody wants to tell the truth about how rich Mississippians continue to get over on their poor black and white citizens.

Brad's mother was a petite blond with a perfect Southern belle aura. She looked at least twenty years younger than his father. Brad looks and dresses like his father, but he is almost three times younger.

Brad introduced his parents as, Samantha and Trenton Pruter. He told them I was the friend from school he had told them about. They smiled and extended their hands.

"It's nice to finally meet you," Trenton said. He gripped my hand and Samantha smiled gingerly. Brad and Samantha showed me the mansion and gave me the history of the most recent renovations. Samantha pointed out the original structure and artwork without dabbing into the history of the plantation.

I waited in Trenton's library while Brad had a few private words with his parents. I lounged on one of two burgundy leather sofas, which sat perpendicular to a large rustic fireplace. The design in the Persian rug and the carvings in the cherry coffee table and mantel piece held my attention for a while. I tapped my fingers and tried to stay out of trouble, but the leather-bound law books that lined an entire wall from the floor to the ceiling fascinated me. One book stuck out like a pointed middle finger. I studied the chandelier and the large cherry desk by the window, but my eyes kept drifting to the tattered book tucked in the corner of the highest book shelf.

I couldn't resist. I pushed the heavy ladder to the end of the book-shelves. I'm afraid of heights, but I climbed each step carefully. Then I grabbed the book, tucked it under my arm and backed down the stairs slowly.

The property of John Winston Pruter circa 1860-1865 was written on the first page. The next page listed his slaves by their first name--Ruth, Bob, Annie, Pearl, Leroy. Their approximate age, size and a general description was next to their name--14-year-old male, built like and ox, scar on left cheek; 15-year-old female, wet nursing tan baby. Notations were made when children were born and who the parents were. There were some notations that listed the father as unknown. Those mothers and their babies were usually sold shortly after they gave birth. The only other slaves who were sold were runaways who had been returned to the plantation. Over two hundred slaves were listed. I was so engrossed in the ledger I didn't even bother to look up when I heard someone enter the room.

The Pruter men or their help had been busy. I was counting the number of women and babies who had been sold when I felt Brad and his father standing near me. I closed the book and sat up innocently in Mr. Pruter's chair. The look in Brad's eyes was like a buck who had stepped into the light of an oncoming car. Fear, indecision, blindness too quickly can only result in panic. I looked from Brad to Trenton. We stared at each other a tense second. I was looking for the Pruter shame. There was none. I stood up too quickly and sent the rolling desk chair flying toward the window. Brad rushed over to prevent it from smashing the windowpane.

"Son, you didn't mention that Gabriella is interested in law," Trenton said. His powerful voice shattered the silence like an alarm clock set two hours early. Cold chills ran up and down my spine. I had a million questions I wanted to ask, but I was dumbfounded. Brad put his hand on the small of my back and nudged me away from the desk.

"You should see how quickly Gabby can carve little blocks of wax into teeth. She has brains, talent and beauty."

There was no shame in Trenton's game when he looked me over. "She is beautiful." He smiled wickedly and said, "But I'll have to take your word on the brains and talent." Then his eyes focused on the closed ledger. Brad picked up the book and put it back on the shelf. My eyes and Trenton's followed each movement.

"I'll show you to your room now," Brad said nervously. "If you're like most women, you'll need some extra time to get ready for the party." Brad was talking to me, but his eyes were on his father.

"Mr. Pruter, you have some interesting books. Perhaps we can sit down and talk about them another time." I said, and Brad almost pushed me out the room.

The pool cottage had an old South feeling as well. It was decorated with the finest Laura Ashley linens, and the Queen Anne bed looked as if it had seen a few generations. It was the most inviting bed I've ever seen. The fluffy yellow comforter with a gladiolus print and white lace trim, and the matching wallpaper, curtains and a silk-screen canopy took my mind off the proof that Brad's ancestors were former slave owners, just as Max had said. I was probably going to be sleeping in restored slave quarters. Although everything about the room had a Norman Rockwell feel of ordinary people on a calm ordinary day, my insides were jumping around like runaway slaves.

"I hope everything is to your likings, Miss Gabby." The sound of Brad's voice brought me out of my reverie.

"Bradley Pruter, where did you find that convenient Southern drawl?"

"Why everyone talks this way in these here parts, Miss Gabby."

I knew he was trying to make light of the situation when I said, "What in the hell have you gotten me into?"

"Don't worry, I'll protect you."

"Is that what your forefathers did when they sold their wenches and their babies?"

"None of that has anything to do with us," he said. His tone of voice sounded more familiar as he raked his hand through his hair, and his cheeks turned bright pink.

"Don't fool yourself, Brad. Change takes a long time, and even longer in Mississippi."

"It was a long time ago." He sounded a bit frustrated or was he irritated.

"Those mothers were penalized for something they had no control over. Their children were outcast, and later pitted against their darker sisters and brothers to keep the race divided. That animosity still exists today. There was so much loathing in Cecil's eyes when he looked at me, I wanted to run under a bush and hide."

"I'm sorry, but I don't understand what all the fuss is about. Things have changed. My family is different now." Brad said.

"I guess I shouldn't expect you, of all people, to understand. It's not your problem, but don't think it doesn't have anything to do with you. It has everything to do with powerful families like yours. You all make the rules, and the rest of us suffer the consequences."

"I'm going to get dressed. You shouldn't worry about things you can't change."

"Denial certainly won't change anything," I shouted.

Brad stepped back. "I'm not in denial. If I could change the past I would. I'll send Cecil over with you a mint julep to calm your nerves. He makes the best juleps in the Delta."

"I stopped drinking. If you were my friend, you would have noticed by now. Big Momma gave me a special blend of tea. Tell Cecil to bring me a cup of hot water and a lemon. Never mind, ain't nothing wrong with my legs, I'll go to the damn kitchen and get my own water."

"Oh, no you will not! Miss Emma doesn't allow strangers in her kitchen. She's already beside herself because the caterers have taken it over. What's the big deal? Cecil can bring you the water."

"Forget it, Brad. I don't want to bother Cecil." Brad shrugged his shoulders and said he would be back to escort me to the party around six o'clock.

I said, "Whatever." He shook his head and left.

Cecil brought me a sterling silver tea pot filled with hot water, several different blends of teas, a couple of wedges of lemon, and freshly baked cookies on a serving tray a few minutes later. I apologized for bothering him. He said it wasn't a problem, but his face said he hated serving little Bradley's high-yellow wench.

𝒬

Sky-blue is not a color I wear often. The blue silk chiffon dress brought out the pink undertones in my skin. Since I was in a Civil War mood, I showed off the pearls around my long neck by pulling my hair up into the perfect *Gone with the Wind* hairdo. The scooped neckline was perfect for my full breasts. I put on a light cover of makeup except for the tomato-red lipstick on my full lips. Pregnancy was still agreeing with me in the looks department. My skin was radiant, my breasts were fuller and perkier, and I had gained some much needed behind and hips.

Brad knocked on my door at six wearing a black tuxedo with a sky-blue ascot. We looked like a couple. Brad's eyes had that dreamy look in them that Max gets when we make love. "You look stunning," was all he said and all he needed to say. I blushed and offered him my elbow.

One hundred distinguished Mississippians were expected including the Governor and the Lieutenant Governor. I wondered if Brad's family were on the side of the bad guys or if they had been helpless good whites as far as the civil rights movements were concerned.

There were three black couples at the party. All three were token black lawyers in Brad's father's firms. None of them were partners although they smiled as though they were being compensated very well. They were all nice to me on the surface; it was obvious that I was Brad's date.

I was received the same by the white and the black couples when Brad introduced me. They all smiled, but their eyes didn't. The only exceptions were the older, bolder, have never had anything to lose because they are rich Southern white men. Their eyes swept across my chest and lingered much longer than is polite for Southern gentlemen. Their eyes percolated with sexual desire, and their smiles and their comments complimented them.

The food was served by a Black service crew who were wearing black pants or skirts, white tuxedo shirts, red bow ties, and white gloves. The catering staff floated around the ballroom of the mansion all evening. Brad's hand felt like it was glued to the small of my back as he ushered me around the room and worked the crowd.

The music ranged from classical, to blues, to country, to pop. I danced with Brad a few times. We were already dancing when the song switched to *Still* by the Commodores. He wrapped his arms around me before I could make an excuse to take a break. My mind switched to Max and Alma, and I couldn't stop my tears from falling. Brad held me tighter. I smudged his tuxedo shirt with my mascara and lipstick. He took me to his father's library when the song ended and locked the doors.

Brad wiped my tears with the pads of his fingers. He was dreamy eyed so I wasn't surprised when his lips covered mine. I was surprised by the way I relaxed and enjoyed his kiss just as I had done Max's all those years ago. I wanted to thank Brad for the many ways he had been my friend without falling in love with him.

After the kiss ended I told him I was sorry. I didn't mean to get emotional on him. He said he understood then he asked me if I felt up to going back to the party. I wanted to wish his father a happy birthday and call it a night.

He gave me his handkerchief. I fixed my make-up and applied some fresh lipstick. Then I wiped my lipstick from Brad's lips with my fingers. He sucked my fingertips into his mouth. I hoped he didn't feel me shiver.

"I'm sorry. I ruined your shirt," I said again.

"It's okay. I'll run upstairs and change. Would you like to come?"

I had a flash of me screwing Brad in my sky-blue silk chiffon dress on the edge of his bed. "I'll wait here." He blushed as though he had read my naughty thoughts. "I won't touch anything." I held up my right hand. "I promise." He smiled again and left.

We chatted with Brad's parents when we returned to the party. Every time we made a motion to leave someone else important strolled over and started a conversation with Brad and his father.

I chatted with Samantha who seemed nervous at first, but she relaxed as the conversation progressed. She was easy listening compared to Maryanne until she said, "I've had a tough time dealing with the feelings my son has for you, but Trent and I aren't going to make the same mistake with you that we made with Ingrid."

I looked for Brad in the crowd. He was across the room. He smiled, and looked at me dreamy eyed. I wondered how he could have those kinds of feelings knowing that I'm in love with Max, and when did I let myself have more than innocent feelings for him?

"Mississippi is changing. There has been a lot of bad blood between the races, but I think it's time we change some of the ways we think. Don't you?" Samantha asked.

"I agree totally." My eyes never left Brad's, and his were focused on me.

"I want my son to be happy. He tells me you all are just friends, but... Gabriella--that's a beautiful name."

"Thank you."

"Are you part Spanish?"

The runaway slaves were active again in my belly. I felt my blood rise to my cheeks. "Brad and I are friends. He is aware of my love for my fiancé. You don't have to concern yourself with my background."

"My only concerns are for my son's happiness." We locked eyes until mine found Brad's across the room again. "I know what I see in Bradley's eyes, and it's a lot more than like." Brad crossed the room and grabbed two glasses of champagne off a tray on his way. He gave me a glass and held up his glass as he called for everyone's attention. A server brought Samantha a fresh glass. The room got quiet and all eyes were on Brad.

"Mother and I would like to thank you all for coming this evening to help us celebrate the birthday of the man many of you have come to respect as a leader in the community, and the man who signs your checks." The crowd laughed. "I would like to propose a toast to my father, John Trenton Pruter." Mr. Pruter joined his wife and me and put his hands around both our waists.

"Daddy taught me everything I know about being the outstanding young man you all say I am. Of course, there is always the possibility that he paid you all to say it." We all chuckled again. "But seriously folks, Daddy taught me to reach out to others when they need a helping hand. He taught me the importance of taking care of and protecting women and children. He was there when I took my first steps, my first drive, had my first date, and when I had my first heartbreak." Brad paused and cleared his throat. He glanced at his parents and me and continued. "Those were all very important lessons, but they don't come close to the lesson Daddy taught me tonight and that is; real men follow their hearts, stand firm on their beliefs, and they are not afraid of change." Brad held up his champagne glass. "To, John Trenton Pruter, and to all of you I say three cheers to a man who believes in his words and lives them every day."

Brad gave his father and emotional hug after the toast. Then Samantha joined them in another hug, and soon Brad and his family were hugging me, and cameras were flashing everywhere. We posed for several pictures for photographers and friends before Brad walked me to the cottage. He kissed me on the lips and I went inside and slipped on the slinky purple night gown I had planned to wear for Max before I climbed into the fluffy bed.

I didn't know if I was falling for Brad or getting back at Max. I opened my Biochemistry book and began reading about the energy cycles out loud to block thoughts of both men. I couldn't concentrate after I heard someone splashing around in the pool. It was November. Didn't the same rules apply for swimming as for white clothes and shoes, and patent leather? Most of my family would say it was a chilly night. I love late fall and winters in Mississippi. I continued to read while I listened to the sound of splashing water. It stopped after a while and a few minutes later there was a knock on my door.

I hopped out the bed and answered it. Brad was standing in the doorway in his red Speedos dripping wet and shivering. A cool breeze whipped by and made me aware of my own nakedness.

"You're going to catch pneumonia, Bradley Pruter."

He smiled and swept his eyes over my almost sheer night gown. "I feel warmer just looking at you."

"You're shivering. Are you crazy? It's forty-five degrees!"

"The water feels great." His teeth were chattering. "You want to go skinny dipping?"

"No thanks. I hate cold water."

"Well, are you gonna let me catch pneumonia or invite me in?"

I stared at him. He had a mischievous look in his eyes, but I thought I could control the situation. "It's your house."

"But it's your call."

"Don't be foolish, Brad, you're standing there with goosebumps all over you."

He pulled me in his arms, covered my lips with his, and kicked the door closed.

21

I knew not what I was doing. I still hadn't figured out when I was being driven by lust, love, friendship, fear or anger. Brad made a trail of kisses from my ear to my shoulders. I held his cold wet body close to mine. He slipped my gown off my shoulders. It slid down my body and teased my flesh like brush strokes of hot flames before it pooled around my feet. Brad smiled. I walked into his arms again to prevent him from seeing my fears, my lust, my shame.

He whispered, "I won't hurt you."

I held him tighter. He held my face between his hands. His eyes asked if we would still be friends. His deep kisses let me know we couldn't have it both ways. I held his damp body as if he was going to slip away. He kissed my neck. I extended it. He slipped his Speedos off. We stared at each other for answers that neither could provide until...

Brad wouldn't hurt me. He had promised. I knew not what I felt or what I was doing. He kissed my lips, my neck, and my hypersensitive pregnant breasts. I knew not what to do. He placed his hand around mine and led the way. We climbed into the big fluffy bed. We kissed and kissed. I knew not what I wanted or needed, but I was hypersensitive to his touch. Would he love me and cheat like Max and Anthony? Are white men any different? Brad kissed my pregnant belly the way I wanted Max to kiss it. Then he moved down and kissed me there! I could only imagine a man giving a woman so much pleasure from the stories my English friend, Hanna Lennon, used to tell me at her sleepovers. I would tell her stories about me and Anthony finger knocking, which was actually better than sex with him, and she would tell me stories about her boyfriend kissing her like Brad was kissing me, which wasn't bad either. It used to sound nasty in high school. But Brad had me whimpering and damn near crying from the pleasure he was bestowing upon me. He kissed his way back to my lips and gave me full body shivers when I tasted my salty-sweet self. It was my first time.

That brought my mind back to Max. He had never ever done what Brad had done. I had no idea. Brad kissed me again and asked if he could? That brought me back to Mississippi. I couldn't make love to him in his bed on his plantation. My ancestors had been raped and sold away by his forefathers. My grandmother had been killed over this type of thing. I was pregnant with another man's child--a black man--a prouder than proud black man. I'm still in love with Max and no matter what happens between Brad and me, Max will still be the father of my growing child.

Hanna and I used to call this heavy petting. We thought we were good virgin girls in those days. We thought this was foreplay and it didn't really count, but it would matter to Max--it matters to me!

I couldn't look Brad in his eyes. I couldn't answer. It didn't matter how far we went. We had already ruined a perfect friendship. I turned away when a tear trickled down my cheek. How did I go from valedictorian and magna cum laude to this? I'm supposed to be smart. I cried for letting myself get pregnant, for putting up with Max's crap, for loving Max, and for this.

"Don't cry, Gabby. I won't hurt you. I promise."

Pictures of young slave girls being raped, and men who look like Max being lynched by men who look like Brad danced around in my head. I saw poor black families working from sun up until sun down as sharecroppers while men like Brad danced to chamber music in their parlors with angels painted on the ceilings. I saw black children in raggedy school houses while the sweat of their parents paid taxes which supported nice schools for whites only. I saw the old four room house we used to live in until the VA approved Daddy's loan so he could build the house my parents live in now. I used to think it was fun to catch the rain in pots and pans, and to feel the wind blowing through the holes in the walls in the winter.

I wanted to hate Brad for not paying my people fairly for their hard work. Where was he when white men like him could have prevented my people from suffering? It's almost a new decade and his family is just realizing that it is time to make some changes.

"Look at me, Gabby. Please don't cry. I'll leave if you want me to go, but please don't cry."

"I can't believe I'm on a plantation in the heart of the Mississippi Delta in bed with someone from the so-called master race."

Brad turned beet red and his thingie went limp. His pupils were fully dilated, and all I could think about was drowning in the deep blue sea that opened in them. I didn't know if I was going to drown in his ocean blues, or if I already had. I didn't know if he was starting to get it or if he was upset because I had blown the mood. He ran his fingers through his wet hair, blew out a breath of air and rolled over on his back.

"It's not like that, Gabby. You can't blame me for everything that happened to your people in Mississippi. That's too much of a burden."

"Look at me, Brad, and tell me what you see."

"I see a beautiful woman."

"What else? What makes me beautiful? Is it my perfect permanently tan skin, or is it my perfectly shaped nose and wide set oval eyes? Perhaps it's my high cheek bones and my supple full lips. Maybe it is my long silky hair with just the right amount of curl. What is it, Brad? Tell me!" I yelled.

"It's all of that and more."

"What more, Brad. Tell me, because all my life I've been the outcast of the people you call mine and the outcast of the people you call yours. Black people look at me and hate me because they see too much of you, and white people look at me and hate me because they see the ugliest part of their history." Brad looked at me as though he was surprised.

"I'm not like that, Gabby. When I meet you, I saw a beautiful woman. The more I get to know you I see a beautiful person. I don't care what color you are."

"Didn't your father tell you to crossover with darker girls so you can't recognize your face when the baby comes?"

"Stop it, Gabby! This is crazy talk. I don't give a shit about your color. I wouldn't change anything about you!" he yelled.

"I want you to understand what the fuss is about, Brad. I want you to understand why I'm angry. I don't want you to continue thinking it doesn't have anything to do with you. Men like you created women like me. My grandfather was a rich white man just like you. I can't say for sure if he raped my grandmother, but I know he made her options very limited. Men like you don't stop there, hell no, you find ways to make us hate each other, and hate ourselves. You may have the privilege of not giving a shit about my color, but I can't afford that luxury!"

Brad stared at the ceiling and looked helpless. We slept together--flat on our back, naked to the world and to each other. There was no kissing, touching, or talking, and no forgetting this time.

🙾

The bright sunrise and the sound of Brad splashing around in the pool woke me up. I showered and dressed quickly in my tomato-red sweater dress even though I figured I was the last person Brad wanted to see. I had nausea, but Big Momma's tea in some hot water from the faucet helped.

There was a knock on the door. I flung it open and stepped to the side, but it wasn't Brad.

"Miss Gabby, Mr. Bradley would like to know if you would like to join him and his family for breakfast or if you would like me to serve you here?"

"Please give my apologies to Mr. and Mrs. Pruter; I'm feeling a bit under the weather this morning. I'm going to pass on breakfast all together."

Cecil's disgusting look quickly turned to one of concern. "Would you like some hot water and a lemon for your tea, ma'am?"

"That would be nice, Cecil. Thank you. I really hate to bother you."

"It's not a problem, Miss Gabby."

"Would you please drop the Miss routine? I'm no different from you Cecil. My momma does the same thing as you and Miss Emma, and it's not what it looks like."

"Miss Gabby, you're Mr. Bradley's guest. It's my job to make sure you're comfortable." He cleared his throat. "I know it's not my business, but Emma thinks you're pregnant with Mr. Bradley's child."

I laughed from my gut. "You're right it's not your business, but it's not his. How did Miss Emma know?"

"Emma just knows these things. I don't know how."

"My Big Momma knew as well. I told you, I'm no different from you." Cecil smiled and left.

I was much nicer when I heard the second knock. It was Brad standing with the hot water and lemon for my tea. He came in, sat the tray down and closed the door.

"I'm really sorry about last night," he said. His head dropped, and I looked away.

"So am I, Bradley."

"Cecil said you weren't feeling well."

I put the tea holder in the cup and poured the hot water over it. "I'm okay. It's just morning sickness." I chuckled. "Cecil and Miss Emma thought it was yours."

Brad turned as white as a sheet of paper and sat in a chair while he digested the news. "You're pregnant? How? Why didn't you tell me?"

"I swallowed a watermelon seed."

"Gabby, I thought I was your friend."

"You are. I was going to tell you last night, but— "

"When are you and Max getting married?"

"I don't know--maybe never."

"He wouldn't walk out on you while you're pregnant, would he? You guys have to work out your differences."

"Right now, I don't have any more words for either one of you."

Brad dropped his head again. "If I had known... I wouldn't have... God, Gabby, I'm sorry..." He stood up. "I'm gonna spend some time with my folks. We can leave around noon if it's okay with you."

❧

The drive home was like the ride I had taken from Nashville two months ago. My heart was breaking the same as it had done when Tammy opened Max's door. I-55 is the flattest, straightest road I've ever seen. I could see for miles, but there was nothing to see except tall pine trees, huge live oaks trees, soybeans and cotton fields, a few livestock and old abandoned shacks. I read Biochemistry to get my mind off Max and Brad. Brad kept his eyes glued to the road. I wished I was driving; at least I could blow off some steam. Brad's Sunday driving was making me crazy. He should have been ready to get rid of me after the way I had treated him. Brad doesn't let anything upset him. It must be nice to live a stress-free life, and to have a father, and friends who can fix damn near anything.

My mind drifted back to the plantation and reconstruction. When I was in school the history books we were provided with said reconstruction was a good time for blacks in Mississippi, but I later learned that even that was mostly lies. Whites were afraid of blacks taking the jobs and getting involved in politics. Many blacks were threatened, their houses and their businesses were burned, they were run off their farms and if they got to uppity many were lynched. They used to call them human barbecues. What kind of shit is that? During the civil rights struggle people died just to obtain decent schools and the right to vote. Big Curtis is so bitter he is a registered voter, but he says after all that, there is nobody worth voting for. He still has nightmares about the things that happened to him when he was a boy and in WWII. When he got home from the war he couldn't even walk around in his uniform without fear. But Belinda says too many people lost their lives in the fight not to take advantage of the right to vote even if you must vote for the lesser of two evils.

When I tell her I shook the Governor's hand, she will probably say, that's good, baby girl, but did you tell him your momma and daddy need to get equal pay for equal work? Black people in Mississippi are some of the strongest and the most determined people on earth. We know about survival, because Mississippi politics are as crooked as all the S's in the state's name.

Brad and Max already have good lives. I won't let them keep me from getting mine. If I stay focused my baby and I will survive. Belinda and Big Momma and thousands of other slave girls survived. I sighed and sank back in the seat.

"Are you feeling sick? You want me to pull over?"

"I'll be okay." I let the seat back and went to sleep. When I opened my eyes, Brad was parked next to Max's Corvette!

22

I hopped out of Brad's car, grabbed my bag and sprinted upstairs. Max was blocking my door. He looked as if he was at a sit-in. His angry bloodshot eyes stopped me dead in my tracks when he looked up at me. Dried tears had made white streaks on his beautiful dark face. I wanted to run into his arms and make everything better, but the love hate in his eyes killed all hope.

Max was gruff, but his tone of voice sounded like someone had stolen the wind from him when he asked, "How could you?"

"How could I what? What are you doing here? I thought you were in Nashville screwing Alma!"

"Where have you been, Gabby?"

"None of your business. You don't give a damn about me and the baby so go back to Nashville and screw Alma!"

"What's with you and this Alma shit? I gave her a ride home. I've been trying to find you all weekend. I called your mother. I staked out Brad's house. I was worried sick about you until I saw you in the paper this morning."

"The paper?" He threw the Sunday *Clarion-Ledger* at me. A picture of Brad, his parents, the Governor and me in living color was on the front page!

"Do you have any idea how I felt when my father showed me that picture, Gabby?"

I couldn't say a damn thing when I looked at the picture. I felt as guilty as I did when I stayed out with Max and Daddy beat the crap out of me, as guilty as I still feel for aborting Anthony's baby, as guilty as I did after I let Brad taste Max's sugar. I just can't seem to get it right.

"I've been worrying myself silly about you, and you've been rubbing elbows and God only knows what else with a bunch of rich white men!"

I flinched. "It wasn't like that. I--I thought you were with, Al-ma." My lips trembled and tears escaped from my eyes.

"I told you I'm being straight with you. I love you. I came to make plans for us to get married Thanksgiving. Why are you doing this to us? Marry me and come back to Nashville with me."

"I--I can't."

"You can, but you won't. You're too busy screwing Brad. I should have listened to my mother. She warned me about women like you."

Tears flooded my eyes. "You know I'm not like that."

"You're practically living at the man's house and now you're in the paper wearing a thousand-dollar low cut dress, smiling from ear to ear, and they have their hands all over you. Where did you get the dress? Did he buy it for you? Are you sure the baby is mine?"

I continued to cry.

"You don't have to answer. It's all part of the seduction, Gabby. Don't you get it? I know you're not that naive. You slept with him, didn't you?" Max held my face between is hands and stared deep into my eyes. All I could do was cry. "Tell me you're not sleeping with him, Gabby."

Guilt and shame won out over words. How could I have been so stupid? I couldn't utter a single word so I continued to cry.

"I should have listened to Mom. Your father even called you a whore." He laughed sarcastically. "You out played the player, Gabby. I really thought you loved me." Tears ran down my cheeks. My lips trembled, but I couldn't say anything in my defense.

"Keep the ring. Pawn it. Use the money to pull yourself out the gutter." Max picked up the paper and shoved it into my chest. "You got what you wanted so leave me the hell alone!" He walked away and didn't look back.

♔

It took all of me not to call Max every night at eleven. Shame filled my heart. There was nothing I could say. The calls in the middle of the night picked up after we broke up. At first I got a dial tone after I said, "hello." Then the caller would moan and groan until I slammed the phone down.

Brad and I were cordial, but we couldn't look each other in the eyes either. He invited me over to study. I made up reasons not to go. After not hearing from Max for a few weeks, and barely talking to Brad I stopped blaming them. I decided to become proactive instead of reactive. When I needed to talk to someone, I called Belinda or Big Momma. And when I needed a hug I went home to visit them or I made up excuses for them to visit me. I learned to study alone. I discovered that reading out loud not only kept me from falling asleep, but it was good for my baby. I read everything Dr. Morgan gave me on becoming a new mother. I was prepared to go it alone.

The morning sickness stopped around the third month. I sent Max copies of my ultrasound pictures with a note.

> *Dear Max,*
>   *I'm sorry I messed things up. I'm taking care of our baby. Can you tell from the pictures that we are having a ___? Anyway, I want him or her to have a better chance than us. I still love you. I know deep in your heart you love me too.*
> *Love Always,*
> *Gabby*

A few days later the phone rang at eleven. The person didn't speak or breathe heavy so I said, "If this is you, Max, please don't hang up.

I didn't do the horrible things you said because I love you and our baby. I miss you. Please talk to me." The line went dead.

I was trying to stick to my budget, but the Firebird's transmission went out. Anthony only charged for parts, but I already knew I would be broke by April. When I got home from another busy frustrating day, the phone was ringing off the hook. I expected it to be another hang-up call. I answered it to stop the noise.

"Good evening, Gabriella. My name is Scott Ford. I'm calling you on behalf of *T&A Magazine*. Do you know our work?" I thought it was Brad playing a sick joke, but I let Scott continue. "I saw you in the mall today. You're a beautiful woman, but I'm sure you already know that." He paused, and I should have hung up but I didn't. "My company is doing a photo shoot at the Holiday Inn this evening. We will pay you up to five-thousand dollars a picture if we decide to use you in our magazine."

I was calculating out the many ways I could use the money in my head. Taking nude pictures had been fun with Max, but the pictures were for our eyes only. I needed the money, but I had to think about my baby, my family, my future, and Max. I was about to tell him I wasn't interested, but something about his voice sounded familiar so I stayed on the line.

"Will I get paid tonight?"

"Sure. We'll take a few nude shots and if my boss likes you, you'll have to sign a simple contract and we'll cut you a check after you take the pictures that will be used in our magazine."

"What if I take the pictures and your boss doesn't like them? I don't get anything?"

"Like I said earlier, you are beautiful, there is no way my boss will not like you."

"How long will it take?"

"One to three hours, but if the boss likes you, you could walk away with twenty grand."

"And if he doesn't like me, nothing? And what will happen to the pictures? I'll have to think about it." He sounded familiar. There was something about his voice that prevented me from hanging up.

"I'll be in room 341 until midnight. We're featuring Southern girls in medical and dental schools so you won't be alone. You're in dental school, aren't you?" I didn't answer because now I was suspicious. Something was not making sense. My gut couldn't make the connection, but it couldn't fully disconnect either.

"Gabriella, this is a great opportunity for you. You could make a lot of money in this business. I could put you with the right people to do movies as well."

"I continued to play along while I tried and failed to pinpoint his voice. I didn't know who Scott was, but he knew way too much about me for comfort.

"How did you get my name and number?"

"I bribed the clerk at The Limited. That sweater you bought is going to look great on you."

I had paid cash! "How did you know I was in dental school?"

"I saw your picture in the paper with the governor. Baby Blue really becomes you so I took the liberty to buy a blue negligee for your shots and some blue satin sheets." Scott's grunt spoke louder than his word. I slammed my phone down when I realized he was the late-night caller!

I'll pay you twenty-thousand dollars to take some nude pictures. It wasn't Max, but no one else knows about the pictures. He could have paid someone to make the call. I doubt if he would, but his mother would. I couldn't remember if I had mentioned the pictures to Brad. I thought about Sara, and the note on my mirror, and I almost wet my panties. Who else would go through this much trouble to scare me? The killer? Christine's husband? Dylan? Who?

☙

I spent Thanksgiving with my family. My sister Agatha came from Germany. She hadn't seen me in six years. Renee, and Hope came from Chicago and Joy came from Detroit. Lorna and Richard, the handsome football player from JSU, came after dinner. They had smiles on their faces, and they couldn't keep their hands off each other. Belinda didn't bother to ask them why they were late. It was the first time all the Oliver girls had been together in ten years. It would have been nice if Max and I had gotten married. The boys even showed up with their rambunctious kids. Things were chaotic but nice. It was my birthday. No one remembered but Lorna, Belinda, Big Momma and Brad. Max used to love spending Thanksgiving with my family.

Hope and Agatha claimed my room so I went back to Jackson alone. When I got to my apartment my phone was ringing. I knew Max wouldn't let me down on my birthday. This was supposed to be our wedding day. I rushed to answer the phone. It was only the pervert or the killer continuing to spook me.

I decided to stop worrying about the killer or Max coming back; they know where to find me. I was determined to get my degree and get on with my life. I made the choices now I must live with the consequences.

Brad and I became best friends again. I didn't spend as much time at his house, but we were back to making eye contact. In some ways, we are better friends after we squashed the race and the sex questions. There was no more hanky-panky though. We hug occasionally, but our relationship is more like a sister, brother thing.

Max sent a card and a five-hundred-dollar check a week after my birthday. The card was a generic--sorry I forgot your birthday. There were no I miss you, or I love you, notations. It was signed, Maxwell. I never call him that.

I encouraged Brad to go out with Rachel. One night while we were taking a break from cramming. He said he wasn't dating for the same reasons as me. I said, "When are you due?"

"At least you have something to account for your heartache," Brad said. "You know what you need, Gabby?"

"No, but I'm sure you'll tell me."

"When was the last time you took a vacation?"

"Try never."

"Your family never took you on vacation? Get outta here!"

"My parents could barely feed us with the money they made. We were lucky to have clean clothes and a roof over our heads."

"You should come with me to Aspen for the Christmas Holidays."

"Are you forgetting that I'm pregnant?"

"Pregnant or not, you need a vacation. You can sit around the lodge and drink cocoa and laugh at my jokes. You need to rest your mind. I heard the next quarter is going to separate the fat from the bacon."

"Let me think about it." My words made me think about the phone calls. I wondered if Brad could do something like that to me--the voice sounds somewhat like his. I haven't ruled out Christine's husband. He put drugs in my punch, and their food made me awfully sick. Whoever is doing this has only tried to scare me so far so I'm not going to let them keep me from doing what I need to do.

A week after I told Brad I would go to Aspen with him and his family, I started having an eerie feeling I was being followed. Lorna thought I was being paranoid. My phone rings as soon as I get home most days. No one answers. And the heavy breathing calls continue to wake me up in the middle of the night. I would call the telephone company and have my number changed, but I'm still hoping that Max will call. Besides, my budget is so tight, when I pulled my name to buy a Christmas gift, I balled the paper up and stuffed it deep into my pocket even though we had agreed not to spend more than twenty-five dollars. I tried to think of a way to tell Brad I couldn't go to Aspen. I felt like a charity case. My pride wouldn't let me go even though it would have been nice to get on an airplane and fly far, far away.

❧

I was at the MetroCenter trying to decide if I should purchase a twenty-dollar tie-pin for Brad when Maryanne approached me.

"Can't decide what to buy Brad for Christmas?" she said sarcastically.

I looked dead into her eyes and saw as much envy as hate. "Excuse me?"

"You know you really ran a number on my baby. He almost failed out of medical school behind the stunt you pulled."

"Stunt?"

"It wasn't enough for you to leave Max high and dry for Bradley Pruter. No, you had to flaunt it and embarrass my entire family. Dr. Brown's wife couldn't wait to tell me how much time you spend at Pruter's house."

"Max left me," I said, but I didn't bother to tell her that Brad and I are just friends.

"Thank God. He finally saw you for the slut that what you are!" I could just hear Maryanne and Julius slinging all the blame on me. "I tried to warn you, but you thought you could do whatever you wanted because you have that hair down to your ass and that light skin." I was surprised to hear Maryanne talk like that in public. Although she had never said it directly she had indicated it enough times for me to get the message. "You're still black, Gabby." She laughed. "Humph. You used to be pretty, but you've let yourself go. You look tired. You've gained a lot of weight. Your hair is even a mess. You did my baby wrong, it's good to see you reaping what you sowed." She chuckled again and walked away before I could tell her I was getting fat because I'm carrying her precious baby's son. I'm tired because of those harassing phone calls in the middle of the night, and I haven't had the time or energy to deal with my hair. It seems as if Max still hadn't found a way to tell his parents the best part of our sorry saga.

I bought the tie-pin. Then I wondered around the mall in vain looking for Maryanne. I wanted to tell her the most important part of the whole sad story. But I wanted to strangle her for turning Max into a man who would walk away from his unborn child because he is a spoiled old fashioned brat!

It was dark when I left the mall. I threw my bag on the seat and flicked on my headlights. A man with dark hair and sunglasses was sitting in a cobalt-blue Buick parked across from my car. He was reading a newspaper and smoking a cigarette--in the dark! He smiled at me when my lights showed his face. I didn't waste any time leaving the parking lot. There had been several reported muggings and a rape at the mall. The car had a UMMC parking sticker on its bumper. I didn't think much about it until I noticed a set of headlights in my rearview mirror. I drove past my apartment. The headlights stayed within throwing distance so I went to Brad's house. A cute red-head with green-eyes answered his door. I panicked.

"I'm sorry, I, ugh, must be at the wrong house," I said. My voice trembled and my eyes followed the blue car as it went up the street and turned around.

"You look flustered--is everything okay?" She seemed friendly enough, but I didn't know how she would react to me being Brad's friend. Our friendship had already caused enough problems.

"Who is it Kelly?" Brad asked as he approached the door wearing an apron. His smile relaxed me before his hello. "Gabby! What a pleasant surprise, I was just telling Kelly about you." He slipped his hand around Kelly's small waist. She smiled. "Were your hands itching?"

"Ears, Brad. I stopped by because I think someone followed me from the mall!" Brad pulled me inside. Then he tried to convince me to stay. I got the scoop on Kelly while he cooked. She was perfect for him. She's a nurse, she's witty, and she didn't seem to be bothered by our friendship. They followed me home after we ate dinner. We made sure my windows and doors were locked.

"Call me if anything weird happens," Brad said.

"I don't want to ruin your evening with Kelly. Thanks for everything, now go home and have enough fun for me."

I prayed for the nightmare to end, but at three a.m. I woke up with cramps, and when I went to the bathroom I was bleeding! I was scared, but I didn't have a second thought about driving myself to the emergency room in the middle of the night. Dr. Morgan was on call. He ran a bunch of tests and did an ultrasound. Then he placed me on bed rest for a week. I'd had a bunch of exams and the added stress of the holidays had compounded with everything else. I didn't argue. I needed a vacation but Dr. Morgan said Aspen was out of the question. It was easy to convince Brad to take Kelly.

Lorna had moved to California with Harold. She called to tell me she didn't have a record deal, but she was spending a lot of time in the studio doing background vocals for other artists. She loved it. She had decided to stay awhile. We tried to figure out who was following me, and why. Lorna thought it was Brad's father.

"Lorna, that doesn't make sense. Why would Brad's father have me followed and what about the phone calls?"

"Maybe he wants to scare you or maybe he just wants to make sure you're legit. You watch the soaps. Rich white people do some crazy shit."

"Brad has Kelly now. What if it's Max?"

"Rich black folks do some dumb shit too, but what could Max gain by following you?"

"I don't know. Maybe he doesn't want me. Maybe he wants the baby. Maybe he's collecting evidence."

"Ummm. I think you have been watching too many soap-operas. Do you really think he would do that?"

"I doubt it. His parents don't even know I'm pregnant. But he loves kids. We had planned to have a large family after we were married and done with school."

"Gabby, what if it's some pervert who thinks you're pretty?"

"Lorna, please don't say that. Those people stalk their prey and torture them before they kill them."

I didn't get any sleep that night. Every time I closed my eyes I re-lived the night Max and I found Sara. I could smell her dead body. I could feel bile in my throat. But it was me in the bed naked with fear in my eyes, slit wrists, blood everywhere and cockroaches crawling all over me. A nude picture of me was taped to the mirror and the note written with my lipstick said: Got you!

23

Self-pleasuring either wasn't hitting on anything, or I hadn't been loved in so long I'd forgotten how it felt. I had planned to use my Christmas break to have a face-to-face with Max. We need to try to work out our problems. My pregnant body needs to be touched in a serious way, but Dr. Morgan made it clear that I could lose my baby if I don't stay in bed and rest. It was the Holidays, and I was stuck in bed all alone with no one to love, but me. I could go home and rest, but I'm not ready to face Daddy, and his I told you so sermon. Doc doesn't have to worry. I'm not going anywhere, and if someone is out there stalking me they might as well take a holiday break as well.

I caught up on my sleep and pleasure reading the first and second day I was bedridden. The third day I called my siblings, but no one picked up on my cry for a visit. They had their own problems and since I'm the future doctor in the family they asked me for advice, a loan, or both. I dialed Max's number and hung up when he answered. I needed to get some things off my chest, so I wrote him a long letter.

> *Dear Max,*
> *I love you too much to stop, which is why I always found a way to forgive you even when you betrayed me. My love for you is longer than time and unconditionally forgiving. I didn't do*

the horrible things you accused me of doing. But if the thought has hurt you enough to make you walk away from me and your unborn son, you are not the same man who protected me from my father's beating, and promised to love and protect me forever. You can't be the man who nursed my wounded soul until I could make sense of my love for you and for my father. You have been as much a part of me as our unborn son since that day. You showed me that you loved me from the brightest part of my soul to the darkest.

Our Baby was conceived with love. That love has been put to the test every day you have been away. There have been times when I tried not to love you, but aborting our baby was never an option. Every day is tough trying to make it on my own. Sometimes I ask myself if it is worth it. I think about our child growing inside of me, and I know without a doubt that it is.

I almost had a miscarriage three days ago. Every day I don't hear from you my burden gets a little heavier. I've been receiving harassing phone calls, and I'm almost positive I'm being followed or stalked. The pressure of these things almost made me lose our child. If you know anything about any of this please stop. If you're not involved please accept my apology.

I want you to be a part of your son's life, but it is entirely up to you. I can explain to him why you're no longer a part of my life, but only you can tell him why you rejected him. If you decide you don't want anything to do with him, my family has agreed to take care of Makai until I finish school. (I hope you like the name.)

Brad and I worked out our race problems and our sex problems and we are better people for it. We slept together, but we didn't sleep together. We decided that our friendship was more important than succumbing to a regretful night of sex. You can hate Brad because we are friends, but don't hate him because you think he took something that was yours. My heart belongs to you only.

Big Momma said because we are young we still have a lot of growing up to do. She said when we made this baby we were acting like grownups. We are still allowed to make mistakes, but we need to take responsibility for them now. You told my father you took full responsibility for our actions, and he gave you a chance to prove it. Can you still prove it?

You probably think I don't love you because I left you alone in Nashville, but nothing is farther from the truth. I've been trying to find a way to help you understand why I need to pursue my own degree. When I went to Brad's family plantation it made me dig into the history of how I came to be. I went back to slavery, reconstruction, the civil rights movement, and personal hard times in my own family. Slavery ended, but as you well know the struggle continued. I don't feel much different from women in slavery times—I'm always struggling, and suffering, and wanting, and needing, and being told, "you can't", or "we want let you," or "you're not supposed to." My suffering motivated me. I can't tell you how good it felt to be the first black valedictorian at my integrated high school. The black community rallied behind me like I was a NBA star.

People didn't expect me to do well. They saw me as the poor pretty daughter of a carpenter and a maid. I was the pretty little girl who was supposed to bat her eyes and marry a nice man who could support me. Max, you knew I wasn't that type when we met. You knew my plans and it suited you perfectly. We had a beautiful relationship for four years. I haven't changed and my heart is still the same. Our plans are still the same, but their paths are in conflict. I'm still the same dreamer you fell in love with. But now you want me to switch gears and become the pretty little girl who bats her eyes and drops her dreams for her man. Max, I wouldn't be happy being that girl. That's not the girl you fell in love with. I must pursue this dream to the end. I need to free myself. I'm not a pretty young slave girl whose master can rape, and use, and

have his way with until he's ready to sell me down the river and move on. I want to make Belinda and Big Curtis proud. I want to make you proud, but I need to earn my freedom first. If you love me as much as I love you—you will feel as free when you kiss me as I do when I kiss you. You are free, but I hope you will always seek the joy in my kiss. I will always seek yours.
Love Always,
Gabby

∿

Lil' Curtis stopped by later that day after he finished working on a construction job at the university. He brought me two Christmas gifts and a small Christmas tree to help me get into the Christmas spirit. We set the pitiful little tree on the coffee table and put it by the window. I decorated it with Belinda's extra ornaments and the crystal ornament my great grandfather had given me when I was a little girl. Mommy had stored it when her grandfather died. I hadn't seen it in years. I used to ask Belinda every day when Big Daddy was going to come home from the hospital? She used to hug me and say, "Big Daddy went to live with Jesus." I used to ask her if I could go visit them. He died right before Christmas, but before he died he sent Belinda to the store to buy the crystal ornament for me.

Big Daddy was the first man in the world that I loved. Big Curtis is a strictly business father. He didn't hug and kiss, like Big Daddy, but he taught us skills we could take to the bank. Big Daddy always gave me hugs, and kisses, and piggy-back rides, and he bought me pretty dresses and ribbons for my hair. He used to call me and Belinda his pretty little red birds because I look the most like Mommy. The red crystal ornament is shaped like a bird. I had begged him to buy it for me. He had promised to buy it for me when he got paid, but he got sick and went to the hospital and never came back. I put it at the top of the tree.

Christmas always makes me depressed. We were so poor we didn't get toys. When things were good we got new clothes for school. There were many years when all we got was dinner, apples and oranges, and maybe a book. Max and I had a few good Christmases, but there was still something deep down inside of me that was sad.

"Don't get all teary eyed on me." Lil' Curtis said. "Have you heard from Max?"

"Not a single word." I dropped my head so my brother couldn't see my shame.

"You want me to get the posse together so we can teach him that he can't disrespect our baby sister? This is still Mississippi. White folks don't give a damn if we kill a brother who thinks he's too good to take care of his kid."

"He'll come around. He loves children." I wiped my face with the back of my raggedy robe. "He's probably busy with school. I saw his mother in the mall, she said he was having a tough time with his studies, of course she blames me."

"Screw his mother. Max better do right by you, there are no bastards in this family, and you shouldn't go through this all alone either." Lil' Curtis frowned. "You sure you gonna be all right?"

"I guess."

Lil' Curtis put two chain locks and a deadbolt on my door, while I finished decorating my little tree. I put the letter in my lingerie drawer instead of giving it to my brother to drop in the mail. I need to find a way to make Max understand why I do the crazy things I do. Time is running out.

Depression had set in when I woke up on Christmas Eve. I had been afraid to go to the mall alone, so I only had five presents under my pitiful little tree. That was still more than the last two years combined. My family is too big to buy gifts for everyone. We have been pulling names since I can remember. Last year I got a gift from Belinda and

Max and a peace offering from Maryanne. I decided to save my gifts for Christmas since I knew I had pulled my own name, and I hadn't bought myself anything. The gifts Lil' Curtis brought were for Makai anyway. Agatha had also given me a gift for the baby on Thanksgiving. Makai was doing better than his mother and his father.

Big Momma and Belinda finally paid attention to my hints and came to cheer me up. Big Momma told me not to worry about Max. She said he would come around then she said she would leave something at my door to help him find it. I was hopeful. I had learned to trust her and Gina. It was clear to me that they knew what they were talking about even though Gina didn't understand it any more than I did. Big Momma on the other hand was a pro.

We drank tea and had old fashion teacakes. They used to make them when I was little. I always wondered why they called them teacakes because they taste and look like sweet biscuits that didn't rise. I put my Christmas dinner in the refrigerator. Makai and I will be having it alone. Belinda and Big Momma put several more boxes under the tree before they kissed me, said, "Merry Christmas," and left.

I curled up on my ugly brown and tan plaid sofa and watched the lights on the tree blink until I fell asleep. Last Christmas Max and I made love by the fireplace at his parents' house while the lights on their large tree winked at us. I had raided the tree at midnight and we made love into the middle of the night. We spent every second of his Christmas break together.

I was totally depressed by Christmas day. I didn't bother to answer the phone or to make my way to the living room to open the gifts. I pulled the covers over my head and stared at the dark light and pretended I wasn't me, and that I hadn't made a complete mess of my life. I pretended that I was the little girl who greeted her Big Daddy with a kiss and a hug, and he loved me enough to pick me up, spin me around and take me for piggy-back rides even though he was tired from working hard all day. That was all I needed from the love of my life when I was four and five years old. Now I need to be thrilled in bed and understood out of it. I still need to be kissed and hugged, but I don't care about pretty dresses and ribbons and gifts. I want to be able to provide for myself and my children. I want to be independent. I want to be free, but I still want Max to love me. Is that too much to ask?

I raided the kitchen late in the afternoon. Makai was starving. I ate Frosted Flakes and my Christmas dinner. I didn't really taste the food. I didn't care. It wasn't for me, it was for Makai. Nothing was for me anymore. I had loved and lost, and now everything was for Makai. The gifts, the caring, it was all for him.

The phone rang. I didn't answer. I was too miserable to talk, and I couldn't deal with any perverts today. I wasn't having a merry Christmas, but I didn't want anyone feeling sorry for me. I put the dirty dishes in the sink.

I curled up on the sofa and watched the lights on my little tree blink while I played with the curl of hair that Max used to call his. I wished I could feel his full lips kissing my belly and kissing me where Brad had kissed. Wishful thinking--Max would never kiss me there. The phone rang again. I picked it up and dropped it back in its cradle. It rang again. I picked up and said, "She's not here," and then I unplugged it.

I knew I was losing it. I didn't care. I hadn't been shut in this long since I got the mumps in second grade. That's when I fell in love with sardines. Belinda wouldn't let me eat anything else, and she took the oil from the sardines and rubbed it on my swollen face then she wrapped my face with a towel. I got the mumps in one jaw at a time. She wouldn't let me go outside to play for two weeks. She said if I went outside the mumps would spread and I would become sterile. I had to look sterile up in my dictionary. I was climbing the walls by the end of those two weeks. Maybe that's why I'm immune to the smell of sardines now. Maybe if I stop eating them Max will come back.

I played with my hair and watched the lights blink on the unopened gifts. There was a knock on my door. I ignored it. It got louder. I figured Belinda had sent Lil' Curtis to check on me. Belinda loves me--I will always be her baby girl.

"Go away," I whispered. I didn't want anyone to see me this way.

"Open this door, Gabriella!"

"Max?" I continued to stare at my little red bird and wish. I was so deep into my funk, I didn't believe it was him. I wanted it too much. Too many things had gone wrong in our lives for it to be Max at my door on Christmas day. I had hoped and prayed too many days and nights for it to be him. At that moment, I couldn't hope any more. It would be too much of a letdown if it was not my Max. Not the one who left me with his son growing in my belly without giving me the benefit of a doubt. Or the one who forgot my birthday, and sent me a generic card with no how are you and my baby doing, or I love you and miss you both. I needed my Max. The one who stepped between me and my father. The one who confronted my out-of-his-mind-with-rage father, looked him in the eyes, and said he loved me from the moment he met me. The Max who declared that if my father needed to beat and kill somebody that afternoon, it would have to be him, because either way, he was going to die loving me.

24

Warm tears slid down my cheeks. I hadn't bathed, hadn't combed my hair, or brushed my teeth the last three days. Even if Max was at my door, I couldn't let him see me like this. I played with a lock of hair, and wished he was kissing me as I sat quietly and held my breath.

"Open the door, Gabby. Your mother said something about some pervert stalking you. Are you okay?"

Lorna and her big mouth; I didn't want to worry my parents with that.

"Open the damn door, Gabriella. I'll kick this motherfucker in if I need to! What's going on? You got a man in there?"

I flinched. Tears flooded my eyes. His tone of voice softened and even cracked. "Are you all right, baby? Why did you, hang-up on me?"

I still couldn't make myself move. I needed my Big Daddy. I played with my hair and wished for things I couldn't have. I felt as helpless as I had felt in second grade. Lost helpless--I don't understand helpless. I thought I was daydreaming about Max.

"Open the door, baby. Please?" Max sounded as if he was talking to a pouting child. "Open the door. Come on, baby. I just want to make sure you're okay."

I wiped my face and drifted toward the door in slow motion. His pleading words drew me closer to him. The sensation of my feet touching the floor never reached my brain. I was walking on his words and nothing else. More than anything, I wanted to believe he was really there. I was sure I was losing it. I cracked the door open as far as the chains would allow. I knew I was a sight for sore eyes, but the worried look washed off Max's face, and he smiled as if he had just make love to me. I looked away and blushed.

"Let me in, baby."

I slammed the door and started hyperventilating. He really was here! I needed to be hugged and kissed. I needed a big girl piggyback ride.

Max banged on the door again. "Open the door, Gabby. Please baby."

My hands shook as I disconnected the chains. "I'm not dressed. I didn't think it was really you."

Max swept his eyes over me and smiled again. "You look terrible. You didn't abort my baby, did you?"

Dr. Morgan was concerned because I hadn't gained any weight between my last two visits. I've been eating, but my metabolism is high when I'm bursting at the seams with nervous energy. I walked away from Max.

"I'm having a bad day. I don't need you to make me feel any worse. I'm still pregnant, but just barely. I almost had a miscarriage. I'm on bed rest, that's why I didn't go home. Besides, Big Curtis is not pleased about our situation." I held up my hand. "Don't say it"

Max pulled me in his arms and squeezed me so tight I could barely breathe. My blue and white plaid flannel gown and my quilted robe with pink and red roses printed on it smelled as bad as it looked. He kissed me while I wiggled and tried to resist him. Then he grabbed me by the butt and started grinding against me. My desires were fully awake as well, but I pushed away.

"Don't even think about it. That's off limits. I can't even drive. I'm going crazy looking at these walls."

Max looked deep into my eyes and played with my hair. "My walls have been closing in on me as well."

"How did we end up like this, Max?"

"We screwed up, but I want you and my baby back so what do you want me to do?"

"I want to be your wife, the mother of your children, and I want you to understand why I have to stay in school."

He stared at me and smiled. "You think we can make it work?"

"We can if we try."

"Why did you hang up on me?"

"Didn't feel like talking or dealing with any crazies today."

"Your mother is worried sick about you. You should call her."

"You can call her. I didn't know Lorna had told her about the possible stalker. At first, I thought you were trying to scare me into coming home."

He smiled when I said home, then he frowned and said, "How long has this been going on?" Max massaged my shoulders and pulled me to him again. He was looking dapper in his dark brown dress slacks, a snug fitting matching turtle neck, and shiny new shoes. He had a fresh haircut, a thick new gold chain and a diamond ring on his finger. The jewelry was probably gifts from Maryanne and Julius, or that heifer Tammy. He had the look of love in his eyes and he kissed my shoulders and ears as though my funk was an aphrodisiac. I got warm chills all over.

"Stop trying to be a hero, Gabby. You need my help. Let me be a man." I flinched but I leaned into him and wished he was kissing the places Brad had kissed.

"I'll try."

"Let me stay with you tonight."

"I'd like that, but you have to keep your hands to yourself."

"Baby, considering the way you look and smell that won't be hard." I hit him on his chest. He smiled and kissed me on the forehead.

"Are you saying you're too good for my funk? Give me a few minutes and some soap and water, and I'll have you on your knees."

He chuckled. "Are those my gifts under that poor excuse of a tree?"

"Those are mine, and if you're gonna talk about my stuff you can go back to the Johnson mansion."

"Can't go before you bring me to my knees. I can't believe you didn't raid the tree at midnight."

"I was depressed. Besides those gifts are for our baby. Sorry, I didn't get you anything."

"I've been a jerk about this, but I want to marry you before the baby comes."

"I'd like that, but I don't want to get married just because we're having a baby."

"Look at you, Gabby. You're not happy here. You could even be in danger. You're barely holding on. Depression isn't good for you or the baby."

"Everything came down on me at once, but thinking that you didn't care gave me the worst pain."

"How could you think that I don't care?"

I pouted. "You didn't call. You didn't come by. And you forgot my birthday."

"I called. I didn't talk. I came by. I didn't come in. I love you, Gabby. I was hurting too. You know how I am about you. I sent you a birthday card and a check."

"Belated, and impersonal. I didn't need a check. I needed an everything is going to be okay hug. Your phone calls and having me followed led to my near miscarriage."

"I didn't have you followed, and I called once a week just to hear your voice."

"Somebody has been calling and somebody was following me."

"It wasn't me."

"It wasn't? A guy called me about taking nude pictures for *T&A*. He sorta sounded like the late-night caller, and he knew a lot about me."

"Baby, there are a lot of crazy people these days. Come home with me where it's safe."

"I wrote you a long letter a few days ago. You can read it while I freshen up. If you still want to stay after you read it, you can."

We went to my bedroom. I gave Max the letter. "Did you tell your parents about the baby?"

Max didn't look up from the letter. "Nope. I didn't think you were going to keep it. How did you know?"

"Your mother called me fat and ugly."

I grabbed the first thing my hands touched in the drawer. Max's attention was on the letter. I didn't want to be in the room while he was reading it. Seeing him had awakened the weak woman in me. He looked good enough to make me act like the whore his mother had accused me of being. I looked in the mirror and saw desperation that had never graced my face before. I took off my tacky robe and nightgown Belinda had given me last Christmas and hopped into the shower.

The water floated over my hypersensitive pregnant breasts and my slightly rounded stomach. I wished it was Max's tongue and hands or better yet his whole body. I dried off and slipped the purple night-gown on that had landed me in a compromising position with Brad. I took my hair out of its braids and let it fall across my shoulders and back.

Max covered the telephone receiver when I walked into the room. "I thought you wanted me to stay. How am I supposed to be good with you looking like that?" His words and his smile made me giggle inside and outside. "Belinda wants to know what time your appointment is tomorrow. I told her I'll take you, but she wants to know the time."

"Ten o'clock."

I slid under the covers. Max hung up the phone quickly. I was surprised when Belinda didn't insist upon talking to me. Max took off everything but his briefs before he slid under the covers next to me. My heart beat quickened. I was as nervous as I had been our first time.

"New cologne?" I asked.

"You like it?"

"I would like anything on you."

"Gucci. Mom gave it to me."

"It's nice," I said as I called Maryanne a witch and that other word that rhymes with it in my mind.

"You smell nice."

"Dial soap and water. I'm on a budget."

"It's much better than the funk you were wearing earlier. Much prettier and sexier too."

"What do you do when you miss me, Max?" I asked as I made myself comfortable in his arms and rested my head on his chest.

"Study and miss you some more."

He stroked my face with his fingers. "Right answer. Have you been good?"

"Yep." He lifted my chin and stole a kiss.

"Me too."

"How risky is it to... you know?"

"You're the doctor," I said as I caressed inside his shorts out of habit.

"We probably shouldn't take any chances."

I moved my hands to his chest and played in his curly chest hair.

"Did you pawn the ring?"

"Nope. I wasn't in the gutter."

"Sorry about that."

"What did you mean when you said you should have known better than to fall in love with a girl like me?"

"A redbone. I didn't plan on falling in love, but I was so nervous around you I was forced to slow down and get to know you first. You're my friend, my lover, my everything. You know how I feel inside. I feel like part of me is missing when we are not together."

"I feel the same way about you. You were a documented womanizer. Everybody warned me about you."

"Don't think Mom and Dad didn't warn me about you." He said as he kissed my shoulder, my swollen breasts, my slightly rounded belly, and then he opened my legs!

I wanted to ask him if he had been screwing white girls. But my mind was split between his parents' warnings, and the way his tongue quickly teased my clit to the busting point. Within minutes my entire body was in a state of bliss.

"I think it is high time we stopped listening to other people, Max, and pay attention... ooh, what are you...we need to listen to our... hearts." He continued to make me giggle inside and out. I couldn't stop kissing him. I wanted to make him a member of the happy camper club as well, but he stopped me.

"Go to sleep, Gabby. I'm not taking any chances with our son. If you do that, I will have to finish the job so deep inside of you, you'll never let me leave you again."

I rolled on my back and giggled. "Good night, Max. Merry Christmas."

He wrapped his arms around me and played in my hair. He probably thought I had drifted asleep when he said, "I love you so much, Gabby, I can't breathe when I think about how badly I've fucked up."

The next morning when he brought me breakfast in bed, my engagement ring was sitting on top of the pancakes. It was drenched with melted butter and sticky syrup. Max got down on one knee. "Let's get married Saturday. We can do the blood work when you go to your appointment. I love you, Gabby. I'll let you decide when you want to move to Nashville."

"Wow! Saturday? This coming Saturday?" I wiped my eyes. "Okay."

He put the ring on my finger, and licked the excess syrup off.

"It's sticky, Max." I said as I flashed a cover girl smile that felt real after so many weeks of faking feeling good.

"Maybe it will help us get it right this time."

I sat the tray on the floor and pulled him into bed with me. I was like a whore and he was like a man who had just gotten out of prison. Our loving was mighty good--mighty good indeed!

We had to shower together, and Max had to drop me at the door so I wouldn't be late for my appointment. Dr. Morgan was running late as usual. He was stuck at the hospital with a difficult delivery.

Some of his patients rescheduled their appointments, but Dr. Morgan told his nurse he needed to see me immediately.

Max and I waited in the waiting room. We played kissing games and made plans to go to a justice of the peace. I wanted to get our families together for a small reception, but Max wanted to take off for a brief honeymoon instead. He wanted it to be our day. He didn't want anyone else involved.

"Mom will take over and plan something grand. Then we'll have to tell them about the baby, and dad will say it's not right for us to live apart," Max said.

"You're right. We should do it our way and tell them later. But I want to tell my parents."

"We'll tell everyone from our honeymoon suite in the Bahamas," he said and he kissed me again.

Max tried to bribe the nurse into telling him why we had to wait. She didn't care how many years of medical school he had, or the fact that Dr. Morgan is his godfather, she wouldn't tell him anything. When I tried to get more information, she scared me even more when she said, "Miss Oliver, I'm not a doctor and these things are delicate. You'll have to talk to Dr. Morgan. I can reschedule your appointment, but if I were you, I would wait."

25

We were ready for some real loving by the time Dr. Morgan strolled in. He was surprised to see Max with me. Julius Johnson and Lester Morgan have been friends since elementary school. They were roommates at Tougaloo and at Meharry. Max has known Lester all his life. He was baffled by his godfather's cold greeting. Dr. Morgan's green scrubs, puffy eyes, five o'clock shadow, and wiry salt and pepper hair looked as if he had been up all night. He was smiles and apologies until he saw Max with me. He switched to a professional more serious demeanor. He knows Max is the father of my baby, and I'm sure he knows Maryanne and Julius don't know that Max did more than smother my fire when they left us home alone that sultry afternoon in September. He's under oath not to tell.

"I need to speak to Gabby alone." Dr. Morgan said.

"Is there a problem with the baby, or do you have a problem with me, Uncle Lester?"

"Alone?" I asked.

"I'll call my nurse in when I examine you, but I need to discuss a delicate matter with you first. Maxwell, you'll have to wait here."

"Can Max come in for the exam. He wants to hear our son's heartbeat."

"Sure," Dr. Morgan said, and then he put his hand on my back and ushered me into the exam room.

The grim look on his face made me over the top nervous. "Is it that bad, Doc?"

He cleared his throat and averted his eyes. "Gabby, this is extremely difficult for me."

Tears welled up in my eyes. "Is there something wrong with my baby? You're scaring me."

"I'm sorry. The baby appears to be okay, but we will have to monitor you very carefully from now on."

I frowned. "What's wrong with me?"

He cleared his throat and whispered, "Your tests came back positive for gonorrhea."

My eyes met his. He cleared his throat again, and I should have known things were going to go from bad to worse. "Your initial tests were negative so you probably contracted it more recently. The last time I saw you, you said you hadn't seen Max. We'll have to inform all your partners."

I was speechless. Did Brad count? Max had given me, and our baby the clap! My eyes clouded up as the devastating news settled in.

"I'm your doctor, Gabby. Everything you tell me will stay in this room, but you and your partners need to be treated immediately."

I wiped my face and pushed back tears as anger took their place. Let's get married Saturday. Let's not tell anyone. Let's go to the Bahamas.

"Anything you tell me will be strictly confidential."

"Max and I had unprotected sex in October shortly after I had the initial tests done. He said he had stopped cheating. I believed him."

"We'll have to tell him, but chances are he already knows if it was that long ago."

"Are you saying he knew he had it and didn't tell me? Is that what almost caused me to have a miscarriage?"

"Gonorrhea can go undetected in women and it can increase your risk of having a miscarriage. We can treat you with antibiotics. Max will need to be treated as well if there is any possibility that you have re-infected him. I've been calling you all week. I didn't get an answer. Have you been resting?"

I didn't hear anything after re-infected. "Max gave this shit to me!"

Calm down--it can be treated. Everything is going to be okay." He patted me on my back.

"I'm sorry, Dr. Morgan. Max and I were planning to get married Saturday. It's not going to be okay. It's never going to be okay." I wiped my face again but it didn't do any good.

"I'm sorry. You and the baby will be okay with antibiotics. I don't know what to tell you to do about Max, but I'll tell him, if it will make it easier for you."

"No. Get him now!" Tears took control of my emotions when Max came in the room. He rushed to my side. If I didn't know any better, I would swear that he cared.

"Please don't cry. Is there something wrong with our baby?" Tears coated his eyes as he looked from me to Dr. Morgan for answers.

"How could you give me the gotdamn clap and not tell me? How could you put your son's life at risk and not say a f-ing word?"

Max's head dropped, but not fast enough to hide his shame. "Uncle Lester, I need to talk to Gabby privately, please."

"Damn you, Max! There isn't shit you can say that will justify the pain you've caused me and my baby," I said as I struggled to remove my engagement ring. It was stuck. All my pregnancy weight so far was in my face, breasts, legs, hips, and my fingers. "Damn you! How could you do this to an innocent baby? I hate you!" I forced the ring off and threw it at him.

He caught it. "Gabby, please let me explain."

"Get out! You've lied to me for the last time." I cried and Max cried. Dr. Morgan tried to calm both of us. I wanted to find a way to forgive him. His loving is sweet, but it is toxic. I need to find a way to get over him. I love him and his unborn child, but I need to be strong enough to walk away and mean it. "Not this time, Max. Not anymore. You almost killed our son. I can't forgive you for that."

"Gabby, I can explain. Please listen to me. Uncle Lester, let me speak to Gabby alone for a minute. Please?" Dr. Morgan left the room. Max sat next to me. He wiped my tears and hugged me, but the tears kept coming like a water sprinkler in the summertime. He stared into my eyes. I let him enjoy the serenity of wrapping a lock of my hair around his finger, but I didn't budge when he smiled at me lovingly--not this time.

"I know this isn't going to sound right, but I found out after we were together in October. Mom and Dad told me about all the time you were spending at Brad's house. I thought you had given it to me."

I stared at Max, but I was speechless. I had never been this upset with him before and this was his defense?

"A couple of weeks later I found out that I had gotten it from a nurse at the hospital who had gotten it from an intern. The intern denied giving it to her so she spread it to as many doctors and medical students as she could to get revenge. She showed up at my house one day and seduced me. It was a quickie. We didn't even take our clothes off. She left after it was over. It didn't mean anything. I was so ashamed I blocked it out of my mind until I couldn't ignore the burning any longer."

"That's it? When were you going to tell me, Max?"

"The weekend you went away with Brad. I thought you had slept with him. I--I thought you all deserved it." He dropped his head. "I didn't think about our baby. I--I was angry and hurt. Dad said it could be Brad's. You had just gotten off the pill. You weren't supposed to get pregnant that quick. I'm sorry, baby. I love you. I couldn't believe you were doing this to me."

I slapped him, and wished for Daddy's shotgun. His face turned to the side. My hand stung. "I didn't take the pill all summer, Max!"

"You didn't?"

"Don't act surprised. I've always given you what you wanted, Max. It's always been about you. What you wanted. What you needed. I wish this baby wasn't yours. I wish I had fucked Brad. At least I wouldn't have to explain why I got screwed by my baby's father. Get out! Get the fuck out of my face. Go! I don't want to hear anymore lies about how much you love me, and how crazy I make you. Go back to Nashville and fuck Tammy, Alma, and I don't give a fuck, but stay the hell away from me! What if you get AIDS the next time? How are you going to explain that indiscretion away? How can you stand there and say you love me, ask me to marry you, and turn around and fuck anything wearing a skirt? I'm sorry, Max but I can't do this anymore."

Max's juicy lips trembled and tears ran down his smooth dark chocolate cheeks like melting ice-cream on a hot summer day. "Please, Gabby, try to understand. I made some mistakes. So, have you, forgive me. This is the last time. I promise. I thought— "

I held up my hand like a stop sign. "Don't think for another damn minute that this baby isn't yours. But as far as we're concerned this slave girl will say father unknown. You denied us so... Fuck you!"

"I never meant to hurt you, Gabby. I love you and— "

Max was trembling and ice cream tears were dripping down his cheeks. I wanted to kiss him and lick his tears until my love soothed our pain away, but I couldn't this time. He had crossed the love/hate line; I finally understood the difference. I held up my hand. "Don't say it. I don't care anymore. Makai and I are better off without you."

Dr. Morgan knocked on the door. I yelled for him to come in. "Get away from me, Max. I'll take the bus home."

Max stood up and stared at me. "Gabriella, please? We can work it out. We have to for our baby."

The door opened and Dr. Morgan stepped in with a grave look on his face. "Max, you need to leave now. Don't worry about Gabby—I'll make sure she gets home safely. This bickering is not good for her or the baby. I left you some antibiotics with my receptionist." Max pleaded with me one last time. I stuffed my fingers in my ears like a child to let him know I wasn't listening. He slammed the door on his way out.

"Are you okay?" Dr. Morgan asked.

"No, but I'll survive."

"I don't want to upset you anymore, but there is one more thing I need to discuss with you."

"Spit it out, the man I love just walked out the door and even I can't forgive him this time, so what else is new."

Dr. Morgan sat down next to me. "I'm too close to you and Max. I love him like a son. I want you and Max to work out your problems. But that's not the position I'm supposed to take as your doctor. I think it will be best if I turn your case over to my new associate. It would be better if I wasn't this involved."

"I didn't know you had an associate."

"He just started. Don't worry you'll like him. He's young and energetic. All the young ladies love him."

"Do I have a choice?"

"I'm sorry, Gabby. I don't want to be in the middle of this. I can't sit at dinner parties with my best friends and listen to them say things about you that aren't true, and I can't set the record straight without breaking my patient doctor obligations."

"Max and his family always get what they want. I'm just a poor girl who made the mistake of falling in love with him. It's okay for people like you all to screw over a girl like me." Laughter built up in my gut. I couldn't stop it even though I was still a shower of tears. "You all are no different from the Pruter men."

Dr. Morgan finished my exam without saying another word. I wanted to hate Max, his parents, and Dr. Morgan. I couldn't keep blaming his parents for raising him wrong. He's a grown ass man. He needs to take responsibility for his own actions, and I need to stop making it easy for him.

Dr. Morgan drove me home. Max was waiting in the parking lot. I searched my bag for my keys. When I found them, I hopped out the car and thanked him for the ride. I walked by Max like he was a cool summer breeze. Even I was amazed by my new coolness. I was on a different mission now. Max followed me to my car.

"Leave me alone. What you did was unforgivable," I said calmly.

"I want to marry you. I want to be a part of my son's life. I love you, Gabby."

"I'll call you when he is born. We can work visitation out at that time. I won't deny him his father. But I am done with you."

"Let's get married. We can make it through this."

"It's over. You've screwed over me for the last time. Makai and I can make it on our own." I got in my car and drove away. Max and Dr. Morgan watched me leave. I went to the pharmacy and filled my prescription and took the first dose on the spot. Then I stopped at McDonald's and brought a happy meal. The coast was clear when I returned to my apartment. The phone rang the minute I walked in. I was prepared to hang up if it was Max or that pervert, but it was Mommy.

"Everything is okay. Dr. Morgan said the baby is fine, and I'm fine."

Max must have been happy to hear that good news. Tell him I said thanks for checking on you last night and for calling me."

"Max had to go home."

"Are you going to come home before you go back to school?"

"Yeah, but not today."

"Baby, is everything okay?"

"Fine. I'm upset with Max, but what's new."

"Maybe you shouldn't be so hard on him. He's not perfect, but he wants to do right by you and the baby."

"Right."

"Your roommate from college called."

I perked up. "I'm not surprised. Gina is like Big Momma about predicting my problems."

"She seems like a nice girl. She said she would call you later today. She's visiting her sister in Jackson. She wanted to see you before she headed home."

I ate my cold happy meal and debated when the phone rang again. It would be nice to see Gina. It was her. We played catch-up, and then we decided to do a girl's night out starting with dinner at the Red Lobster in Highland Village.

PART FOUR

"God gives the hardest jobs and leaves the
hardest decisions up to women."

Belinda Oliver

26

I scrubbed Max's filth off me and shampooed and dried my hair. I prefer to let it air dry, but this is no time to catch a cold. I put on my red sweater-dress, applied a light cover of makeup and practiced my honky-dory smile. If the slaves picking cotton in the pictures at the museum could fake a smile, so could I. I flashed my cotton-picking-smile one more time before I left to meet Gina and Gretchen. Max was still in my parking lot. I walked by him again without acknowledging his presence. He followed me to the restaurant. He drove away while I hugged and kissed my girlfriends.

Gina had relaxed her gigantic Afro and cut her hair into a lopsided bob. Marriage seemed to be agreeing with her. Gina was the rebel amongst us. She always pushed us to fight for our rights and stand up for our beliefs. Even though black women have always worked their asses off Gina believed that we still needed to be down for women's rights.

Gretchen is the tannest of the three of us. She can still pass the paper bag test and she has enough Afro centric features to avoid the high-yellow and big-red nicknames which were often bestowed on Gina and me. Gretchen's cat eyes are her claim to fame.

Gina is the whitest of our bunch, but she doesn't make any bones about claiming her blackness and celebrating in it. I'm comfortable with myself. Most people think I'm mixed because of my hair. My family is loving and very diverse looking if nothing else. We were too damn poor for me to cop a holier-than-thou attitude. Gretchen used to be the kind of light-skinned sister who made others automatically hate all sisters who look like us. I thought she had changed, but as soon as we were seated she said, "My grandmother showed me a copy of your picture in the paper with the Governor and the Pruter Family. Bradley Pruter is a knockout. So, how did it feel to be around all that old money?" She giggled. "Never mind the money. How was he?" she whispered.

"Brad's money is no different from Max's except his was stained with our ancestors' blood, and Max's family's money was made from our ancestor' ills. Brad is a true friend and Max is a great lover if nothing else."

"Girl, Max was bent out of shape for weeks behind that picture. You looked like Hollywood glamour in that dress and those pearls. You must have had a hard time explaining that love/lust look in Brad's eyes to Max."

Sometimes I hate the way Gretchen calls me pretty. I'm sure she meant it in a nice way, but it felt like she was blowing sand in my eyes. I made eye contact with Gina when Gretchen rolled "Max" off her lips as if she was familiar with his dick. I was ready to kill Max. I took a sip of water and looked Gretchen dead in her eyes and said, "I hope you didn't let him cry on your shoulders because you know the man is mine."

"Oh, no, girlfriend. I would never go there." Her eyes shifted so I didn't believe her. "I look out for my sisters. I swear--I tell all those hussies that Max is head-over-heels in love with you. He might mess around every now and then, but he is definitely yours... He showed me your picture." I flinched, but she held my stare. "It's beautiful, but so are you." She struck more nerves than I wanted to address to be convincing. Our waiter interrupted just in time.

"Can I start y'all ladies off with a cocktail this evening?" our young bubbly waiter asked.

"I'll have a Tanqueray and tonic," Gina said. Gretchen ordered a Sprite and I ordered sweet tea. Max used to be nervous about me hanging out with Gina after I told him I had made out with her. I think he was afraid her free-spirit would rub off on me. The guys on campus loved her including Max. Oh, I was the pretty one, but Gina was the sexy one. She was the one the guys pursued.

Some girlfriends seal their lifelong friendships with a drop of blood. Gina and I sealed ours with a kiss that lasted all night. We both needed to be loved that night so we loved each other. We were pouring our hearts out to each other one minute talking about our fathers, and I don't know who kissed whom first, but it happened. It was different, strange and sweet. It was like masturbating with a girlfriend. She reassured me that she was still a virgin and I was still Max's girl. We were curious and we didn't have to be anymore. It only happened once, but I still feel a closeness to Gina that goes way beyond our secret. I trust her the way I trust Lorna. We have a shared history which goes beyond sharing a few kisses with another woman. We share a history that only a sister as pale as Gina whose heritage has been questioned as many times as mine can understand.

We ordered dinner, and when our waiter left, Gina stared Gretchen in her eyes and said, "So, Gretchen, who have you loved lately?"

Gretchen's cat eyes clouded up and she burst into tears. Gina turned three shades of red, but she got up from her seat and rushed over to give Gretchen a hug. Gina can be brutally honest sometimes, but she has a soft heart. She can't handle it when honest feels mean. I couldn't move when I saw the same agony in Gretchen's eyes that I had seen the night I found her in the shower barely hanging on to life. I didn't know how much I cherished her friendship until we almost lost her. It was the memories of her near fatal abortion that reminded me of what I had done. It prevented the thought of aborting again from ever entering my mind.

"Where did you get these beautiful cowrie shell earrings you're wearing like an African queen," Gina asked her. "Did you know those shells were once valued more than gold by some tribes. You're a queen, Gretchen, so don't worry, sugar, you're gonna find your king soon."

"You guys don't know how much I miss you. I'm not as strong as you all."

"You're a queen, Gretchen, and that means that you don't have to compare yourself to Gabby and me. Learn to live up to your potential instead of ours. We make lots of mistakes just like you, sugar," Gina said. She kissed Gretchen on the lips. I flinched and even felt a tinge of jealousy. "You're lucky I love you, girl. We're sisters, and sometimes that shit ain't easy, but we're in this for life--I didn't intend to stir up any bad memories." She kissed Gretchen again and sat back in her seat.

"I've been thinking about cutting my hair. I love your haircut, Gina. I can't believe you got rid of your Afro," I said.

"Girl, black folks are scarce in Connecticut where I live. I figured I'd fry my hair and blend my white ass in."

"Now you sound like Gretchen."

"You all are always picking on me. I can't help it if I'm not as pretty as you guys. Don't cut your pretty hair, Gabby. I bet Max won't let you anyway."

"Gretchen, you get your hair done every week. My father wouldn't let me cut my hair, but Max doesn't control me."

"We're not picking on you, Gretchen. We're trying to help you focus on what is important. Nice hair and clothes don't make the woman. It's what's in here," Gina said as she pounded her overly exposed left cleavage. "We love you because we know that under those beautiful clothes, and behind your beautiful eyes, you have a heart that hurts the same as ours." We all made eye contact--we all knew she was referring to the night Gretchen tried to kill herself.

Gina reached for our hands. She held them while she said grace. Dinner was pleasant after we got off the subjects of, men, skin color, and hair. Gina hated Connecticut, she loved dental school, and she loved being married. Gretchen liked dental school at Meharry, there were a lot of potential marriage candidates there. She thought she had found the one, but a couple of weeks into it she found out he was married and had a family in New Jersey. She knew she wasn't strong enough to play with sharks--she hadn't gotten over her near death experience with the last one.

I spent exactly twenty-five dollars on dinner, tea, and tips. Gretchen had a long drive back to Freehold. I offered to drop Gina off at her sister's apartment in Lorna's old neighborhood. She was on my case as soon as Gretchen pulled away.

"What's wrong, Gabby, and don't give me that nothing bullshit."

"Max and I broke up for the umpteenth time, and this is really it."

"What about the baby."

"Max has done some horrible things, but I still love him. He says he loves me, but he keeps messing up."

Gina put her arms around me, and led me to my car. "Love is funny that way. Sometimes you don't know how deeply you are in love until it hurts."

"Make it plain, Gina. I'm not in that cosmic world as deep as you."

Gina chuckled. "When we love a whole person, and they love a whole person, that's a lot of loving. When you love all of Max, you love his mother, his father, and all the things, and loving they have given him. Then he has to do the same for you."

"I said make it plain, it's been a long day."

"For example: How does Max feel about his mother and father?"

"He loves them. He wants us to be a mirror image of them."

"And how do they feel about you?"

"They hate me. No, hate is too strong a word. They don't think I'm good enough. They think I'm being silly about school. I think I see your point."

"Wait. I'm not finished. How does your family feel about you and Max?"

"They think we should have gotten married a long time ago."

"So now you know why you keep holding on, and why you keep holding out. Talk to Max and let him figure out why he loves you, and why he continues to cheat on you."

"You're good. I didn't know you majored in psychology."

"I didn't. But I'll take a check."

"It's in the mail." I hugged Gina and kissed her on the cheek. We promised to stay in touch. The phone was ringing when I got home. I ignored it.

৯

Max showed up at my door with a gold wedding band between his teeth when he smiled. He was wearing a blue suit with a red rose pinned to his lapel. And when he gave me the bouquet of red roses he had hidden behind his back, he was as smooth as Billie Dee in Mahogany. I was wearing my flannel gown and flowered robe. I had cried myself to sleep for the third night in a row so I couldn't help myself when I realized it was Saturday.

Cold air whipped around the corner. I pulled my robe tighter, but I didn't invite him in. He removed the ring from his mouth and tried to give it to me.

"No. I won't tolerate your cheating anymore. It hurts too much."

"It won't happen anymore. I love you. Let's get married today."

"No, Max. The proof is in the pudding. You're a liar and a whore." He flinched and his jaw muscles flexed. "I won't allow you to hurt me and my baby anymore."

"I love you, Gabby. Let's get married." His tone of voice trembled and his eyes begged. I looked away.

"I love you too, but it's not enough anymore. I need you to be totally committed to us. Our son and I deserve more than you can offer. I'm done. You can't hurt me anymore."

Max placed my engagement ring in my hand, closed my fingers around it and kissed my hand. "You're my wife, Gabriella, your father said so." He turned and walked away. Then he turned around and faced me again. "You're carrying my son. You are my wife," he said sternly. He leaned toward me and stole a kiss while I was processing his words.

"Maybe you should get counseling, Max. If you want to marry me, you'll have to change. Stop listening to your parents and listen to your heart."

"My parents don't have anything to do with this. They don't even know about the baby."

"And why is that? Will it make you less of a man in their eyes, or will it give them proof that I'm not good enough for you?"

He took my hands in his and squeezed them as he stared into my eyes. "Baby, I just want to do things right."

"You need to keep your dick in your pants. Why are you afraid to tell your parents? Is it because I'm just another one of your whores? My father said it. Your parents said it. You even said it." Max looked away. I refused to let him see me cry. "You made me this way. I did whatever you wanted me to do to please you, and now you're ashamed to tell your parents what you've done to me. Why should I marry you? Leave me the hell alone, Max!"

"I love you, Gabby. You make me so crazy." He pulled me in his arms again and kissed me. I kissed him but I didn't embrace him. "You are my wife--my life!" He touched my stomach. "This is my baby." He stared into my eyes, and he played with my hair. "I need you, Gabby. Please don't give up on me. I'll be back and I will get it right."

I went home for a couple of days. Max's last visit had made me depressed. Belinda pampered me and feed me until it seemed as if food was going to come out my pores. Anthony stopped by. He got all choked up when I told him I was pregnant with Max's child.

I still hadn't gained but ten pounds, and it was so well distributed that only people who know me well noticed. I cut my hair into a short sassy cut like Gina's. I wanted to start the New Year with a new look and a new attitude. It's time for me to take control of my own life. Big Curtis had a fit about my hair. I didn't care. I was living for Gabby for a change.

GLORIA F. PERRY

I stayed with my parents until New Year's Day. Big Curtis sensed my pending depression and went light on the lectures. He even gave me a few hugs. I was touched when he showed me the rocking horse he was making for Makai. My parents were looking forward to having a baby around.

I would have gone back to my apartment, but I didn't want to take a chance on getting sentimental if Max showed up. We always made sure we were making love when the clock struck midnight. One year we made love in the Holiday Inn bathroom while everyone else including his parents partied outside.

January was cold and lonely. Brad loved my hair and my new attitude. School kept me busy. Brad and Kelly were a couple, and we were still friends. Brad invited me over, but I made excuses not to go.

Max called once a week. I wouldn't talk to him until he told me he was seeing a therapist. He didn't have a problem as far as actively going out seeking other women. He had a problem resisting them when they sought him out. He was working on his resistance and trying to break mine down. I listened to his stories and his pleas. There were many cold and lonely nights. It was nice to hear his voice. We mostly talked about school and about how I was feeling. Max seemed to be concerned. He was breaking me down a little at a time, and anyway, I couldn't stop loving him while his seed was in me. Hell, I never stopped loving Anthony.

27

I was too embarrassed to go back to Dr. Morgan's office. I skipped my January appointment and transferred to another office. When they discovered that I didn't have insurance, they cancelled my appointment, and referred me to the free clinic. New patients had to wait three months to get an appointment, or they could walk-in for emergencies. I conceded to defeat, and went to see Dr. Dayton in February. He was a tall almond-colored man with hazel eyes like Gretchen's. His eyes stripped me naked when he said, "Gabriella Oliver, a beautiful name for a beautiful mother to be."

I do have a weakness for men who can make my name sound exotic. Dr. Dayton sang it like Marvin Gaye. I thought, flirt, but I relaxed and climbed back on the examination table. Dr. Dayton smiled and started reviewing my chart.

"Not married, hmmm."

"Engaged," I said. I had gotten used to saying it around school. I still wear Max's ring. There is no point in getting bombarded with questions.

Dr. Dayton's teasing smile turned to a frown as he continued to read my records. "My, my, you have quite a history. Did you complete your antibiotics?"

"Yes, I did," I snapped.

He raised a brow, and put my file back into the chart holder. Then he sat on the little stool and said, "Put your feet in the stirrups and push to the edge of the table."

All my muscles got tight when he put the large speculum in and stretched me open. "Relax, Gabriella."

"Let me ramp that thing up your ass, and we'll see if you can relax."

Dr. Dayton chuckled and said, "Sorry, I should have known you were a feisty one." It wasn't so much what he said, it was the way it oozed with sexual innuendoes that made me want to get up and run.

He poked around a few minutes, took the cold speculum out and put a couple of fingers in and moved them around. When he touched my clitoris, my muscles tightened again. I wiggled and tried to avoid his efforts, but he massaged it until I was hot in the face.

"What are you doing?" I asked when my heart began to race. I've been finger knocked enough times to know this was no ordinary exam. Dr. Dayton smiled and pressed his free hand down on my stomach, but he continued to tickle my spot with his fingers. My feet were digging into the stirrups. I wanted to kick his gotdamn teeth out.

"Is there something wrong, Doc?"

"Nothing so far," he said with too much of a grin for him not to know he was crossing the line. "You have a family history of fibroids. I--I was just checking." He removed his slimy fingers and smiled at me again. I was leery of him, but before I could put my shock into words he had raised my gown up to my breasts and rubbed jelly on my stomach. Then he rolled his monitor around my slick belly until we heard Makai's strong heartbeat. I smiled and forgot about my pulsating clit.

"Wow, he or she has a powerful heartbeat."

I giggled. "He."

"So, you want a boy?"

"Big Momma and the ultrasound confirmed that it's a boy. Big Momma is never wrong."

Dr. Dayton wiped the gel from my belly and exposed my breasts. He raised a brow and I could tell from the look in his eyes that he couldn't wait to touch Max's joy mountains.

"What are you doing?"

"A breast exam."

"Dr. Morgan already did one."

"Relax, Gabby. I do a thorough exam on all first-time patients. Dr. Morgan is an excellent doctor, but I'm responsible for you now." He rubbed and massaged my breasts for five minutes. Each! He pinched my nipples and did everything but climb up on the table and suck me off. He did a final pinch of my left nipple and said an excited, "Great!" He smiled. I burned inside.

"I don't anticipate any more problems. We'll check your blood at each visit. If you have any questions or concerns, or if anything unusual happens, you can call me anytime." He smiled and gave me a card with his home number written on it. "Anytime."

I told myself he was just doing his job, even though I felt totally violated. Maybe I was just over reacting to an obviously handsome man. I wrapped my arms around myself while he filled in the lab slip for my blood work.

Dr. Dayton gave me a blue and white paper. "You're gaining weight very slowly. I think it would be a good idea for you to sign up for WIC. You're not dieting, are you?"

"I've been eating three squares a day complements of my mother. I eat at least three fruits a day. I'm eating better than I've ever eaten. I'm naturally skinny. Max thinks I look great pregnant." I threw the Max part in just in case he was getting ideas.

"You look great, but you're pregnant. Stop by to see the nutritionist after you do your blood work. I'll see you again in a month."

I dressed quickly even though I felt like I needed a cold shower. Sign up for WIC, next I'll be signing up for welfare. Max is going to pay for my prenatal care. It wasn't necessary for him to feel me up and down like that.

By the time, I left the office I felt totally humiliated. The lab tech saw that I'd had an STD and treated me like dirt. And the nutritionist made me feel as if I was lying about my eating habits. I'm one of those lucky people with a hyperactive metabolism. Dr. Dayton wouldn't have taken those liberties with me if I was married, and had insurance. If Max and I were married none of this would have happened.

When Max called to see how my visit had gone, I was deep into an "all men are dogs state," but he reminded me that it isn't so much that he is a dog as it is that he doesn't have any resistance when women freely give him whatever he wants. I was too angry with myself for not speaking up to talk. I couldn't deal with him after I had been finger knocked, caressed, put on WIC and told to sign up for welfare. My family may have been poor, but we were never a part of the system!

The following Friday Dr. Dayton called my emergency number at school. Everything was going through my head when I got his urgent message. Did I have one of those resistant strains of gonorrhea? What if they found something else? What is wrong now? I didn't wait until my break to return his call.

"Dr. Dayton, this is, Gabriella Oliver. I got your message."

"Thanks for calling me back so quickly. You didn't tell me you were in dental School. Congratulations."

"Thank you. Is there a problem with my lab results?"

"No, no, your lab results were fine. The nutritionist said you were upset when you left the other day. It must be hard for you going through this alone. I just wanted you to know, I'm your doctor and I'm here for you if you need anything, or have any questions."

"Thank you, Dr. Dayton."

"Jared. Dr. Morgan filled me in on your case. We will be working closely together to make sure you get the best care available. Keep your head up. Everything is going to be okay."

"Thank you."

"However, I would like to review your case with you. My philosophy is to make sure my patients fully understand what I'm trying to do for them."

"My next appointment is March sixth."

"Since you are so far along, I don't want to wait another month to make sure we are both clear about your care."

"I don't have much free time with school and all."

"Why don't you let me take you out to dinner? I have some concerns about your weight. It will give me a chance to observe."

Alarms went off in my head, but since medicine is supposed to be becoming more patient friendly, I agreed to go. Dr. Dayton picked me up at my place because we couldn't decide where to meet.

My black sheath dress had gotten snug and my red sweater dress was dirty. Max had sent me a box of candy for Valentine's Day and a dozen roses, but he hadn't bothered to call. My mind was on him when I pulled on my blue pleated skirt, a pair of opaque tights and the sky-blue Angora sweater I bought from The Limited. I couldn't button the skirt but the sweater was long enough to cover my slightly bulging stomach and my opened button. My hair had grown out of its cut. I twisted the back and put it in a French twist, and let the side curls hang down.

Dr. Dayton picked me up at seven. I didn't invite him in. We went to a new Italian restaurant called Lombardo's.

Our dinner conversation turned personal quickly. I steered it away from me by allowing him to talk about himself. I pretended to be interested. Jared was born and raised in DC. He went to school at Howard. He only planned to be in Mississippi long enough to work off his government loans. Mississippi was way too slow, and the women were too unsophisticated for a city slicker like him, (his words not mine).

I stuffed myself with Lasagna and salad. I was okay with him thinking I was a hick. Jared's pompous talk confirmed that I hadn't imagined the unprofessional manner which he had treated me. As the evening progressed, it started to feel like a date—one I was past ready to end. He had polished off four glasses of wine. He kissed my hand, and started divulging his sexual preferences. Every time I tried to change the subject, he twisted it right back to sex. I skipped dessert. It was late, and I just wanted to go home and kick myself for giving him the benefit of the doubt.

I was quiet when he drove me back to my apartment. He insisted upon seeing me to my door. I didn't intend to let him in, but he said he needed to use the bathroom. He admitted that he had drunk too much wine. While he was using the john, I went in my room and took off my shoes and tights. The tights kept rolling under my little belly and the shoes were uncomfortable with the tights.

He asked for a cup of coffee to help him sober up so he could drive home. I didn't have any coffee. I offered to make him tea. He sat on my sofa and made himself comfortable. I filled my teakettle, and put it on the stove. Then I habitually started Prince's *Purple Rain* CD that was already in my stereo. Jared looked through a picture album of my family that was on the coffee table. He called me over and asked me about a picture of my five brothers. I sat next to him and while I was putting names to the faces Jared locked me in his arms and kissed me. I put my hands on his chest and tried to push him away. He grabbed both my wrists with one big hand, and reached under my sweater, and unhooked my bra with the other! Our eyes meet. He had a sinister grin on his face. My brain raced to find a way to escape, but my body froze. He unzipped his pants, and pulled out his junk. I wiggled and tried to free my hands. He held my wrists so tight, my fingers felt numb. He pushed me down on my sofa, and pent my arms over my head. I couldn't stop him. He was too big and strong. I like it when Max does that, but this was insane! He held my wrists together with one hand while he ripped my panties off with the other. Then he laid on top of me like I had given him permission and whispered something about how good he was going to make me feel. The heat of his breath on my ear gave me cold chills. I didn't want to risk harming my baby. I pleaded with him to stop. I was somewhere between panic and shock when Jared forced my legs open with his knee.

He kissed and rubbed anything and everything he could get his free hand on. I couldn't remember what my ninth-grade health teacher told us to do in a rape situation, but I refused to let shock shut my brain down. Is it better to fight? Didn't she say something about rape being about power and control, and not the sex act itself. Is it better to be passive because the rapist gets off on the struggle? Or did she say always fight? Jared licked my breasts, and moved what I hoped was his fingers in and out of me. I struggled and pleaded with him to stop. I remembered my teacher saying date rape is the most common type. No one ever seriously thinks it will happen to them. I placed myself in another body while Jared had his way with the one on my sofa. I refused to let him see me cry. His eyes glazed and I noticed his sinister smile again. His eyes rolled up. I screamed, "Noooo," as loud as I could, and bucked and shoved him off me with my feet. He recovered quickly and penned me down again. "Stop!" I shouted. We continued to struggle. I kicked and screamed as loud as the teakettle squealing on the stove. He gripped my wrists again. I snapped my legs shut and crossed and locked them with my feet. It took all my strength to hold them together. Jared laid down on me again and rubbed himself against my bare thighs. He grunted a few minutes later, and sprayed semen all over my skirt and legs. The teakettle continued to whistle and blow steam. Jared let my arms go. I pushed him off me and scurried away.

"Get out! How could you do that to me? You're my freaking doctor! How could you violate me like that?" I ran to the kitchen and grabbed the teapot from the flame. Most of the water had evaporated from the pot so I couldn't douse him with scolding hot water if he continued to pursue me. I didn't have a gun, but I had knives. I opened the silverware drawer and pulled out the sharpest knife I owned. "How could you do that to me?" I cried.

Jared tucked his shirt in and closed his trousers in a rush. He still had that evil smirk on his face that showed no remorse.

"Get the fuck out of my house. I should call the police and the Medical Board!"

"You weren't complaining when I was giving you what you needed," he said in an arrogant tone.

"I didn't fucking want to have dinner with you, and I sure as hell didn't want or expect that from you." I threw the knife at him. "Get out of my house, you pervert!"

He ducked and the knife went over his head and stuck in the wall.

"You took advantage of me. You read my chart. You knew about my problems with my fiancé. You raped me in your office and you raped me tonight!"

I reached in the drawer for a butcher knife. Jared made a quick dash for the door. I aimed and threw all my anger. The knife made a loud thump as it dug deep into the center of the door when it closed. It shook but held steady. I was amazed. A split-second sooner and it would have been digging into Jared's back.

I was too damn angry to cry. I snatched the knives out the wall and the door, aimed and threw. Again, and again I pulled the knives away from their intended targets. I had discovered a new talent. I ran the cold sharp blades over the bluish-green veins in my wrist. Sara couldn't have killed herself. I was ready to kill that mother sucker, but that isn't the same as killing yourself. I have too many undiscovered talents for that shit.

Someone was fighting and arguing outside my door. The voices sounded familiar, but I shut it out of my mind and headed to the shower.

28

I was determined to complete this thing that had turned my story book world upside down. I didn't worry about Max, Makai or the pesky night caller. It wasn't that I didn't care; I just couldn't deal with my screwed-up reality. Of course, I skipped my obstetrics appointments. I still loved and wanted my baby, and Max, but I couldn't go back to Dr. Morgan or Jared, and with school, I didn't have the time to go to the free clinic and sit all day.

Life passed at a slow-poke pace. Pregnancy, school, and being alone consumed, exhausted and frightened me. The late-night phone calls were stressful. Not hearing form Max since before Valentine's Day was devastating. And dealing with what Jared did to me was overwhelming. Gina sensed my depression, but I was too ashamed to share. I felt so stupid. I cut everyone off, but the more I tried to ignore everything, the more I mentally berated myself, and it swallowed me whole.

I kept my pregnancy a secret from my classmates until almost my eighth month by wearing bulky clothes and coats. The second trimester had been a breeze compared to the first, but with Makai kicking around and turning in my belly I felt as pregnant as I looked. Six weeks shy of my due date I called Dr. Morgan and begged him to see me. He was pleasantly surprised to hear from me. He didn't ask any questions about Jared. I was relieved. I didn't want to lie or relive anything about that night or my visit with him. He asked me to come to his office after my last class. He had replaced Jared with Dr. Karen Carr. He wanted me to meet her.

Dr. Morgan greeted me and took me to a room when I arrived. "You look great. How do you feel?" he said.

"Thank you. I feel okay. I'm getting close."

He smiled. "I thought you had switched doctors."

"You know my feelings about switching doctors."

"I'm sorry I forced Jared on you. The last thing I wanted was to make more problems for you and Max. Vicky and I weren't blessed with children. She has spoiled Max as much as Maryanne and Julius."

"Have you spoken to Max? How is he?"

He was shaken after he damn near killed Jared outside your door. He almost went to jail you know."

I didn't know anything, but I wanted to know more without putting Dr. Morgan in a precarious position again.

"Is Max okay? Is that why Ja—" My heart suddenly felt heavy when my mind flashbacked to what Jared had done. I had gotten good at blocking everything I couldn't deal with out of my mind. It takes all my energy to cope with my internal turmoil, and present responsibilities. I hopped from the table, pushed my tears backwards, and ran for the door.

"Wait, Gabby! It wasn't your fault. Several patients had complained about him coming on too strong." I stopped and looked Dr. Morgan in his eyes. "I record all my telephone conversations with my patients so I can make notes in their charts later. My memory isn't what it used to be. Anyway, Jared used my phone when he called you. He dropped the charges against Max when I played the tape for him. After he ended the call to you, he made lewd remarks about how he had gotten off touching you. He was explicit about how he was going to have you either willingly or kicking and screaming, with the second option being his preference. It was all the proof we needed."

"Why didn't anyone call me?"

"We didn't want to upset you."

"I see."

"Jared was reassigned to the Indian Reservation in Philadelphia."
My mind took off like a jet as I tried to decipher this new information. I kept running into turbulence. Max knew. He hadn't called.
What did all that mean? Shouldn't I be angry that everything was
taken care of without anyone consulting me? Is being reassigned going to stop Jared from taking advantage of someone else? Exactly how
much does Max know?

"Why did Max assault, Jared?" I asked.

"You don't know?" Dr. Morgan asked.

"No… I completely shut down for a while." Tears pooled in my
eyes, but I needed to know. "Does Max know what Jared did?"

"He was there. He beat Jared, but he wouldn't admit to doing
anything wrong."

"Oh, my God!" Max's initial reaction must have been awful. "He
thinks that I wanted Jared to… I had heard the tussling outside my
apartment. I was too distraught to react to it. Did Max hear the tape?"

Dr. Morgan nodded. The irony of being in love with a cheater is
that it is easy for Max to cheat because my love is so strong it is easier
for me to forgive him than to leave him. Does that make me strong,
or am I weak?

"Well, the good news is you're doing fine, and it won't be much
longer now," Dr. Morgan said as he completed my exam.

"I guess I should count my blessings. At least school and my baby
are great."

"Gabby, I'm glad you're back. I didn't mean to upset you. I thought
you had talked to Max."

"It happened so fast, I didn't know what to do… I blamed myself."
I tried to push the tears backward, but they came down hard as reality crashed in my mind.

"It wasn't your fault. Jared was totally out of line."

"I was too ashamed to talk to anyone about it. He made me feel
uncomfortable from the start. I should have said something. I should
have told Max. Jared held my wrists so tight, I had bruises for months.

It happened so fast. I couldn't think. I couldn't get away. I couldn't believe he was doing that to me. I still can't believe it happened to me. I tried to block it out of my mind."

"It wasn't your fault. He abused your trust as well as mine. I feel awful that you and Max had to suffer because of my mistake for forcing him on you. You and Max have a full belly right now. Let's just make sure your baby is okay."

We listened to Makai's heartbeat--that always makes me feel better. "Doc, if you see Max tell him we need him."

"You will have to tell him, Gabby. You need to tell him everything. He's hurting as much as you. It would be better if I wasn't that deeply involved. I told you about Jared because I was partly responsible."

Guilt had worn me down so I didn't make a stink when I realized Dr. Morgan was trying to ease his own conscience. "Thanks for telling me. Since I only have a month or so to go, will you see me to the end? Please?"

Dr. Morgan smiled. "It will be my pleasure. If I see Max is it okay to tell him that his babies are doing okay."

"Tell him at least one of them is."

"You're a fighter, Gabby; if you love Max as much as I think you do, call him."

❦

That night at eleven I picked up the phone, and dialed Max's number. My heart pounded while it rang. I had carefully chosen the right words to say, but when he answered, I knew no words could change what had happened, and my words suffocated in my throat until they were as dead as the telephone line. I managed to say, "Hello," the next night, but when Max said, "Gabby?" I pressed the button until I heard the dial tone pounding in my ear like the musical prelude of an Alfred Hitchcock episode. Max had heard what he had heard, and he had heard what Jared told him. If he wanted to hear my dying words he wouldn't have taken three months and counting to call.

Makai was doing okay so I continued to block Max out of my mind. I had gone from glowing to bloating in a matter of weeks. I wasn't in a hurry for Max too see me anyway. I can't wait for my pregnancy to be over even though I'm praying for a delay since my due date falls in the middle of finals. My belly is big and round and my navel sticks out like a button. My neck has turned dark and my cute nose has blended into my high cheekbones. I move slower with each passing day, but Makai was kicking up a storm. I wanted to believe now more than ever that if Max could feel him kicking, and hear his son's heartbeat, he would know my love for him is everlasting. He would even forgive me for not telling him about Jared after my initial visit.

♪

I hadn't been so glad to see Friday since Max and I started our weekend lovemaking marathons. I'd had a rough week. Makai had been kicking around like he was getting ready to make his mass exodus. I flicked on the TV and listened to the local news while I warmed one of Belinda's dinners. The news was filled with senseless murders, drug busts, and Mississippi crooked politics. Jackson was quickly becoming a very dangerous place to live. When I sat down to eat a composite sketch of a familiar looking guy flashed on the screen.

"The Jackson Police Department is looking for a man fitting this description for questioning in connection to the Catherine Walls case." A male with long dark hair, a Mets baseball cap, and dark sun glasses covered the TV screen. "The man in this sketch was seen coming from Catherine Wall's apartment hours before her boyfriend, Dennis Lane, discovered her mangled body. Miss Walls is the fourth murder to fit this pattern since early September. Jackson police now believe they are looking for a serial killer. This man is believed to be armed and extremely dangerous. Please call the police hotline at the bottom of your screen if you have any information regarding this case."

I reached across the table and turned the sound up. "The suspect drove away in a late model blue Buick. If you have any information about this crime please call (601)873-9110," the pretty blonde reporter said, and chills ran up and down my spine.

"The police would also like to question the suspect, in connection with the murders of three other women." Pictures of the other three victims flashed across the screen--one was Sara! "All four women were last seen shopping at local malls. Miss Wall was a nurse at Hinds General Hospital. Police questioned Dennis Lane. He is not a suspect at this time." My heart skipped two beats, and I almost had Makai when the phone rang.

"Gabby, are you watching the news?" Brad asked.

"Oh, my God, Brad, that could have been me!"

"You should call the police and tell them about your close encounter."

"I'm scared, Brad."

"Do you want me to come over?"

"No, I'll be okay. I don't have any plans to go out."

"Lock up, and if you need me, don't hesitate to call."

I checked to make sure I was securely locked in my prison before I sat back down to finish my dinner. I wish I hadn't told Belinda I was gaining too much weight from eating her homemade biscuits. Makai has been kicking me all week for depriving him. I took a bite of food and as I was savoring it a picture of Julius flashed across the screen.

"Dr. Julius Johnson, a prominent physician and community activist was shot in his office around noon today by a disgruntle patient. Lillian Baker, Dr. Johnson's long time nurse told Action News that the patient was upset when Dr. Johnson refused to renew a prescription for Percocet, a pain medication which can quickly led to dependence and abuse by its users. The patient returned several hours later and shot Dr. Johnson three times before he turned the gun on himself. Dr. Johnson was taken to the University Medical Center by Life Star helicopter. He underwent five hours of surgery to remove three small caliber bullets from his shoulder, arm and leg. He is in critical condition."

I put my chicken between two slices of bread, and stole bites while I slipped on my sandals, grabbed my keys and student ID badge, and rushed to the hospital. I stormed into the waiting room of ICU as if I owned it and Max. He was sitting with his head hung down. Tammy was rubbing his back. She had enough clay-colored make-up on her face to plant a garden. Her tears had made rows down the center of her cheeks, which made her look like a sad chocolate clown.

Max looked up when I stormed into the room. He smiled, but I stopped dead in my tracks. Tammy looked at me and my swollen belly as if I was dodo. I wanted to laugh when I saw her clown-face, but it wasn't the time or the place to finish the cat fight she started in high school. Max's eyes were damp, but he smiled as he walked in slow sexy motion to greet me.

He pulled me into his arms and hugged me despite my protruding belly, wide nose, ugly maternity dress, and what I had let Jared do to me. Makai did a somersault and kicked hard. Max placed his hand on my thin orange and yellow sundress where all the commotion was, and then he covered my lips. I returned his kiss with every loving emotion I owned. I didn't care about Tammy and Jared. I kissed him for Makai and me. We wanted to let Max know we wanted to come home.

"I saw the news. Are there any changes? Are you okay?"

"I'm scared, Gabby." I flashbacked to the first night I slept on his blue sheets. He still loves me enough to share his fears. He played with the spiral curls in my hair.

"Your hair grew back?"

"Yeah," I said, and I wished I could have him back as well. I stared at the fear in his eyes while he toyed with my hair. He probably stared at my fears as well.

"I wish I hadn't left you alone in Nashville last August. I should have come home when we found Sara."

GLORIA F. PERRY

He threaded his fingers between mine. Tammy continued to stare at me like flies swarming around a pile of manure.

"How do you feel? You look tired," Max said.

"I had a busy week. Where is your mother?"

"Uncle Lester and Aunt Vicky had to take her home. The doctor had to give her a sedative."

Tammy continued to look at me with evil eyes. I was happy with Max's kiss and the love and concern in his eyes. I smiled and offered her peace. She can offer Max a shoulder to cry on, and he has taken her up on her offers, but his eyes still tell me his heart belongs to me. I know her look--I see it every time I look into Anthony's eyes. I also know you can like someone strongly, but you can't squeeze love out if it isn't there.

"I just stopped by to see if you needed anything," I said. Then I turned to leave.

"Wait!" He squeezed my arm. "Can you sit with me for a little while?"

"I don't want to intrude," I looked at Tammy and offered peace again.

"You're not. Please stay." His eyes begged. I smiled. He sat beside Tammy and patted the spot on the other side of him for me. Makai kicked again. I may have been hiding my excitement about kissing him on the outside, but my insides were jumping around like freed slaves. Max put his hand on my belly and smiled.

"He's an active little guy, huh?"

"Like his daddy," I said mostly because I didn't like Tammy's nasty attitude. I was trying hard to be nice to her and supportive of Max.

"I'm surprised you're not hanging out with Brad tonight," Tammy said. "Your car has been at his house every other night this week."

I rolled my eyes. "Brad was kind enough to be my Lamaze partner."

Tammy's blond hair and heavy make-up had thrown me off back in August. It took me a while to put the puzzle together before everything clicked. She isn't the only one who did their research. Lorna checked her out for me before she left her job at State. Tammy's

228

father is head of the English Department at JSU. He had a local talk show on WOKJ on Saturday Mornings and Tammy came on to talk about her experience in Jack and Jill. She and Max have traveled the same social circles since they were kids. They both went to St. Agnes High. They were in Jack and Jill, and Max escorted her to her debutante ball and to his junior and senior proms. He had other girls in-between, but he was always there for Tammy. I'll bet my last dollar that she was his first. I may have to learn to deal with her so I continued to send her peace. Makai kicked. Max smiled as he rubbed my stomach.

"Promise me that you will call me when it's time," Max said. He continued to rub my belly.

"Sure," I said. Sparks that I thought I would never feel again after the fiasco with Jared began to stir in my girly parts.

He half smiled and gazed into space. I doubt if he heard what Tammy had said. She opened her mouth to say something else, but I looked at her as though I would jack her ass up. Then I sent her some more peace and love her way. I stood up and announced that I was going to the chapel to pray.

"I'll go with you." Max said. He stood up. "You wanna come, Tammy?"

"No, you guys go ahead. If the doctor comes I'll come and get you."

Max laced his hands with mine as we walked silently to the small hospital chapel. Several people were already there praying. The room was lit by the soft glow of red candles in tall red glass jars. The room smelled like sandalwood burning. Max and I slid into the back row. The chapel had three short rows and an altar with a stature of Jesus nailed to a cross surrounded by candles. Max got on his knees. I sat next to him on the red crushed-velvet bench. He held my hand and closed his eyes. We prayed silently for ten minutes, and then he got up, made the sign of the cross and sat next to me. We held hands and he rubbed my belly like a bottle filled with a genie for another ten minutes. Makai kicked a few times. The dim candle light and having Max next to me had calmed my spirit. I realized that I hadn't relaxed in months. I rested my head on his shoulder. He stared into the candle light and toyed with my hair. After we left the chapel he walked me to my car.

"Thanks for coming," he said. We kissed, and then he rubbed my stomach again.

"If you need a shoulder and a friend, I'll be home."

"Don't forget to call me," was all he said as he backed away.

29

My doorbell rang around midnight. Max's voice surprised scared and excited me all at the same time. Makai had been kicking up a storm since Max kissed us goodbye. I had showered and shampooed my hair, and put it in four braids so it could air dry. Makai and I had an ice cream snack. We were still too wired to go to sleep. Max had that look in his eyes even though he had walked away as if he wasn't interested. The doorbell rang again followed by a loud knock. Max yelled, "It's me, Gabby, let me in!"

"Me who?"

"You know, me, the guy who loves you, but who keeps messing everything up."

I cracked the door and left the chains in their hooks. I don't know why I was playing coy when all I wanted to do was jump his bones. I would have pounced on him in the chapel right in front of Jesus nailed to that cross if we had been alone. "Do you think you can get it right this time?"

Max smiled. I was wearing a white sleeveless T-shirt and blue bikini panties. The apartment was hot. All the windows were closed and locked, but I hate sleeping with the air conditioning on. Pregnancy had turned my nipples and areolae darker so they were probably visible through my thin T-shirt. Max swept his eyes over me. That look was in his eyes and smile. I wasn't sure if he was smiling at my exposed belly button or my ripe nipples, but I clumsily unhooked the chains.

He definitely had that look in his eyes, but he stuffed his hands in his pockets like a nervous little boy instead of sweeping me up in his arms and devouring my pleasures.

"Well, are you gonna come in?" I asked. He stepped inside. I closed the door, locked it, and put the chains back into their slots. "How is Julius?"

"It's still touch and go," he said as he rocked on his heels and surveyed me sheepishly.

"As much as Big Curtis and I bump heads God knows I would be a basket case if somebody shot him."

"Mom totally lost it. Her whole world is Dad."

I slipped my arms around Max and hugged him. "He's going to be okay." Max put his arms around me and nervously rocked us like ocean waves. "Did you eat? Belinda sent me dinner. I lost my appetite when I heard about Julius. I can warm it for you. Mommy's food is good medicine for the soul."

"Thanks." He continued to rock me. I made a motion to go to the kitchen, but he tightened his arms around me. "Let me hold you for a little while first." He leaned his head into the top of my head and took a deep breath. "You washed your hair?"

"Yeah, it's still wet."

"Do you ever wish I was here?" Max asked.

"All the time."

"I used to wish you needed me like Mom needs Dad, but after seeing her breakdown today, I'm glad you're independent. I would never want you to be in as much pain over me as she was today."

I tightened my arms around him and rocked us. "I'm in pain, but my blues ain't like hers."

"I haven't always been straight with you, Gabby, but I've always been very much in love with you. When I saw Mom lose it this afternoon, I knew it was more than her whole world revolving around Dad; her whole world is Dad."

I tiptoed and touched my lips to Max's. He held my face between his big hands and stared into my eyes. "That's a lot of pressure to put on a man."

"That's too much pressure to put on anyone. What your parents have is special in its way, but times have changed and people have to change as well."

"I finally understand why you took the scholarship," he said as he undid my braids.

"I'm from a different class. Working is a basic instinct for women like me. Come on." I slipped my hand in his. "Let me warm your food."

My legs were tired, and my ankles were swollen, but I didn't want him to worry. I wandered around the kitchen while he watched. His smile made me forget all about being pregnant. The twinkle in his eyes made me feel sexier than ever. I warmed the dinner and we chatted while he ate it.

Julius was resting when Max left the hospital, but he wasn't out the woods yet. Max was just as worried about Maryanne. I let my hair hang over my chest to keep him from staring. His stare gave me warm chills that I wasn't sure if either one of us could handle. He touched my belly and talked and kissed it when Makai moved around. And we kissed and stared at each other until we both had to look away.

"I have a new talent you wanna see?" I asked to break the monotony.

"I don't know if I can stand it tonight. You have me pretty roused as it is."

I giggled. "This will un-rouse you." I gathered up my knives and stood in the hallway and aimed for the door while Max watched. Each knife stuck in the center of the door.

He clapped for me and said, "Wow, how did you discover you could do that?"

My face went blank, and so did his as I thought about Jared. How could I have been so damn stupid? Max walked over to me and hugged me.

"I have to go check on Mom."

I walked him to the door. He kissed me lightly. "When Julius is better, I'd like to see if we can work something out."

"I'd like to work something out before Makai gets here." He kissed me again. "I'll call you if there are any changes." He touched my belly and said good-night to Makai before he slipped out the door. I was disappointed.

His kisses got me through the night. Makai was quiet the next morning; maybe he was sad like his mother. I stayed in bed and studied. Belinda called around noon. I told her about Julius. I didn't bother to tell her about Sara and the man in the blue Buick. I didn't tell Max either; I didn't want them to worry.

There was a knock on my door around three o'clock. I pulled my flowered sundress on over my blue panties and T-shirt and rushed to the door. I thought it was Max until a man's voice yelled, "Police, open up!"

I cracked the door and left the chains on. "Can I see your identification please?" The officers showed me their badges and photo identifications; I wouldn't know a real one from a fake one, but theirs looked authentic to me. "What can I do for you?" I asked calmly but sweat was already trickling down my back.

"We need to ask you a few questions about Sara James's murder."

"Murder? They said it was a suicide."

"There have been some new developments; we need to ask you a few more questions. Can we come in or would you prefer to come down to the station?"

I could feel my wet T-shirt sticking to my back. "I'm not dressed; can you give me a few minutes?" I asked. I closed the door before they could answer. I run to my bedroom and put on my bra and sandals and called Brad. Then I sat on the sofa and waited for the officers or Brad to knock on the door. Five minutes passed before the officers knocked again. I opened the door again and flashed a phony smile.

"Sorry for taking so long. I had to use the bathroom." I rubbed my stomach. "This is my first."

"Miss Oliver, we don't have all day. We just want to ask you a few routine questions, and depending on your answers we will be out of your way." I took the chains off the door and let the officers in. One was young, handsome, and the same color and size as Max. His name was Jerry Young. The other officer was about the same height and size. He had black hair, blue eyes, and a sharp nose and chin. His name was Gresham Harris. They were dressed in street clothes, which was why I had asked to see their badges.

"You have a lot of locks for one door Miss Oliver," Officer Harris said.

"I've had a lot of scares for one woman, sir."

"What happened to your door?" Officer Young asked.

"I like to play with knives," I said before I thought about the connotations. Harris and Young looked at me as if I was a suspect. "I throw them. Would you like to see?"

"That won't be necessary," Harris said, and after he read me my rights he took out the sketch I had seen on TV and showed it to me. "Miss Oliver, how long have you known this man?"

Brad knocked on the door and yelled for me to let him in. I didn't hesitate. Brad hugged and kissed me on the cheek. Then we all sat at my small table. Harris showed me the picture again. I studied it for a few minutes.

"I don't know him, but I think he followed me from the mall on December twentieth."

Harris and Young looked at each other and made leery faces. Officer Young frowned when he noticed Brad holding my hand and rubbing my back. I was shivering.

"Miss Oliver, did you report the incident?"

"No sir, but when I saw his picture on the news yesterday I had planned to call, but then I found out that my fiancé's father had been shot." Harris looked at Young in a knowing way again.

"So, you had two opportunities to file a report and you didn't, Miss Oliver. Are you having, or did you have an affair with this man," Harris said as he pointed at the sketch.

"No sir. I went to the mall to do some Christmas shopping. I ran into my fiancé's mother. We had words. She's not to fond of me. When I went to my car, that man was parked across from me. He had on sunglasses, but I'm almost certain that is him. He was reading a newspaper. It was dark." I pointed to the picture. "When I turned on my lights he smiled at me. I didn't like his smile. When I drove off I noticed that his car had a UMMC parking sticker. I have a student sticker his was an employee. I vaguely remember seeing him around school. Sometimes when men try to get my attention, I try to blow them off without being mean, but some of them think a little kindness is more than it is. Anyway, I drove away, but I think that man followed me. I was afraid to go home so I stopped at Brad's. Brad and Kelly came home with me. Later that night I almost lost my baby. That's why I remember the exact date."

"Miss Oliver, can you tell us why this man has nude pictures of you all over his walls, CDs with your name written on them, a bedroom set and a stereo, which can be traced back to your credit card, and the silk scarf you were wearing in some of the more provocative pictures? We have records of you all's late-night phone calls. You're a beautiful woman, Miss Oliver. Those pictures were obviously taken for and by someone special. This is a murder investigation. If you're withholding information we will trace it to you sooner or later, so why don't you tell us what you and Adler are up to, and stop wasting our time," Harris said.

"We think you're living some kind of a double life. We think you and Adler Hutchinson were lovers," Young said.

"Lovers! You have got to be kidding. I don't know that man! I think he followed me but I'm not one hundred percent sure."

"You say you like to play with knives. You and your boyfriend could have been acting out your sick sexual fantasies when you all killed those girls and cut them up? The first victim was your roommate," Young said.

"That's enough!" Brad shouted. "There is no way, Gabby, is involved in any of this."

With everything that had happened to me, I didn't even react to the officers' accusations. I thought Max had taken the pictures when he went back to get my clothes. A flashback of Sara lying in her own blood, the look of her eyes forever suspended in a state of shock, her exposed body, and that smell flashed through my mind. I hopped up and ran to the bathroom and threw up. Brad and the officers followed me. I rinsed my mouth and went back to the kitchen.

"I was in shock after Max found Sara dead. I spent the weekend at Max's parents' house. I rubbed my belly--this is my proof. Max went to the apartment that Saturday and brought most of my things. My brothers had just moved me in so I thought I could leave my stuff in the apartment until I found a new one. I stayed with Max's parents until I found this place. When I was ready for my stuff it had been stolen. I didn't bother to report it because I thought Dylan had taken it."

"I thought you said you didn't know Dylan." Officer Harris said.

"I said I didn't know the apartment was in Dylan's name until I was told that night. Sara hadn't asked me to sign a lease. Dylan was Sara's boyfriend."

"Why didn't you tell us this before?"

"Sara kicked him out shortly after I moved in, and at the time you all said she had killed herself."

"Do you have this man in your custody?" Brad asked.

"No, Mr. Pruter. Someone saw his picture on the news and called us. He split before we got there. We searched his place and all we found was Miss Oliver's pictures and things. His phone records led us back to Miss Oliver."

"My fiancé took those pictures. I stole the book from Max when I moved out because I didn't want them to fall in the wrong hands." I chuckled but I felt more violated than I had with Jared. The phone calls, the feelings that I was being watched rushed to my mind. I suddenly remembered seeing the blue Buick and the man in the parking lot at school several times. "I was being stalked, wasn't I?"

"Maybe? From the looks of his apartment, he thinks you're pretty hot stuff, but you never know what people like that are thinking," Young said.

"Do you think he is planning to kill me? Some pervert has been calling me in the middle of the night for months, now we know it was him."

"Did you report the calls?" Harris asked.

"No, I thought it was my fiancé trying to scare me into coming home."

"Miss Oliver, do you live alone?" Harris asked.

"Yes sir. My fiancé is in medical school in Nashville."

"We ran a profile on Hutchinson and judging from the shrine he made with your pictures and belongings, he had, and probably still has plans for you," Harris said.

Tears dripped form my eyes that I didn't feel coming. I was visibly trembling. I can't wait to have this baby so my hormones can balance out, and I can control my emotions better. Brad put his arms around me. He tried to reassure me.

"We didn't come here to alarm you, Miss Oliver, but we're dealing with a very sick man. We'll send an undercover officer over to keep an eye on you until we catch Hutchinson," Young said.

"What if you don't catch him?" I asked.

"We will." Both officers said.

"Miss Oliver, did your roommate know this man," Harris asked.

"I don't know. I didn't really know Sara all that well." I thought about the last words Sara had spoken to me; *I don't know how you do it, if Dylan wasn't around I would be fucking some nigga off the streets.* I had suspected Christine's husband all these months.

After the cops left, I cried on Brad's shoulder until Makai started kicking around. There was a thunderstorm brewing and a tornado watch. I promised to stay home, but knowing that my life was probably on the line made me want to make things right with Max before it was too late.

30

I showered and put on my most flattering maternity dress, if there is such a thing. It was a navy-blue sheath dress with a scoop neck and a hip length beige lace vest. I'd filled a picnic basket with turkey and peanut butter and jelly sandwiches, potato chips, juice and my sharpest butcher knife. It was steamy hot. Dark clouds loomed low in the sky, which was a perfect description of how I felt. I sat the basket on the floor and stuck the knife under my car seat. Then I checked around for perverts and zoomed off. It started to pour as soon as I turned the corner. The wipers were on, but I still couldn't see--my eyes were raining. It was Saturday so I was lucky enough to find a parking space near the hospital entrance. I made a mad dash for the door.

Max was sitting alone with his head hung down. He walked across the waiting room to greet me. "What's wrong, baby?" He asked. He wrapped his arms around me, and led me to a chair.

"How is your Dad?"

"He had surgery again this morning to stop some internal bleeding. He's in recovery."

"I brought you some sandwiches." I gave him the basket and wiped my cheeks. "It's pouring outside."

"Dad is going to be okay. His situation is touch and go, but he's gonna make it...he has to." Max put his hand on my stomach. "How's my little boy doing today?"

I smiled despite everything when Makai kicked for his father.

"What's wrong, Gabby? I don't want you getting upset over Dad. He's tough, he'll be okay."

I squeezed Max's hand. "How are you holding up?"

"I'm hanging in there. Aunt Julianne came up this morning to be with Mom. She's a basket case."

I squeezed his hand again. "Max, the police have the nasty pictures we took... they think the man who took them is a serial killer, and I'm fairly sure he has been stalking me." I sniffled and Makai kicked me hard. "I know this is a bad time and all, but I thought you should know, just in case something happens to me."

"Whoa! Back up. A serial killer!"

I told Max everything I had learned from the police visit. "I thought you had taken the pictures when you went to get my things. The photo album was in my lingerie drawer."

"No, it wasn't there, I looked. When you took the pictures, I thought you didn't want to be with me anymore."

"I thought the pictures would be safer with me. I should have never agreed to let you take them in the first place."

"Baby, those are beautiful pictures of our love for each other. There is nothing pornographic about them."

"So why do I feel so violated? Some pervert has been calling me for months. At first I thought it was you trying to scare me into coming home. What are my parents going to think?"

"I showed some of your less revealing poses to Dad. He said they were beautiful works of art. He said you're beautiful, and that I had a great talent because I had made you even more beautiful."

"Big Curtis is gonna disown me when he finds out. Those officers looked at me like I was the playmate of the year."

"That's because you're beautiful. Last night when I saw you looking all cute in your underwear with your stomach protruding, and your lips pouty from our kissing, I thought what a great picture that would make for our collection."

"Never again, Max."

"Baby, you're always saying how we shouldn't let other people tell us how to live. You used to love taking those pictures. Yes, most of them were nude shots, but they are all tastefully done. You once said I made you feel beautiful and free in the pictures."

"You did, but now—look at the mess they are causing in the wrong hands."

"You're more beautiful than ever, and if you won't let me dictate what you do, I know you're not going to let some pervert make you ashamed of your beauty or our love."

"Max, I don't wanna die in a bad way."

"Baby, I'm not gonna let anyone hurt you or come between us."

"I wish I had stayed in Nashville with you."

"I miss you, but you're doing what you thought you had to do. You're too full of life to let me or anyone else steal it from you."

"You mean it, Max?"

"Yup. I understand why you did it. I wish things had worked out the way we, I had planned. I was mad as hell when you left. I thought it was over when I couldn't find the pictures. I know how determined you are, that's what I like best about you."

A tall red-headed doctor wearing surgical scrubs came into the waiting room. "Mr. Johnson, your father is out of recovery. He's resting, but if you and your wife would like to visit him for a few minutes, you can."

Julius was hooked to IVs, heart and blood pressure monitors, a catheter and oxygen. If it wasn't for his fingers and mouth twitching occasionally, I would have thought he was dead. His lips were ashy white, crusty, and swollen. His skin was purplish, and his nails were yellow. Seeing him made me realize why I had chosen dentistry. Max kissed Julius; I followed his lead.

"Dad, it's me and Gabby. You hang in there. My son is gonna need his grandpa to teach him the ways of the world," Max said and his voice quivered.

"You told your parents about the baby?" I whispered.

"I told Dad. Mom doesn't know," Max said. "Dad, Mom is pretty broken up about you being in here. I know how much you love her.

You should get better for her. She won't be able to find her way with-out you, none of us will…" Max squeezed my hand, and then he kissed Julius again. "I'll be back to check on you later. Try to rest and get better." Max's voice quivered again. His eyes clouded up. He squeezed my hand and led me out the room.

His tears came down the minute we were outside the door. My eyes clouded up as well. "What if he's not around to see Makai? He's been rooting for us to work out our problems even though he wouldn't say it."

"Seeing Julius lying there hooked to life support was scary enough to make me want to make the most of life while I have it. Maybe Makai will give Julius a reason to hold on. He certainly has been my inspiration."

"I need to talk to his doctor. I'll be back in a few minutes." Max kissed me and walked away.

I had been free of Max and his lies until Makai started to kick around. Now he claims to understand me, and his eyes and kisses are filled with love. He's all choked up because Julius may not be around for our son. Hell, I didn't think he was going to be around for Makai until yesterday. Max smiled when he came back and saw me daydreaming about us being a real family.

"What are you thinking about?" he asked.

"When we loved each other so much nothing else mattered."

"Shit matters, Gabby, but it doesn't mean that I've stopped loving you, or that I've given up on winning your love and trust back. A great philosopher, Mr. Big Curtis Oliver, once told me, 'Life gives grown folks many twists and turns, boy, if you want to pretend that you're grown with my daughter, you better learn how to deal with the hard shit when it comes, cause if she's anything like her momma, she's gonna keep you on your toes.'"

"And Mommy always says, 'If you can't stand the heat, stay out of the kitchen.' I stood up. "There's a tornado watch. I should get home before the weather gets too bad."

Max walked me to my car. The sky was sunny and beautiful to the east, and dark and gloomy in to the west. It was muggy, and it felt more like August than late April.

"I'm gonna check on Dad again." He stuffed his hands in his pockets and locked his eyes on me. "I was wondering if I could stop by later?"

"I'd like that." I smiled wickedly and held his stare. "I'll make spaghetti and a salad. It'll be like old times."

He smiled and said, "You have a date, Mrs. Johnson." He kissed me and waved goodbye.

"Bring your camera and tripod," I said as I started my engine. He smiled again. I blew him a kiss and drove away.

Rain was coming down in sheets when I got to the supermarket. The wind was gusting, lightening was flashing, and the thunder was bombing. I decided to wait the storm out in the store. The possibility of getting together with Max made me forget about the tornado watch. It seemed as if everybody and their daddies were in Jitney-Jungle picking up the ingredients for a romantic dinner. The lights in the store blinked. Within seconds the store was dark. The store manager asked everyone to remain calm. Little kids and babies cried all around me. Makai even kicked as if he knew everything that was happening. My eyes adjusted to the dark quickly. Some people were putting food, and other items in their purses and diaper bags. My money was thin, but with my luck, I would probably get arrested, and end up on the cover of the *Clarion-Ledger* again. A generator kicked on and dim light lit the supermarket. Five minutes later the manager announced that they could resume checking out customers. It was Saturday, the store was packed, and the lines were black Friday long. By the time I got checked out, it was dark, but at least the storm had subsided.

GLORIA F. PERRY

I pulled into a parking space and popped my trunk. The apartment complex was totally dark. It had started raining again. I reached under the seat to get my umbrella. Someone snatched my door open, and a funky hand covered my mouth before I could sit erect!

"Do what I say, and I won't hurt you!" a man's familiar voice said. He poked a sharp object against my back with enough force to let me know he meant it.

I couldn't scream. This time I would fight to the end—I didn't have any other options. My hand was on my umbrella. I continued to feel around for the butcher knife. I tried to bite the man's hand after I got a firm grip on the knife. He bitch-slapped me with his free hand before I could take a stab at him. Then he pressed his knife into my back until he was at the brink of drawing blood. My blood. My baby's blood!

"Why are you bothering me?" I mumbled into his dirty hand.

"I've been watching you for months. I was looking for you when I killed your roommate."

I almost peed on myself when he said that. The mere thought of Sara made me want to vomit.

"You wouldn't hurt a pregnant woman, would you?"

The sharpness in my back eased up a little, when the man said, "Sure I would. Baby killers always make the news." I could hear a smile in the way his voice changed. Every word was filled with love—a very dark psychopathic love.

My mother-to-be-do-whatever-the-fuck-you-must-do-adrenaline kicked in. I tightened my hand around the knife and eased it from under the seat. I was ready to fight crazy with crazy!

"You were supposed to be mine. Bradley Pruter has lived like a king, and I've struggled all my life. Do you think that's right, Gabriella?" My mind was full of questions, but I focused on trying to find his weak spot. His dirty hand still covered my mouth.

"I'll say one thing for my little brother; we have the same taste for half-bred whores." His tone of voice was filled again with venomous love. I chanted real love, trumps fake love—it must—I will save me and my baby.

Now I knew why the man in the dark glasses looked familiar. "You're Brad's brother?" I mumbled. "Does he know? Brad has a kind heart. He told me he always wanted a brother..."

"Shut the fuck up. He's my half-brother, of course Trent denies everything. But he loves Bradley enough to accept a piece of ass like you. The Pruters treat me and my mother like trailer trash."

He pressed the sharp object into my back again.

"This isn't Brad's baby—we're just classmates, and friends, and nothing else," I managed to mumble.

"I said shut the fuck up, and get out the car!" The point of the sharp object pressed against my zipper, and my spine. The pain was more than I could take. I bit his hand again, this time I could taste blood. He pushed the knife deeper into my metal zipper—I was wearing one of Hope's homemade dresses with a real zipper. When he repositioned his knife, I jolted up, spun around, and swung my knife for his neck. My goal was his carotid artery.

It was dark, but I could see the surprise in his eyes when I knocked his switchblade from his hands, and lunged toward him like a mad woman. My tomboy days of wrestling with my brothers, and playing any kind of ball they played came in handy. Adler dodged the blow by grabbing my knife with his hand. I got queasy when blood dripped from his hand like a slaughtered hog. I screamed, and let go of the knife. I screamed again, and picked up his knife, and pierced his shoulder. My strength must have been coming from my strong will to protect my unborn child because I was scared as crap.

Adler dropped the butcher knife. "I'm gonna kill you, whore bitch!"

When he bent, and reached for the butcher knife, I stomped his hand with my heel, stabbed him again in his back-shoulder area, and rammed my knee into his mouth and nose like a head butt. I had seen Sara; I didn't want to end up like that. I could feel the rage in his eyes even though it was dark. Warm pee ran down my legs and reminded me that I had to fight. He lunged toward me again like a raging bull.

"You like it rough. Well, that's exactly what I had in mind. I'm gonna fuck you until you scream like your roommate. Then I'm gonna cut your pussy and your baby out right before I kill you. I bet the newspaper will print that."

A car with blinding lights roared into the parking lot. Adler hesitated when he looked toward the bright light. I picked up the butcher knife. The car continued toward us like a speeding train. Adler turned and ran toward a white pickup truck parked in the corner of the parking lot. I aimed and threw the butcher knife.

"You picked the wrong sister to call bitch whore!" I shouted. The knife hit his shoulders before it fell to the wet ground again. He yelled, but like the others it couldn't have been more than a skin prick. Cutting through skin and clothes was harder than I thought. The car continued to speed toward him. Adler grabbed his shoulders and stopped to pick up the knife. He looked toward me, and the approaching car again, but he continued to run toward the truck. The light reflected off his knife on the ground. I picked it up.

The car made a squishing sound when it stopped. Max hopped from his car. I gave him the knife. He grabbed the tripod and chased Adler. He hit him over the head with his tripod. Adler wobbled and fell face first into a large pothole. Muddy water splashed high into the air. Max jumped backwards.

"Run, Gabby! Call the police. I'll stay here and make sure he doesn't get away."

"Be careful, Max, he has a knife!"

The extra weight didn't slow me down one bit as I ran up the stairs. I asked for Detective Young or Harris. Detective Young scolded me for leaving without telling him my whereabouts. They had sent an undercover officer over, but I had left before she arrived. "Will you please shut up and let me get a word in edgewise." I shouted into the phone. "Adler is in my parking lot with a lump on his head." My heart was pounding against my chest. Warm pee stung the shaving nicks on my legs as it trickled down them again.

"I'll see who is in your area. Someone will be there soon. The storm knocked out half the power lines in North Jackson. It's been a busy evening."

I dried my legs and changed into a pair of dry panties before I went back outside with a flashlight to make sure Max was okay. He had penned Adler to the ground and sat on his back. He had ripped Adler's shirt and used it to tie and bandage his hands together. Every time Adler screamed a bitch whore obscenity, Max dipped his face in the mud hole.

Two police cars arrived at the same time. Adler looked in my direction while he was being handcuffed and said, "I should have slit your throat back in September instead of letting myself fall for your naked pictures. I'll be back for you. Believe that. I'll find you wherever you are and the next time you will end up like the others."

Max hugged me tighter and whispered. "It's over baby. He's just trying to get into your head. Don't give him that power."

Detective Young read Adler his Miranda Rights, but Adler continued to spit out bitter obscenities about me, Brad's father, Sara and his other killings.

Adler was a security guard at the university. He had given me directions to the office of minority affairs where I first met Sara. He said he followed me to Sara apartment and watched my comings and goings for two weeks before he made his move. He had let himself into the apartment, but my door was locked that night, and Sara's wasn't. He was just planning to rape her. But according to him, she made him kill her—they all did. He laid low for four days after he killed Sara. He waited for the gotdam newspapers, and the news to report his crime, but there was nothing. He let himself into the apartment again. He found Sara the same as he had left her. That's when he decided to wait in my bedroom for me. But Max was with me. Max discovered Sara's body before Adler could make his move. He wrote the note on my mirror and sneaked out the window with the rest of my nude pictures while I was screaming, and crying, and making a commotion about Sara. He laid low again after the papers said Sara had committed suicide. Every time he saw me and Brad talking, and hanging out around school, he wanted to harm me to get back at his father and Brad. He had a special thing for me and my pictures. He wanted to make my murder extra special. He went out and raped and killed other girls who looked like me. He was angry when he saw the picture of me and Brad in the newspaper. And when he noticed that I was pregnant, he was even more determined to rape and kill me like the others. Raping and killing Bradley Pruter's girlfriend and baby would surly cause pandemonium in the newsrooms, and the police department. The newspapers and the newsrooms would finally be forced to report the gory details that linked all the crimes. He wanted everybody to know he was a notorious serial killer, and Trenton Pruter's oldest son. He even confessed that he should have banged my half-breed ass, and cut my pussy out like he had done the others. He'd had plenty of opportunities. He continued to shout obscenities until he was out of hearing distance.

Max hugged me. I thought he was rocking me in his arm, until I realized I was shivering. It was still muggy and eighty-five degrees.

Detective Young patted Max on the shoulder. "You did great. I would have been tempted to kill the son-of-a-bitch if this was my lady." He swept his eyes over me. Max frowned.

"The thought crossed my mind, but I have too many people depending on me to be stuck in jail. I want to be around for this little guy we have in the oven. Gabby, had done all the hard work before I arrived."

Detective Young's smile moved to my protruding belly. Makai felt like a rotisserie chicken rotating around in me. "So, you're the photographer, you're one lucky son-of-a-gun."

Max looked deep into my eyes, and smiled. "When can we have our pictures back?"

"They're evidence, but since Adler more or less confessed, justice should be swift. Don't worry, by the time me and my partner finish with him, and the paperwork, we'll have more than enough evidence to close this case. Alder won't be seeing the light of day for a long time. Don't worry about him spoiling any of your plans. I'll need a statement from you all before we go, and then we will be on our way."

Max took the grocery bags from my car. The apartment was sultry hot, and so was I. No power meant no AC and no way to cook. Max opened the windows. The air outside was just as sticky hot. I lit candles and placed one on the kitchen counter, the dining room table, and the coffee table.

Max took off everything but his boxer shorts. Sweat glistened off the hair on his chest and around his navel. He kissed my shoulders and slipped my dress off. Then he lifted my hair and twisted it into a knot. He pressed himself against my damp white cotton panties and I remembered that I had peed on myself twice. He turned me in his arms and kissed my lips.

I looked deep into his eyes. "Let's take our time and get it right this time." He nodded and gave me his T-shirt. I took a shower and dressed in it, and a pair of red cotton panties.

He rested on my sofa while I prepared the salad. We ate salad and bread, and drank the nonalcoholic wine he had brought. We stared at each other lovingly and tickled and rubbed each other's legs, hands and feet. Then we sat outside on the balcony and watched the stars, and the moon reappear as the clouds dissipated.

Max moved the candles to the bedroom and set up the tripod. I posed for a few side shots in my panties and his T-shirt. I took a few shots with my hair in two long braids. Then I took the braids out and took the T-shirt off. Max said I looked like a not so innocent teenage mother. We did nude shots together while he covered me with his hands and mouth or by pressing our bodies so close we looked like ebony and ivory keys on a grand piano. The room was sultry sticky hot and so was I.

Resisting each other was impossible. The room got hotter as the candles flickered, and hot molten wax dripped on my furniture and between my legs. The camera continued to click and we continued to kiss and take our time. When I couldn't take anymore warm chills, I pushed Max on the bed and grabbed the camera. I clicked a few pictures, and then I loved him until we were both one continuous trembling hot chill. The camera was on the bed next to us. I snapped his picture when he got that look in his eyes that let me know he loved me without a doubt if only for a split second. He was still trembling and his arms were covered with gooseflesh when he took the camera from me and snapped my Kodak moment. I rolled over on my back and we wallowed in our sweat and love juices. After we returned to earth, we got up and converted my bathroom into a dark room. Max kicked me out. He didn't want me smelling the chemicals. We had reclaimed each other again in pictures. We made love again and it was sultrier, sticker, and hotter than the first time. I drifted to sleep afterwards, but I jolted myself awake when I heard myself snoring. Max was lying next to me. The room was still sultry, sticky hot. The green light on the alarm clock was flashing, but I didn't bother to get up and turn on the AC. I liked being sultry, sticky, hot with Max.

The phone rang at eleven-thirty the next morning. I was in the middle of a sexy dream. Detective Young was the last person I wanted to converse with on a hot Sunday morning, even though he was the bearer of news that couldn't wait.

31

Our night of loving had been a much-needed sweet escape from reality for both of us. I was groggy and incoherent when I whispered, "What?" into the phone. Max turned over and told me to go back to sleep.

"I hate to disturb you this early in the morning," Detective Young repeated. "I thought you would like to know that it's over. Adler is dead."

I sprang up in the bed. "Dead!"

Max sprang up, "What! Who died? Is that Mom?" I shook my head and used my eyes to let him know that it wasn't his mother.

"After we attended to Adler's wounds he was still talking shit, excuse my language. We put him in the cell with a couple of big ass niggas, excuse me--we figured they would shut him up y'know. Anyway, he had been sodomized and beaten. We found him this morning hanging from his bunk with his pants wrapped around his neck."

"Wow!" I wiped sleep from my eyes. "May I have my pictures back now?"

"You'll have to come down to the station and sign a release."

"I'll be down later today." I hung up the phone then I kissed Max.

"What's up, baby?" he asked as he stretched.

"I'll be right back." I had an urgent need to pee.

Pregnant pictures of me in ecstasy were hanging in the bathroom to dry—proof of my undying love for Max—proof that Max had loved me even though he hadn't asked me again to marry him.

I took the pictures down from my lingerie line. Then I carefully poured the developer and the fixer back into their plastic containers, and the rinse water from the third pan into the toilet. I took another private look at the pictures while I sat on the throne. Then I freshened up and climbed back into bed with Max.

"I can't talk right now, Mom," he said as he waved me away.

I wrapped my arms around him and kissed him anyway.

"I'll meet you at the hospital in a half-hour," he said, and then he slammed the phone down and directed his crumple up face, and bad mood my way.

"It's over, Max," I blurted out.

"What? I didn't do anything, Gabby. I swear, baby."

"Not us silly, we've been given yet another chance. Adler died the hard way. It's over. We can have our pictures back. I won't have to tell my parents. I won't have to feel embarrassed about something we did that is this beautiful." I gave Max the pictures from the night before.

We take all our pictures in black and white to capture our emotions, and our true essences. Colors sometimes distort our view of the world and ourselves. Colors are beautiful, but when things are black and white we're forced to see the gray areas. We're forced to take a closer look. We can see things the way they are instead of the way we dress them up to be. Max looked over the pictures in the morning light, which is different from the candle light so close to the heat of passion.

"We're good at this," he said.

"Yep, but it's deeper than the pictures. I love you, Max." I wrapped my arms around him again and kissed his cheek.

He shook me off with a stretch and a yawn. "I was sleeping good, baby. That was the best sleep I've had since you left me in August."

I stole another kiss. "Hopefully it will be like this from now on."

He picked up his watch from the night stand. "Gesh, I have to go. Mom is feeling better today. She's going to meet me at the hospital." He kissed me and got up.

"Max, what couldn't you talk about now?"

He stopped in his tracks and flashed me that hateful corkscrew stare again. "What did you do to make my mother hate you?" His tone was bitter and accusing, and I didn't miss how he had changed the subject.

"I stole your heart, and she thinks I'm not good enough for you. That's why I stayed in school. I want you to be proud of me. I want your parents to know I'm perfect for you."

Max sat on the bed next to me. "Mom can be a prude, but it's more than that. She flies off the handle with the mere mention of your name. Baby, I need to know what really happened when you were living there?" He stared into my eyes and played with my hair.

"I ran into her at the mall. She was rude and I wasn't exactly pleasant. I was upset when I left the mall. It was the same day that Adler followed me to Brad's, and the same day I almost lost Makai. Did you tell her about the baby?"

"Dad knows, but every time I bring your name up, Mom calls you derogatory names and leaves the room."

"I was angry with you for not telling her about our baby. She called me fat."

Max laughed. "You got angry with Mom because she called you fat? You're pregnant baby—you're supposed to be fat."

"I wasn't angry because she called me fat and ugly. I was angry with you because you were ashamed of me because I got pregnant."

"Baby, I wanted us to be married before we started our family. I didn't mean to make you feel ashamed." He kissed me and gave me a hug. "Dad knew, but when you wouldn't marry me and come home, I never found a good way to tell Mom."

"Makai will be here in another month. Do you want me to go with you to the hospital to tell Mommy Dearest?"

"No! Let me deal with her and Dad first. Dad has been upgraded to stable. I'll sneak away at lunch and go with you to get the pictures. I'll probably go back to Nashville tonight." Max kissed me and went to the bathroom. Twenty minutes later he was gone.

He called at one o'clock. He couldn't meet me for lunch. I told him I loved him. He said he would see me later. He called from Nashville at midnight to let me know he had gone back. Maryanne had insisted. He said he had stopped by while I was out. Maryanne seemed to be feeling much stronger after she found out Max was counting on me for support instead of her. He didn't get around to telling her about Makai.

෪

Brad had read about Adler in the Sunday *Clarion-Ledger*, but of course none of the things Adler had said about Brad and his father were printed in the newspaper. I didn't bother to mention any of it to him. I didn't see any point in stirring the pot now. I'm sure the paper didn't have any desire to go head-on with the Pruters.

The pictures were returned in good condition. They were still professional and tasteful pictures even though Adler had tried to turn them into something vulgar. A week later I was back into the routine of school. The pictures of Max and me loving each other were the only proof I had of our night of undying love. He called every night. We made small talk about Makai and Julius and skated around our issues and feelings. He didn't mention getting married although it was clear that he had plans for our son.

A week or so later I ran into Maryanne in the hospital cafeteria. Max still hadn't found a way to tell her about Makai. She stared at me and my protruding belly for a moment without speaking.

"We need to talk," I said.

"It looks as though it is a bit late for talk."

"We should at least try to get alone. I love Max and he loves his unborn son." Maryanne's eyes bucked and she leaned on the table for support. "I'm sorry if I said or did something to offend you, but I hope your feelings for me won't keep you from loving your grandchild."

Maryanne's coffee shook in her hand. Her eyes looked as though they were going to pop out their sockets.

"Why are you ruining my son's life?" she finally asked. "How can you stand there and say you love him, and do this to him?"

I took a deep breath and coated the bile in my throat with honey like Belinda used to do castor oil. It tasted just as awful, but I knew it was for the greater good. "I don't want to fight," I said sweetly. "Max and I have issues, but my love for him and our baby is not one of them. I'm gonna have his son in a month or so. Perhaps if we had your blessings we could solve some of our problems."

"How can my blessings help him now? He's unhappy about what you're doing to him. He won't even talk to me about it."

"He said you blow up every time he mentions my name. Max and I can't be happy in whatever we decide to do about our son until you and I accept our roles in his life."

Maryanne sat in an empty chair next to the coffee machine. "When are you due?"

"Middle of June if I'm lucky."

"I knew it was more than you leaving him that was making him distraught. I hated the way he obsessed over you after you left him. I couldn't stand it. Every time I turned around you were at Pruter's house. My poor Max almost lost everything when your picture was in the paper. Julius had to talk to the dean to keep Meharry from kicking him out of school. I couldn't stand by and let you ruin his life. Yes, I told him you were a slut every time he brought up your name. Why did you leave? Why won't you marry him?"

I thought about Max in his blue suit with the ring in his mouth. "I love him. I want to marry him. A lot of things went wrong for us.

Every time we tried to make them right another hurdle was thrown in our path."

"Don't give me that bullshit! You walked out on him. You threw Pruter in his face. Pruter has moved on with that pretty red-head. Now you want me to believe that you're having my grandchild. Do I look like a fool to you, Gabby? I tried to warn you, about those men."

"Maryanne, I'm trying to reach out to you! I want you to be a part of your grandchild's life, but if that attitude is all you can offer, then forget it. I'm done."

She said, "Humph," and I stormed away. There was no way I was going to let her see me cry.

Two days later I went to see Julius before he left the hospital. Max had said his father was doing much better and the doctors had said he would be able to go home in a few days. I didn't bother to tell Max I had run into Maryanne.

Julius smiled when I walked in. "You look great, Gabby. How is Makai doing?"

"Max told you his name?"

"He pretty much tells me everything. Maryanne and I were sorta hard on you, but we don't run Max's life as much as you probably think. He's learning from his mistakes. God knows he's made plenty with you, but make no mistake, my boy loves you."

I kissed Julius on the cheek the way I had done the day he was unconscious. "I suppose I've made my share as well." Makai kicked. I put Julius's hand on my belly and let him feel his grandson move. "But keeping our baby wasn't one of them."

Julius smiled. "I can't tell you what to do, but Max will make you a fine husband if you let him."

I sat on the bed next to Julius. "He hasn't asked lately." I looked away and bit down on my lip. "He probably would have moved on after I left Nashville if it wasn't for Makai."

"Max is used to having things his way. He's a perfectionist. But trust me, he loves you. The only thing stopping him from doing the right thing is you."

"We don't talk about our feelings anymore. Maybe we've pushed each other to far apart. Maybe we can't fix it anymore."

Julius continued to rub my tummy even though Makai was quiet. "Max wants to do what's best for you and Makai."

"I love Max. I didn't get pregnant to hurt him—this wasn't some disparate attempt to hold on to him."

Maryanne walked into the room. Makai kicked again.

"He's an active little rascal," Julius said.

"I was sick the whole time I was pregnant, but Max was a beautiful baby. I don't know how you manage school and being alone. Do you mind, Gabby?" Maryanne put her hand on my stomach. Makai kicked hard. We all giggled.

"It hasn't been easy, but I'm more determined than ever to do what I have to do. Max understands why I do it. It's probably going to get harder after Makai comes, but I can't quit. I'm not a quitter."

"I thought about what you said the other day. Max is sure about Makai, and you, so I guess we should at least try to act like family." She looked me dead in my eyes and said, "But, I'm warning you, I'm not going to let you do anything to hurt my son."

I half smiled and rose from the bed. "Brad and Kelly are having a few friends over for dinner to announce their engagement. I'm sorry I have to rush off." I waited for a reaction from Maryanne, but I was pleasantly surprised when I didn't get one.

Pink and blue balloons that looked like storks carrying babies were on Brad's mailbox, and cars were parked everywhere when I arrived. Dr. Brown's nosy wife told me to park in their driveway so I wouldn't have to walk too far in my late pregnancy state.

My classmates yelled, "Surprise!" when I walked into the house. I was touched by their show of love and support. At that moment, I knew I couldn't quit or take a year off. This was my class. They had not only accepted me, they made sure I had everything I needed for Makai.

Max ordered a crib with the trimmings. Big Curtis put the crib together, painted the room, and hung wallpaper with red, yellow, blue and green clowns on it to match the comforter for the crib. Daddy finished the little red rocking horse for Makai, and a matching red rocking chair for me. Everything was perfect. I was ready to take on my new role as a mother as soon as I finished my exams. My water broke at three in the morning--two days, and two exams before I completed my first year of dental school!

32

I had been having Braxton-Hicks contractions since I took my Dental Anatomy exam. At first I thought it was the usual nervous stomach problems I always get when I take final exams. A cramp jolted me awake, and something warm and wet gushed out between my legs. My tolerance for stomach cramps isn't worth anything. I knew immediately that focused breathing wasn't going to cut it when Makai was ready to make his grand entrance into the world.

I was scared. It was the wee hours of the night, and I was home alone. It was too early to call Belinda and Big Momma, and I didn't feel right about calling Brad even though he was my Lamaze partner. He's still my ace, but he's living with Kelly now. Max still hasn't mentioned marriage, but he and his parents are anxiously waiting.

I pulled the wet sheets off my bed, and hopped to the bathroom with the bundled-up sheet between my legs like a snowball maxi pad. The contractions felt like gas pains. They griped my insides in the middle of the night, and bit into my gut. I knew if I didn't move fast, I would have more than air in your pants.

After I recovered from my first real contraction, I called Dr. Morgan's answering service. It was 3:15 a.m. Max and I were about to move to the next phase—parents—single parents? I didn't know which one scared me more. I jumped when the phone rang at 3:30

a.m. I had forgotten it was the middle of the night, and I was in the middle of a life changing event. I turned the lamp on to shed some light on the situation. Dr. Morgan's new associate, Dr. Carr, was on the line.

"My water broke. I'm all alone. I'm scared, what should I do…" I rattled off quickly. Then the tears came.

"Calm down. You're going to be okay."

"Okay." I sniffled then I took a deep breath.

"Is there someone you can call?"

"Max, but he's in Nashville."

"Can you call a neighbor to bring you to the hospital?"

"Do you think I can wait until six to call my mother?"

"How do you feel?"

"I'm okay, until the contractions come."

"Is there someone close by who could bring you to the hospital?"

"I could call my Lamaze partner."

After I talked to Dr. Carr I showered and shaved. I hadn't shaved my legs since the last time I saw Max. I couldn't see them so I pretended that no one else could either. After I cleaned up and got dressed, I called Brad.

"I'm sorry I, uh, woke you up. I thought you said you got up at five before exams to cram?"

"Gabby, it's four o'clock. What are you doing up this early?"

"Having the baby."

"How can you be so calm? I'm on my way," Brad said right before the line went dead.

I stopped telling Max that I still love him after he skated around his feelings one time too many. I'd asked him if he still loved me and he had said, "What do you think?" Now, that's a bullshit answer if I ever heard one. I've been secretly pissed off at him since that night, because I think he is more concerned about Makai than me. What if we end up in a custody battle? Things have changed. I punched in his number on my princess phone. The train is about to pull into the station and we are both going to be responsible for our little passenger from this point on. Max answered in a groggy sexy tone.

I spoke quickly. "My water broke, the contractions hurt, I miss you, you should be here, are you coming?" My heart pounded as I caught my breath and waited for his answers.

"Are you okay? Calm down."

I was hyperventilating into the phone. "Don't take my baby away from me. I'll be a good mother. I swear."

"Claim down, Gabby. Nobody is gonna take our baby. Did you call Uncle Lester? Call my parents. Mom can take you to the hospital. You talk a good game, but I know how you are when pain hits you. Don't try to drive yourself."

"Will you stop being a fucking doctor for one minute and get your ass to Jackson if you're coming!"

"Stop screaming, baby. I'll be there as soon as I can."

"Max?"

"Yes, Gabby."

"Be careful," I said instead of telling him how much I love him, and need him here with me.

"I will. Our son needs me."

"I need you as well. I'm scared, Max. I'm sorry I yelled. I didn't mean to mess things up for us. I'm sorry."

"Ssshhh, I love you, Gabby. We both made some mistakes. But we're in this together from now on, okay?"

"Okay. I'll see you later," I said through clenched teeth when another contraction hit.

"Hang in there until I get there. Do your breathing exercises until the pain eases up. I'm on my way. I love you."

Max hung up when Brad pressed on my doorbell. I called Belinda and asked her to meet us there. Brad and I left at five o'clock. I was doubled over in pain when we finished with the paperwork. The nurse wouldn't let Brad go with me when she discovered he wasn't the father or a relative.

"Brad is my Lamaze partner," I pleaded. "I'm too scared to go alone."

"You said your mother and the father are on their way." The nurse said.

"Yes, but he's coming from Nashville, and she's coming from Hot Springs."

"It will be too confusing when they get here if Mr. Pruter goes in with you."

Another strong contraction hit me. I doubled over again. "I don't give a fuck how confusing it gets, Brad is the godfather, he was my Lamaze partner, I'm scared to death and he's coming in--got it," I said through clenched teeth.

Brad looked as scared as me. Then he looked at the nurse and said, "This could get real ugly. If I were you I would do whatever she says."

I rolled my eyes at Brad. "Are you going to show us where to go or do I have to wheel myself," I said as the contraction dug deeper instead of easing up. I let out a loud screech which sounded like one of my love calls.

The nurse picked up the phone and punched in a few numbers. "I need an orderly, stat!" she said.

Brad rubbed my back. "Focus and breath, Gabby. Do it the way we did it in class. He, he, he, he." I chimed in, and we breathed together.

I imagined the ecstasy I had captured on Max's face in the photographs. I focused on his face, his eyes, his smile and the passion and love that had brought us this far. The love that was about to give us a son. I wanted to see that look on Max's face when our son was born. I want to know that nothing has come between us and our passion. I want to believe our love is as strong and as enduring as the look in his eyes. I want to believe that our love has made it through the cheating, the interfering and the separations. I want to believe that our passion and our love child will make our commitment to each other real. Solid. I didn't know how badly I wanted our bond to be forever until my water broke. Everything from this point on is about our future.

"Breathe, Gabby. He, he, he, hee," Brad said.

I flashed him a fuck-off look even though he was trying to help. We had discussed our feelings about using breathing and focusing to ease the pain. I had decided that it was a crock of shit. But when I focused on my love for Max, I forget about the pain for a moment. "I'm sorry. I was focusing, I just forgot to breathe."

Brad continued to rub my back. "It's gonna be okay. Max will get here in time."

"I'm not worried about Max."

"Yes, you are."

"Fuck you, Brad, you don't know everything."

"I know you better than you think."

"I'm sorry about the F-word. Thanks for being my friend, but you don't know me better than you think." We laughed, and I wondered for a split second if we could have been more than friends.

Belinda and Dr. Carr arrived at eight. I sent Brad downstairs to take his Biochemistry exam. Dr. Carr examined me. The contractions were thirty minutes apart and getting stronger with each episode. I wanted to have all natural birth, but as soon as Dr. Carr arrived I begged for epidural anesthesia. My cervix was only dilated four centimeters and Dr. Carr said I had a way to go. The nurse hooked me up to a fetal monitor that showed the baby's heartbeat, and a sonogram that showed the position Makai was in as he got ready to make his grand entrance.

The gadgets and my moaning and sometimes screaming freaked Belinda out. She had delivered me twenty-two years ago at her doctor's office while I was in the breech position. She didn't have monitors or anesthesia, and Daddy wasn't allowed in the room. Belinda used to tell me I survived birth and I could do anything my heart desired--I believed her.

Belinda couldn't stand seeing me in pain. I told her to go check on Big Momma. She left promptly. I was stuck with Nurse Patty. Her alligator skin was as tan as mine and judging from her white hair she probably should have retired ten years ago. I figured I was doing her a favor by pushing her to that realization. She should have been resting by a lake or the ocean instead of holding my hand while I called Max everything but a child of God for not getting to Jackson fast enough. He was supposed to be by my side. I need to see his face so I can focus!

By the time the anesthesiologist came I had ran out of derogatory superlatives to call Max so I started on Julius and Maryanne. Then Nurse Patty looked at me wrong so I started on her.

The anesthesiologist told me to curl over so he could feel my vertebrae. I curled in a knot and the next thing I knew I was throwing up all over the place. It stunk like sardines. I was embarrassed so I cursed Max. More nurses rushed into the room. Someone cleaned up the mess and wiped everything but me down with something that smelled like bleach and lemons, but worse. Nurse Patty helped me change into a clean gown. Dr. Carr came in and checked me again and ordered an antibiotic. Another nurse came and turned my arm into a pin cushion before she could find a vein to start an IV for the antibiotic. No one could or would answer my questions about why I needed it. I was starting to wear Patty down with my foul language. I wanted to know what infection I had and where the hell it had come from. Everyone was tight lipped. I cursed them all out. I was already hysterical when another contraction hit me. "Where the fuck did the anesthesiologists go?" I asked as I tried to get up from the table to go find him. I was too hooked up to go anywhere.

"Calm down," Nurse Patty said.

"Let's trade places so we can see how calm you will be!"

"The doctor will be back in a minute. Hang in there, honey. Why don't you breathe with me," Patty said sweetly?

"F breathing. What's taking you so long, Max? I need you."

Nurse Patty held my hand and rubbed it. "I'm sure he will be here soon, dear. Let me help you in the meantime."

I wanted to apologize to Patty, but I was too embarrassed. The anesthesiologist came back after Nurse Patty had calmed me down. I curled in the fetal position again. Someone washed my back with an antiseptic soap. Then the doctor walked his fingers down my spine again. He wiped something cool and wet around my lower back that numbed my skin. Then he pressed a little harder and told me to take a deep breath. Something sharp pricked me between the pressure spots and less than five minutes later I couldn't feel anything from my waist to my toes. I freaked out again, only this time it was internal agony. I was helpless. Totally helpless!

I couldn't feel the pain that had been bad enough to make me call everyone I love including my mother, and the people who were trying to help me awful names. I could feel a vague squeeze and when I looked at the monitor, I knew it was a contraction. Dr. Carr checked me again and said I was five centimeters. She reassured me that Max still had plenty of time. I asked about the IV. I had an infection. I wanted to know where it came from, and if my baby was okay. She reassured me that the baby was fine, but she was very secretive about the infection. That pissed me off. I had heard about people picking up strange infections in hospitals. I was not taking it lightly. I wore poor Patty out, and I still didn't have any answers.

Patty squeezed a chair beside my birthing table and all the monitors. She held my hand and tried to comfort me. When she perked up at around two o'clock, I thought it was time for her to go home. I was about to apologize when she hopped up and said, "You must be Max. Gabriella has been telling us about you all morning."

I looked sheepishly at Max. Damn, he looked good! He smiled broadly when Patty told him I had been talking about him. I grinned timidly and prayed that Patty was too much of a Southern Baptist to repeat what I had said. Max walked over and kissed my chapped lips. I held his head and tongue wrestled with him until he pulled away. He smiled at me coyly.

"Hey, Baby," he said, and a mischievous smile graced his handsome face. Then he looked at the monitors and the IV.

"Hey yourself. You missed most of the fun, but I'm glad you're here."

"What is the IV for?" He knitted his thick eyebrows and stared into my eyes again. The look of passion was there or was it compassion? Did he care about me or were his concerns only for his son?

"They think I have an infection. I missed my Biochemistry exam this morning." I felt a squeeze and looked at the monitor.

Max leaned over me and looked as well. "I see they gave you something for the pain."

"Yep, an epidural. Max, I don't need another doctor."

"He kissed me again. "I'm just checking everything out."

"Well, ask me how I'm feeling?"

He chuckled, and Nurse Patty smiled in the background. "How do you feel?"

"I'm better now that you're here." I glanced shyly at Patty.

"We could have used you around nine o'clock. Gabriella was having a rough time," Patty said.

Dr. Morgan smiled when he busted into the room, and saw Max holding my hand. "Gabriella. Maxwell. If all goes well, you all will be parents soon. How are you feeling, little lady?"

I glanced at Max and smiled. "Better. Much better."

"Dr. Carr went home so if you hurry up, I'll have the pleasure of delivering my grand godson. Let me check you and see how you're progressing. First babies tend to take their time you know."

"He was waiting on you and Max to get here."

Max squeezed my hand. I felt a flutter in my belly and in my heart. Not even the strong anesthesia could keep those feelings from surfacing with me being this close to Max.

"Gabby, you're dilated seven centimeters. Things are going to sped up now."

"Since you guys are here I don't have to hold back any longer."

"Max, you need to scrub if you want to help," Dr. Morgan said. Max left and Patty slipped back in his place.

"Thanks for staying with me. Forgive me for saying those nasty things about you."

"Hush, child. You're gonna need your energy in a bit."

Max came back ten minutes later dressed in blue scrubs. He exchanged places with Patty again, and leaned over and kissed me on the forehead. I asked for ice chips. He feed me ice and fluffed my pillows. I could feel the squeezing more now with each contraction, but it was nothing compared to the pain I had felt earlier so I didn't say anything.

Two hours later I could out and out feel the contractions even though I couldn't feel my toes. Dr. Morgan announced that he could see Makai's head. He said he was going to give me an episiotomy to facilitate a rapid delivery and prevent tearing. Max left my side to go watch the procedure. He returned a few minutes later and announced that Makai had curly hair like mine. Dr. Morgan told me to push each time I felt the tight squeezing. At first Max held my hand and repeated for me to push whenever Dr. Morgan said. Max had little beads of sweat on his nose and his hands were sweating. His excitement showed in his eyes, and the tone of his voice. When Dr. Morgan announced that the head was coming, or did he say crowning, Max disappeared behind my cocked legs. There was a tent of covers draped from my midsection to just below my knee. Max and Dr. Morgan were talking below the tent. I tried to pull the covers away so I could see what they were doing. They said my little tent needed to stay in place to keep everything sterile. Every time I tried to pull it away Patty would put it back in place.

"Push, Gabby," Max said from behind the tent. I tried to rise on my elbows. I wanted to see. Patty gently pushed me back down, and told me to push.

"Come on, baby. Push!" Max grunted the words out as if he was doing the pushing. "He's almost out, Gabby! Push, baby." I could hear excitement, love, lust, and joy in his tone of voice. Come on, baby. Come with me he liked to say when we make love. I pushed up, and pulled the drapes from my knees. I needed to see Max's face. I wanted to see his ecstasy. Patty pushed me down and replaced the covers. I felt a long squeeze. In my heart of hearts, I knew it was the big one.

"Come on, baby. That's it," Max said in the same sensuous tone. "That's it, Gabby. You did it, baby," he said, and then I heard Makai's strong cry.

"I be damned--he looks like you, Max," Dr. Morgan said.

"Gabby, he looks like me," Max said, and if pride had a sound, that was it.

"Let me see. Give him to me."

"Hold on, baby. "I'm gonna cut the cord," Max said, and he took the sound of pride to a higher level.

"We're gonna clean him up a little then you can see him," Dr. Morgan said.

"Look how big his balls are. Are they supposed to be that big?" Max asked, and he took the sound of pride to the highest level. I guess he figured he had something to do with the size of his son's balls.

"Give me my baby and leave his balls alone," I demanded with the finesse I had earlier in the morning.

"Hurry up you guys, Gabriella's ugly side is starting to resurface," Patty said as she chuckled.

"Why did he stop crying? Is he okay?"

"He's fine. Are you planning to breast feed?" Dr. Morgan asked.

"Yes," Max answered.

"May I see him now?"

"In a minute," Dr. Morgan said.

"Are you sure he's okay?"

"He's beautiful, Gabby. But he doesn't look anything like you."

"That's because you doubted me, Max. May I see him?"

"In a minute," Dr. Morgan said.

"What's taking so long?"

"We're examining him while you expel the placenta. He weighs nine pounds. Wow he is twenty-three inches long," Dr. Morgan announced.

"Yeah, yeah, now give him to me!"

"Hold on, I have to check your placenta and stitch you up," Dr. Morgan said.

"He's perfect, Gabby. He got a ten on his second Apgar," Max said, and the look of ecstasy was in his eyes when he finally gave Makai to me. He kissed me gently on my crusty lips before he handed him over. "You did great, Baby. I'm so proud; I don't know what to say." Max smiled and wiped tears from the corners of his eyes.

I looked at Makai and all I saw was Max. Max's skin color. Max's dreamy eyes and long eyelashes. Max's lips, and of course Max's balls. I closed my eyes and silently prayed that we would work our problems out because it is going to be impossible to look at Makai's face and not see Max. I don't ever want to resent him because he reminds me of his father.

Makai started a sucking movement with his tiny lips when I held him close to my heart. Max smiled a knowing smile when Makai got his little fingers caught in my hair. I didn't know if it was my milk coming in or flutters of love in my heart when my son cried. I was overwhelmed with loving emotions. I wasn't surprised or ashamed when tears escaped from my eyes.

"Don't cry. I'm here," Max said. He kissed me again and again. "I'm a father now. I want us to be a family. I'm not going to lie and cheat us anymore. I promise."

The tears kept on coming. I put my finger in Makai's hand to avoid looking at Max. His little fingers made a ring around my finger. I wished it was Max's band of gold. I wished we could be a happy family. I wanted him to ask me to be his wife, but he stopped short of popping the question.

I tried to concentrate on my son's little hand. Makai squeezed my finger and blinked at just the right moment. I smiled and wiped my tears. He has been with me for nine months. According to all the books I read; he knows my heart beat. He knows my voice. He knows my cry. It's amazing how much they come here knowing. He knows, and I know, that I will love him no matter what happens between Max and me.

"We have to take him for a little while," Patty said. "We'll take you to recovery until the feeling returns to your legs. A nurse will bring your baby to you after you're assigned a room." She took Makai and walked away. Max followed her.

I continued to cry in recovery. I didn't know if I had postpartum depression or if they were tears of joy. All I knew for sure was that I was scared.

33

Gina and Gretchen are Makai's godmothers. I called them first. Gina couldn't wait to see Makai so she could spoil him, and Gretchen couldn't believe he didn't look anything like me. I called Lorna and gave her Makai's statistics after I got Gretchen off the phone.

"So, my nephew looks like his daddy, huh?"

"He looks like he spat him out. Max is so proud, Lorna, I swear I could see his chest expanding and a halo around his head. You should have heard him talking about my baby's balls."

Lorna chuckled. "So are you gonna marry Max now. The way you were talking about kissing him I doubt if you will make it six weeks."

"I've decided not to let him touch me again unless I'm his wife, and he hasn't asked."

"Famous last words. Do you remember Richard, the football player I used to hang with at JSU?"

"Yep. The one that you couldn't get enough of."

"The one who couldn't get enough of me. Anyway, the Forty-Niners drafted him and he asked me to marry him!"

I screamed into the phone. "Are you gonna do it?"

"Hell, yeah, he's the best I ever had, and he's gonna be rich. I'm taking his ass to Vegas next week."

"But do you love him? And what about Harold?"

"You love the shit out of Max and look what it got you. Harold is my manager—he's business."

"Lorna, I have to go. The nurse just brought Makai in. I'm gonna nurse him for the first time. I'm so excited!"

"Wait--I have some more good news. It looks like today is the Oliver girls' big day."

"Okay, but hurry up. My boobs are full."

"Zora Huston one of the girls I used to do background with, signed a deal with Arista to do her first album. She asked me to do back-up for her. We've been working night and day on her project. She's going to be hot, Gabby. I can feel it. She made me promise to tour with her when the time comes."

"That's great. I'm so proud of you. I miss hearing you sing. Will you make Makai a CD?"

"I'll hook him up with the best soulful lullabies he will ever hear."

"Soulful lullabies?"

"*I Want to Be Free, Ain't No Mountain High Enough, Shining Star,* don't worry—he'll love it. I'll be home for The Fourth. Tell Makai not to worry, Auntie Lorna will be there to spoil him soon." She chuckled again. "If his daddy doesn't act right I'll bring him to California so you can finish school. Babies love me. I'm proud of you, too, Gabby. Our dreams are coming true—ain't no stopping us now!"

"I love you, Lorna, congratulations. Call me from the chapel."

"Girl, you know you're my number one fan. I wish I could have been there to hold your hand until Max got there."

"You would have slapped the mess out of me with the way I was cutting-up."

Lorna's laughter and her words rang in my head long after she hung up. I survived. There will be other challenges, but nothing is going to stop me. I have a child to raise and support--I can't stop now.

The nurse gave me a wet pad to clean my nipples before and after nursing. She said I could use mild soap and water when I go home. She also gave me a cream to apply to my nipples just in case they get sore and cracked. She said most women give up on nursing because their nipples get sore. The nurse reassured me that the benefits outweigh a little pain. I cleaned my nipples before I put it in Makai's mouth. She instructed me to put as much areola in as possible to lessen the pain. Makai's sucking reflexes were strong. While he suckled, and nourished his body from mine, I got a wonderful euphoric high. I was already emotionally in love with my son. It was different from the love I feel for Max even though it was just as strong and wonderful in its own way. Now I have another love lust thing to figure out.

The door opened. Max walked in. "Say cheese."

He snapped a picture of me nursing Makai then he leaned in and kissed me long and hard while our son continued to nurse. Max tickled Makai's foot and said, "Hey, little man, let go of daddy's titty."

I giggled, and stuck my finger in Makai's mouth to prevent him from pulling when I removed him from my right breast, to switch him to the other side. Thin white milk ran down his chin. He smiled like a drunken man with no teeth. Then he burped and started sucking again. Max threw a diaper over his shoulder and burped him again. He gave him back to me when he cried. I offered him Max's other titty. He was a happy camper again. Max looked jealous even though he said he was thrilled that I was nursing our son. He sat on the hospital bed next to Makai. He played with my hair while Makai continued to nurse.

"Gabby?" Max said softly. I was happier than I had been since I left him in Nashville last August. I looked at him and smiled when he called my name.

"Let's get married," he said. He looked deep into my eyes. I got warm chills.

"Okay," I said softly while I fought to push back tears and lost. I kissed him while Makai suckled from my breast.

"Please baby. I know I haven't always shown you how much I love you, and how much you mean to me, but I did a lot of growing up while you were carrying my son. Baby, I don't deserve a woman as strong, and as beautiful as you, but I swear to you, if you'll marry me, I'll make up for all the times I did you wrong. Please, baby, you humbled me completely today when you pushed this little man into the world. You have given me so much happiness, and I keep breaking your heart. But no more!" Max got down on one knee. "I don't love anybody but you. You're the only one that can make me crazy enough to get down on my knees and beg like this."

I giggled through my tears, and said, "Yes, Max, I'll marry you."

"Please, baby, please, I'll never hurt you again. I swear. I love you, Gabriella Oliver. I love you... Only you."

I giggled. "Okay, Max. The answer is yes. Didn't you hear me the first time?"

He burst out laughing. "I love you, Gabby. I've been practicing my speech since Christmas. I didn't want to waste it. I mean every word of it though. Baby, I just wanted you to know how I feel." He smiled broadly before he stood up and backed out the door. "I'll be right back." He had a catfish smile on his handsome face before he disappeared behind the door.

I nursed Makai until we were both punch drunk from the ecstasy we were giving each other. Two hours later Max woke us up when he rushed into the room. He had on his navy-blue suit with a white rose in the lapel. He was carrying a large white box with a gold bow and ribbon. He smiled and the light hit the wedding band between his teeth. It was so shiny and bright it looked like Harold's three gold teeth with diamonds.

I giggled and said, "Come here." Max sat on the bed next to me and Makai. He had drifted back to sleep, but he continued to suckle occasionally.

"Open the box," Max said as he took Makai.

"What is it?"

"Open it and see." I untied the pretty bow. Max turned his back when I lifted the top from the box. It was a white silk and lace dress with a plunging neckline, and a matching veil. "It's perfect, Max."

"Mom found it at the bridal shop in the mall. She said it is bad luck for me to see it. Put it on and I'll be back with your preacher at eight."

"That's an hour from now."

"An hour too long for something we should have done years ago." He kissed me and gave me Makai. "I love you," He said before he disappeared again.

I was speechless. A few minutes later Belinda and Big Momma came to help me get dressed. They had on their Sunday best. They already had flowers pinned to their dresses. Big Momma gave me her pearls and a scripture, 1 Peter 4:8, which reminds us *above all to love each other deeply, for love covers a multitude of sins.* Belinda gave me a blue garter belt and a girdle. She made me promise to stay in school, and she promised me that she and daddy will always be in my corner. I put on a light cover of makeup and undid my braids. I was still soft in the middle but the girdle Belinda gave me took care of that.

Big Curtis and Max's parents arrived with Max and Reverend Bond at eight. We didn't have music but *Stay in My Corner,* and every time Max had cheated or lied to me, and all the times we had loved each other, and the many times he had begged for forgiveness all played in my head. I couldn't think of one moment through the thick and the thin that I didn't absolutely love him freely. Our love isn't perfect, but it is strong. We survived even when our love slow burned like a small flicker of candle light. We survived because of love.

Reverend Bond performed the ceremony. Our families congratulated us and Maryanne reminded me that I had obligated myself to keeping Max happy. I reassured her that I didn't have a problem with keeping him happy if he obligated himself to me and our family only. I was still hooked to an IV. It had been a long day. Max and I spent our wedding night in the hospital bed with Makai close by. Makai woke up every two hours to nurse, and for diaper changes. The realization that there is more to parenting than having a cute healthy baby didn't take long to sink in. We were both frazzled after our first night of being officially married parents.

Max went back to Nashville the next morning to finish his second year of medical school, and to study for part-one of the medical boards exams. Makai and I went to my apartment two days later. A week later I passed my other exams with flying colors. I wanted to stay in dental school in Jackson, but things started to fall apart as soon as Max went back to Nashville.

34

My landlord didn't want to hear any more sob stories, and my money hadn't been right since April. Makai was only three weeks old. I called my husband and asked him for rent money. We had only spent one married night together. Instead of loaning me money, Max begged me to come to Nashville and spend the summer with him. The movers took my things to his parents' house. Makai and I were in Nashville the following day at sunset.

Max added my name to his checking account. I went out and brought Pampers, lobsters, candles, new sheets and condoms. It was his birthday and I wanted to give him some love. But when I gave the house a thorough cleaning, I found a cowrie shell earring like Gretchen's wedged between the cushion of the sofa, and wiry strains of bleach-blond hair were tangled in the crocheted pillows on the bed. I tossed the earring and hairs in the trash. My mood did an about-face even though Gretchen had gotten married and was pregnant. I wasn't worried about Tammy--she will always be a thorn on my rose, but the rose is mine. I called Gretchen. She was out shopping. Chance was so excited when I told him to tell Gretchen Makai and I were spending the summer with Max, he invited us over to have dinner with them.

Gretchen was obliviously deeply in love with Chance, but something about Max seemed to make her nervous. I was shocked when I discovered just how pregnant she was, and that her husband was the same Chance who had asked Lorna to stop singing in nightclubs, marry him, and have his children last summer.

I didn't mention the earring, the hairs or sex to Max. We consummated our marriage two weeks later after he decided to support my decision to stay in school. We enjoyed each other and our son the rest of the summer. I forgot about the earring and the past, and concentrated on loving my husband and my son. Max made Makai and I feel like the most important people in his world. Everything was great until it was time for us to go back to Mississippi.

My plan had been for Makai to stay with Belinda and Big Momma, but Big Momma got sick, and Belinda had enough on her hands taking care of her. Max gave me a choice between staying in Nashville, or moving in with his parents. Maryanne was more than happy to take care of Makai. She loved her grandson enough to tolerate me. The thought of not seeing him every day made my heart ache so I moved back into the Johnson mansion.

I was the other Mrs. Johnson, but Maryanne treated me like a stepchild. Living with her was like trying to ice skating on a rocky road. We were in conflict about everything including our mothering skills. She spoiled Makai rotten. She hated that I was breast feeding. She had the audacity to call me Elise the cow! She decorated the bedroom closest to hers for him so I couldn't hear him crying in the middle of the night. Then she tried to give him formula, but thank goodness, my baby wasn't having it. She decorated everything in his room baby-blue, and she threw out the rocking horse Big Curtis had made because it clashed with the room. And when I brought it back inside she called it a homemade piece of junk!

I had to bite my tongue so many times it was amazing that I could talk. She even had a hissy fit when I disciplined Makai. Spanking and yelling at him was totally out as he got older and into everything, but she didn't believe in time-outs either. She didn't like it when my family and Brad visited. Belinda ignored her. She always brought enough of her home cooked goodies for Julius so he was always glad to see her.

Brad was serious about being Makai's godfather so he spoiled Makai rotten as well. Max decided that he should get to know Brad better since he was special to Makai and me. They started playing golf together, and Max became so obsessed with beating Brad at his own game that they soon became best friends. Max was Brad's best man when Brad and Kelly got married. Their picture made the society page of the *Clarion-Ledger* with a caption listing Max as Brad's best man and Makai as his godson.

Maryanne bragged about the picture for months. She finally forgave me for the sky-blue dress fiasco, but she continued to pick at me about little things. She hated when I brought Makai and me clothes from Kmart instead of some swanky, overpriced store in the mall. I didn't feel right living off Julius and spending up his money. But Max always took her side. He told me not to look a gift horse in the mouth. I was sure he had heard me, or someone in my family, say those words, so I knew there was hope.

Big Momma taught me how to use positive mind control, which isn't much different from living in denial, but it wasn't long before I was thankful for Maryanne's help and hospitality. I learned to mutter witch-bitch under my breath while I had a big ass smile on my face. After I learned to control my reaction to life's little setbacks, the years went by quicker.

I survived with Max's love, and help from our families. Max came back to Jackson after he graduated. He worked in Julius's office, and postponed his residency until I graduated the following spring. We were finally happy and together. I was so excited about having him home; I let him convince me to stop taking the pill three months before my graduation.

My life had finally come full circle and I thought I would be happy forevermore when three-year-old Makai ran up to me after I received my degree. He presented me with a bouquet of roses and said, "Mommy, I proud you, Daddy too." I picked him up and gave him a bubble kiss on his lips, then I pulled up the sissy sailor suit Maryanne had dressed him in and bubble kissed his belly. We giggled until tears flowed from the corners of our eyes. Max joined us and stole a few kisses of his own. Max's eyes were twinkling with love and pride, and his kisses told me just how much he loved us.

We had stopped by his father's office on the way to my graduation, and confirmed that we were pregnant again. The office was closed so we got a quickie before my ceremony. I had an extra-large smile in the pictures Max, Belinda, Lorna and Big Momma were taking of me—Dr. Gabriella Oliver-Johnson!

Maryanne and Julius gave us a combination graduation going away party. Big Curtis and Belinda and my brothers turned it into a real party. Belinda brought gumbo and her blues records, and Daddy brought his homemade corn whiskey and a deck of cards per Max's request. Maryanne seemed to be embarrassed until Brad's parents told her they were having a fantastic time. They said the food, the card game and the music were great. They wanted to know who her party planners and caterers were. Belinda and Daddy started a Soul Train line out by the pool. Max and I, and the Pruters joined in. Julius had drunk too much corn whiskey. He was all over Lorna. Maryanne got off her high horse quick when she saw Julius whisper in Lorna's ear. Before the night was over Maryanne had kicked off her Cinderella slippers and let her hair down like the rest of us.

We left for Boston two days after my graduation. Maryanne kissed me and gave me a hug when we left. She made me promise to take care of her boys. Max was excited about doing his obstetrics and gynecology residence at Brigham and Women's Hospital. We wanted to get settled before he got bombarded with his medical studies again.

I hadn't planned to be a full-time wife and mother while we were in Boston, but Max was busy with his studies, and we saw him when we saw him. Michelle and Michael were born on Christmas Eve. The twins had been a difficult pregnancy. Working had been out of the question. They looked like me. Michelle slept well, and she rarely cried. Michael was the opposite. Max adored our children and it wasn't long before I let him convince me to have another one. I figured we might as well complete our family while I wasn't working.

I hated Boston. The winters were too cold, I hated the snow, the people were too snooty for my taste, they talked funny, and Max was rarely home. My world was centered around my children and Max. I don't know if I was trying to make-up for all the times I had been selfish, or if I enjoyed being a mother and pleasing my husband. Max was in seventh heaven when he had time for his family. I finally felt free and totally committed even though this was not how I had pictured it. Makai made lots of friends when he started school, and as much as I hated Boston, I hated taking him away from his school and friends. I could only pray that life for Max and me would remain as sweet as it had been in Boston.

By the time, we moved back to Mississippi four years later we had Makai, Michelle and Michael, Miles and one in the oven. We were planning to live with Max's parents until after the baby was born. Max didn't want me to have any added stress.

Maryanne adored her grandchildren. She had flown to Boston to help me out with each of them. She spoiled the boys and she treated Michelle like a goddess. I was surprised since Michelle looks so much like me.

Max rented a car at the airport and instead of going straight to his parents he took us for a drive in the country. Michelle, Michael and Miles had fallen asleep when Max turned off the main road. He drove slowly up a long winding driveway to a humongous brick house surrounded by live oaks with hanging moss, tall pines, pecan trees, and magnolia trees. The house had double porches, stately columns, double doors with cut glass on each side, and stunning large arched windows. Multi-colored azalea bushes were everywhere and the smell of sweet magnolias filled the air. I screamed and woke my babies up when I recognized the house. It even had the perfect location in the country—halfway between his parents and mine.

"How did you know," I said as I stuck a bottle of breast milk into Myles's mouth.

"Last Christmas Lil' Curtis showed me the plans you drew in your high school drafting class. He said it was your dream house. I asked him if he could build it. Do you like it?"

My brothers had gotten together and formed The Oliver Brothers Construction Company. Their motto is: We've built everything from outhouses to mansions--if it can be built we're the brothers to do it.

I kissed Max on the cheek, "I love it. I can't believe you pulled it off without me finding out. You're still sneaking around on me I see."

Max's laugh was filled with pride. "It was easy."

"Can we afford it, Max? We've lived off your parents long enough."

"I got the rest of my inheritance from my grandfather when I graduated, and I sold the house in Nashville, and your brothers let me have the family plan, and of course Mom and Dad pitched in a little extra for their grandchildren. Lil' Curtis was on a mission. Dude was calling me every week about some fancy change he knew you or the kids would like. It was his dream house to build."

I kissed Max again. "You guys did all of this right under my nose?"

"Nope, dude was paging me at the hospital. Let's go inside."

Miles had just gotten the hang of walking. He let me hold his hand while he climbed the four steps to the porch. When Max opened the double front doors, Makai, Michael and Michelle took off running. Miles wasn't far behind them. Max scooped me up and carried me across the threshold. The rooms were huge. I loved the hardwood floors, and the way the light came through the large windows. We found our way to the master bedroom suite. Max gave me the details about how Lil' Curtis had convinced him to add his and hers walk-in closets and vanities. He said he wanted me to have the whirlpool bath and the fireplace, but the marble was my brother's idea. I loved it. I started undressing Max so I could show him how much when the kids interrupted.

"Mommy! There's a treehouse, a playground, and a pool in the backyard. Can we go outside? Can we? Please?"

"Sure, we can," I said as I tried hopelessly to slip my swollen feet back into my shoes. I sat on the steps of the back porch and watched while Max pushed swings, and played in the sand and pool with the kids.

Our furniture didn't come for three days. We slept in sleeping bags and on cots because the kids refused to leave. The kids loved camping out in our new home, and Max and I didn't have any complaints.

Max joined his godfather's practice. He was a hit from the moment he walked into the office. He was rarely home, but when he was, he played with the kids and made sure I was happy.

I had been out of school four years and counting. I had gone through hell to get my degree, and I hadn't practiced dentistry a single day. Dentistry and medicine had changed. AIDS was here to stay. Minority and poor communities were being hit the hardest. I was torn between my children and trying to have a career. I had a lot more respect for Belinda and Big Momma who didn't have a choice. They not only took care of their families, they also took care of the families they worked for. I joined Brad's practice in Jackson on a part-time basis six months after Melissa was born, and I worked at the free clinic against Max's wishes. I had more than I dreamed I would ever have.

I quit my part-time job at the clinic when my boss hugged me, and whispered how he wished he could take my husband's place in my bed. He licked my ear and grinded into me. He grunted like he had come in his pants. Then he walked away like nothing had happened. No one was around. I left and never returned. I don't know what Max told him, but I got paid for six months. It wasn't about money. Max said when you can't hurt people for the bad things they do, sometimes you can settle for the next best thing.

My life felt complete. I was happy and free until Big Momma died two-days shy of her one-hundred-and-tenth birthday. Big Curtis had a heart attack shortly after Big Momma passed. Daddy survived, but now Belinda spends most of her time taking care of him. Lorna and Richard filed for a divorce after Lorna's career blew up, and she refused to settle down to have kids. She finally admitted that Miz Inez, the baby killer, had messed her up. She was okay with living vicariously through my kids. She was especially fond of Melissa who she claims looks like her. Melissa definitely has diva lungs, and a diva's attitude like her aunt.

Women were still throwing themselves at my husband, the rock-star ladies' doctor. Sometimes I take the keys to his Corvettes, and make Max drive the Mercedes station wagon with the child safety seats. He loves playing father can do it all, and even I must admit that he does it well. He also loves his work. I wished he didn't have to work so much. He swears that he got all his womanizing out his system before Makai was born. We had been married ten wonderful years and I was open to having more kids when Max's dick problems blew up in his face, and things went to hell again.

35

Max and the kids ran into Gretchen while they were shopping for Maryann's birthday presents. Makai said Michael had a stomachache so Gretchen volunteered to stay with him, Michelle, and Myles while Max took Michael to the men's room. According to Makai, Max and Michael were in the men's room when Gretchen mumbled something about Max making her abort his other brother. Max got paged while he was in the men's room with Michael. He dropped the kids off at home and rushed back to the hospital without noticing that Makai was upset.

Makai ran to his room and slammed the door. He is more spoiled than the others. I thought he was upset because Max had to go back to the hospital. I didn't get overly concerned about his tears until I went to his room to tell him dinner was ready.

He had cut the pages from his dictionary into threads, and broken toys were scattered all over his room. After Makai told me what Gretchen had said, he asked me if Max had told me to abort him? He is old enough to understand that Max and I got married on his birthday.

I hugged him and said, "Sugar, your daddy and I love you and that is all that matters."

"Is that a yes or a no answer, Mommy?" he challenged.

"Your father and I were in medical and dental school in different states. He wanted me to drop out of school and marry him. I refused, so yes, we were having a rough time, but he never told me to abort you."

I didn't cry in front of Makai. I was devastated even though I didn't know if it was true. I had found an earring like hers. I never questioned Max about it. Boy, did I feel like a fool. I paged Max. He called me an hour later. He said something about a full moon, a full house, and not coming home until morning.

I imagined him fucking Gretchen and probably others on the many nights he was unavailable for his family. She was my friend. I loved her like my own sister! I always suspected that she had a thing for Max, but I always thought she valued our friendship more.

All kinds of crazy thoughts went through my head as I packed Max's clothes and sat them in the garage in the middle of the night with a note that said: *You would be better off staying with your parents until I figure this out. You can see the kids whenever you like. It will take me a while to understand how you could fuck Gretchen.*

I was so angry, I went back to the garage and cut Max's underwear until they looked like they had been through a paper shredder. Then I ran over his new golf clubs with the station wagon. I stuck a note to the clubs that said: *Since you weren't here, I took my frustrations out on your clubs. How could you fuck my friend? Never mind--I don't want to know how you could be that damn lowdown.*

I conked out around three. The phone and the garage door woke me up a few hours later. Max was in the garage on his Blackberry.

"What did that bitch tell you?" Max asked.

"If she's a bitch, what in the hell does that make you?"

"Baby, I'm tired. Can I come in? We can talk about this after I get some rest."

"Gretchen told Makai about the abortion you forced her to have."

"What! I oughta kill that crazy bitch!"

"Don't yell--my head hurts. You can talk to Makai later today. He's pretty upset."

"Baby, may I please come in? It was a long..."

I hung up. He called right back. "Go to your parents, Max. If you come in here, I promise you it will not be pleasant. Go away. You can come back this afternoon to talk to the children. Don't forget to tell them you will be staying with your parents for a while," I said before I hung up again.

Max came over at two o'clock. I gave him a disgusting look and walked out. It was a rainy afternoon. The mall was swimming with shoppers. I got caught up in the flood of people, and decided to run up his credit cards. Max is an excellent provider and since we didn't need anything I bought my parents a living room and dining room set, and a comforter and matching curtains for my old room.

Hope and her two sons were unloading a U-Haul truck full of their stuff when I got to my parents' home. I didn't get the details, but it looked as if they were there to stay. Hope hasn't worked in years, she's not very helpful around the house, and she won't cook for shit. I decided not to burden my parents with my problems.

Anthony stopped by when I was leaving to go home. He sensed something was wrong, and since the truth was coming out I agreed to go somewhere with him so we could talk. His wife and daughter were out of town. We ended up at his house. I could always talk freely with Anthony if nothing else. The conversation was easy while I was telling him about Max even though I was all tears. A hug, a back rub, a reassuring I understand led to a kiss, and we ended up talking about why things had gone wrong for us while he played his old Al Green albums on his new stereo in what he called his man cave.

He played *I'm Still in Love with You* and we danced, and kissed like old times. I made a motion to leave when I detected those old-style stars in his eyes, and the comfortable way his arms always gave me peace. He said the words I knew in my heart were still true, and his kisses were sweeter than I remembered. Daddy wasn't breathing down our backs, but the truth was still burning my throat. I sat on his pullout sofa bed. He sat next to me and unbuttoned my blouse. My breasts had his attention. It felt like old times.

"I had an abortion," I blurted out. I looked away. My heart beat quickened, and I don't know if I was dizzy because letting go of my burden had made me lightheaded, or if I wanted to tread the old murky water I was in.

Anthony touched my breasts with his rough mechanic's hands, and moaned, "Pixie and Dixie." He had nicknamed them that the first time we were together. "It's been a long time."

"Did you hear me, Ant?"

He continued to please me in ways he had never been able to achieve before. Then he unzipped my jeans.

"No girdles?"

"It wasn't a miscarriage, Ant."

"I didn't think that it was…"

Our eyes met. "You didn't?"

He tugged my jeans and my French lace bra and panties off. "I couldn't understand why you wanted me to hate you. I couldn't understand why you hated yourself."

A tear escaped, and another, and moans--his and mine. Anthony stopped kissing me in places that belonged to Max now, and simply held me. The nightmare I'd had about Max pouncing on Gretchen flashed through my mind, and I began to cry again. Anthony held me and soothed me. He undressed and we lay together on his sofa bed in his man cave, and listened to Al Green. We held hands and stared at the ceiling for a while. Then we kissed for a while. And when it felt right in a naughty way, but wrong in every other way, I rolled on top of him, and fucked him with an abandon.

"You're changed, smarty pants," Anthony said, "But I ain't mad at you."

He had a sly grin on his face. I was still panting more from my disbelief for what I had just done, than from the thrill of it all. Anthony rolled me over, and made slow love to me before I could recover. I ruined Anthony's best when I cried Max's name.

We agreed that what we had done was more about closure than the possibility of any future get-togethers. Evelyn was pregnant again after fifteen years. Anthony still doesn't believe in divorce, and nor do I, which was why his goodbye kiss hurt so deeply fifteen years ago. We dressed in a hurry like we used to do back in the day. I was nervous, but to my surprise I didn't feel as guilty as I had thought, or as avenged as I had hoped. I was still shooting mad at Max and Gretchen. An old burden had been lifted though. My old festering questions had been answered. Now I could deal with my current problems with Max with a clear head.

Anthony walked me to the car. Don't forget to wash your sheets before Evelyn and Toni come home."

"I will, but tonight they will remind me of you, and what we let slip away. Gabby, I…"

"Me too, Ant." I kissed two fingers, and touched them to his lips. Then I flashed an innocent smile. "Evelyn is a lucky woman, and…"

"Your heart belongs to Max now. Go home and give him a chance to explain, but don't ever breakdown and tell him about tonight. I will never regret loving you." I nodded and went home.

36

Max was blocking the kitchen door when I got home. He glanced at his watch. It was midnight. He couldn't hide the worried look in his eyes. I wiped the smirk from my face before I pushed pass him.

"I put the kids to bed," he said. "Hope said you left three hours ago." He cleared his throat, but he couldn't hide the quiver in his tone of voice when he continued. "J.C. Penny called. They wanted to let you know they can deliver your furniture to your parents' address on Wednesday." He stared at me and begged with his eyes. I was still feeling devilish enough to let his ass suffer.

He cleared his throat again. "I was worried. I didn't know what to tell the children."

Guilt entered my mind, but I flashed Max a blasé look, and sat the bed-in-a-bag, and my new curtains down. "I'll deal with the kids tomorrow. I have rum raisin ice cream. You can have some while I run down your new house rules."

I still had Anthony's spit and cum all over Pixie, Dixie and Trixie. Lorna had been only partially right about that first dick thing. Now it is clear to me that I did what I did years ago because I was never in love with Anthony like I am with Max. Knowing that I'm still in love with my husband, I sat down calmly with him and outlined a plan for us to carry on with our lives with as little trauma to our children as possible. He could pretty much come and go as he pleases, but he couldn't spend the night, and our bedroom would be off limits until I decided otherwise.

Max wanted me to go out on dates so we wouldn't have to discuss any of this in front of the children. He wanted to go out once a week. I agreed to once a month until I'm no longer mad enough at him to do something else crazy.

It seemed as if Max was always working and rarely home before I put him out. I didn't think that the kids, or I would miss him as much as we did. The kids drove me crazy with questions about when he would be coming home. He always read them their bedtime stories and tucked them in. He loved to help with their baths. He used to take Makai to his little league practices, and help him with his homework. When he comes by, I retreat to our bedroom, or go out shopping. I'm just so angry with him.

My goal was to hear his side of the story when I picked up the phone and called him. It was late, the kids were sleeping, and I was lonely, and horny as hell. Max was on call so naturally he thought something was wrong with me or one of the kids when the hospital paged him. I lied and said I had a headache. I said I had run out of Tylenols, and I didn't want to leave the kids alone while I went to the store. Max sounded sexy sweet when he said he would bring me some as soon as he got a break.

I wasn't ready to deal with what he was probably going to tell me about him and Gretchen, but the longer I postponed it, the easier it was getting for me to just accept his love, and get on with our lives. Max will do and say whatever it takes to be close to me and his children.

I looked in the mirror and said, "Gabby you have to get this over with before you let Max back in your bed, or it will bug you forever." Then I told myself that I looked terrible so I took off the T-shirt and boxer shorts I was wearing, and put on the sleazy red teddy from Frederick's of Hollywood Max had given me for our anniversary.

Max rang the doorbell instead of letting himself in. He smiled at me cockeyed, and I knew that he knew I had lied about the headache. I invited him in, but he said, "I better not." He gave me a bottle of Motrin, chocolate kisses, and a pint of Cherry ice cream. He must think I have PMS. During that time of the month I'm just as subject to attack him for no good reason as I am to jump his bones.

"I, ahhh...I'm on call."

It pissed me off that he saw right through my attack camouflaged as a seduction. I should have skipped the three-inch fuzzy slippers. "Well, ahh, thanks for bringing me these." I held up my bag of goodies, and forced a smile as I attempted to close the door.

Max blocked it with his foot. He frowned when I looked up at him. "Was this a test, Gabby?" I held the bag up again and shook it. No words came. "I blew it, didn't I?" Tears coated my cheeks. Max closed the door and left.

After my failed attempt at getting Max to sweep me off my feet, and make me forget what he, and I had done, the first month went by in a haze. My energy was sapped from dealing with the kids mostly alone. It was getting harder and harder to get out the bed in the mornings due to a lack of sleep, and too much wine. Max came by every day, but I continued to use that time to retreat to my room and rest. I was too confused, distraught and angry to confront him after what I had done with Anthony. I even tried to get out of our first monthly date. Max wasn't having it. He took the kids to his parents' house, and then he came back and threatened to knock the door down if I didn't come out.

We went to T.G.I. Fridays in Highland Village. He poured his wine, dine, and seduce Gabby charm on so thick it turned me off instead of turning me on. I didn't know if it was the food or my nerves that made me feel sick. By the time, I convinced Max to take me home, I wasn't sure if he had changed, or if he was even remorseful when he said, "I have never loved anybody but you, Gabby. I've done some things that I am truly ashamed of, but I have not cheated since we got married. I swear."

"So, are saying you slept with Gretchen before we got married?" Max turned toward me. I held his gaze, even though he was driving. His eyes got misty for the first time all evening. "Just tell me why?"

He stared straight ahead and the muscles tightened in his jaw when he said, "It wasn't like a love thing if that's what you're worried about. I was lost after you left me. Everything was falling apart. I was failing out of school. I had nightmares for months after we found Sara like that. I couldn't get that note threatening you out of my mind. I wanted you to come home so bad I couldn't concentrate on anything else. I wanted to keep you safe. My dreams, our dreams, were slipping away, and I couldn't do a damn thing about it. I was afraid. I couldn't figure out how to make everything right again with us or school, so I shut down. I was stoned out of my fucking mind for days after I saw your picture in the paper with Brad. Just the thought of him touching you while you were pregnant with my child nearly killed me. I was angry. I was hurt. I didn't care about anything anymore. My life was fucked-up, and I didn't know how to fucking fix it. I couldn't fix it without you. I was high more often, than not. I had pretty much shut completely down when Gretchen came to my house to help. We drank some whiskey and smoked some herb and…"

"And what?"

"Honest to god, Gabby, I don't know how it happened. All I remember is being on top of her calling your name, and her crying when she told me she wasn't you."

The taste of puke coated my mouth when I pictured what Max had said. He had confirmed it! "Did you rape her?"

"Hell no! I was fucked up, but I would never force myself on anyone, Gabby. You know me better than that. Gretchen and I both agreed that we had made a mistake. I promised myself that night that

I would never cheat on you again, and I haven't, not even when I was going through that shit with Jared. That motherfucker had the nerve to brag about how much he enjoyed you. Sick motherfucker! I hope he gets raped every night he spends in prison. I didn't want to believe what he did, but I had heard and seen some of it with my own eyes and ears. Yes, I beat that motherfucker bad enough for him to press charges. That's the most violent I have ever been in my life. I had to protect your honor. I had heard your screams. I didn't see you for months after that. I couldn't, but I never considered being with anyone else. I had to get myself together, I couldn't afford to shut down again. You have to believe me." I could tell from Max's tone that he was getting frustrated, but I wasn't about to let him blame me this time.

"Did you force Gretchen to have an abortion?"

Max looked at me with begging eyes. "I didn't force her to do anything, baby. It's her body, it was her choice. You were pregnant with Makai. I told her that you were pregnant, and that we were going to get married."

"She told Makai that you forced her to have an abortion!" I yelled.

"I didn't force her. We agreed that we didn't want to hurt you. An abortion was the only way to take care of our mistake. Baby, it was a long time ago. I love you. We have five beautiful children and a wonderful marriage. Tell me what I need to do for you to find a way to forgive me. I've beat myself up about this for years. In some ways, I'm glad it is finally out in the open. I hated myself for hurting you. Keeping it a secret form you, was one of the hardest things I have ever had to do. I don't want to downplay your anger, but I'm a better man, father and husband because of that mistake. What's done is done so what are we going to do now? Have I failed you and the kids in any other ways? Haven't I been a good husband and father?"

My mind returned to our breakups before Makai was born. "I may never be able to forgive you or Gretchen!"

Max pulled the car into our driveway and turned the engine off. Then he took my hands in his as tears pooled in his eyes. "I'm sorry,

Gabby. I've tried to be the husband and father you and our children deserve. I was young and stupid." His voice cracked. He paused to clear his throat. "There has to be a way for you to forgive me. Tell me what I need to do. Please don't stop loving me, Gabby."

"I'm trying to make sense of this, Max. All I want from you right now is the truth. Did you invite Gretchen to your house that night?"

"Absolutely not! She came to see what she could do to help me and you get back together. One minute she was telling me how much she knew you loved me, and the next thing I remembered was her telling me that she wasn't you, and a month or so later she told me she was…and neither one of us wanted to hurt you. We mutually agreed to take care of it. I gave her the money. A few months later, she told me she had married Chance. And we finally got married. I thought everything had worked out for the best for everyone."

My mind reversed back to the time when Max and I were separated while I was pregnant with Makai. My overactive imagination didn't need any more details to add to the nightmares that were already causing me to have sleepless nights. I've been waking up in cold sweats after dreaming about Max having orgies with Gretchen, Gina, and me, and me running to Anthony and screwing him like a two-dollar whore. Then I have flashbacks of Gretchen barely clinging to life. I told her I loved her, and I meant it. I told her I needed her to pull through it as much for me as for her. We promised to always, always no matter what, no matter whom to be there for each other. We promised God that we would never ever walk down that path of doom again under any circumstances. We were sisters fighting the same battle to survive the sins of our pasts, and I couldn't for the life of me understand how she could have done that again?

"Did you take Gretchen to have the abortion?"

"I gave her the money. She told me she would take care of it."

"Have you ever seen River, Max?"

"I can't honestly say that I have."

I busted out laughing. All my life I've taken Daddy's advice and picked battles that I could not only survive—I chose battles that made the victories worth the fight. I was in a fit of laughter and tears.

"It's not funny, Gabby, you have to let me come home!"

"Shut up, Max, I'm not finished, and you're not coming home until after I talk to Gretchen. And I'm telling you right now that your stories had better match, so if there is anything else you need to tell me, you had better come clean now, if you want to come home."

"She had no business bringing that mess up after all these years. I called her and cursed her out. What in the hell was she thinking saying something like that in front of a child? It's no telling what lies she will tell you. I'm not gonna let our future depend on her crazy ass!"

"My head hurts. I'm going inside and go to bed, Max. Do you want to add anything else? I don't feel so good."

"I saw a look on your face when I mentioned Jared that concerned me. I know we never talked about it, but I don't want any more secrets between us."

"I'm just glad he finally got what he deserves."

"So am I, but I need to get it off my chest, and your eyes say you do as well." He cleared his throat and his jaw muscles flexed again. "I came to your apartment that night to propose again. I thought the Gretchen mistake was behind me, and I had gotten myself back on track at school. I was in therapy, and I had finally figured out that the only way to embrace my dreams was for me to embrace yours. There really is no me without you, Gabby. You tried to explain it to me, but I had to learn the lesson the hard way. And boy did I fuck things up. We needed each other for either of our dreams to work, we still do. When I got to your door that night, I heard a man's voice. I was about to leave when I heard you scream. I climbed onto your balcony. I saw what Jared was doing to you. I saw you struggling, but I know you, and it also looked to me like you hesitated. I tried to open your slider door. It was locked. I could see that you were afraid. In my heart of hearts, I know you didn't fight him off like I know you could have because you wanted to protect our baby. I beat him until he passed out. He wouldn't admit anything. He said you invited him in. He said you were lonely and you wanted him. He said he couldn't believe how wet you were for him. I don't want to know, but if you need to tell me, you can." Max's tone of voice had gotten thick and tight. He cleared his throat again when I didn't say anything. "Dad, Uncle Lester, and I didn't want to chance stressing you out. We took the easy road. We knew he was lying, but we dealt with Jared without involving you or Mom. They made me promise to give myself, and you, some time and distance to heal. I couldn't afford to mess up with you or school anymore. I hated leaving you to deal with it alone." He cleared his throat and took a deep breath. "I needed to hold you in my arms, and make sure you were okay, but they made me wait. We waited a couple of days to see what you were going to do about Jared. You didn't report or say anything so we cut a deal with him. That look on your face says that ... I'm sorry, Gabby."

"He raped me! He abused his powers as my doctor. He abused his powers as a man. We all abused our powers by setting him free to do it to other women." I said, and I couldn't stop the tears that coated my cheeks. "Thank God for the women who were brave enough to speak up, and put his ass in jail. If ten women spoke up, imagine how many other poor women suffered in silence like me for ten years." Max reached for my hand and kissed it. "I blamed myself for months for being too embarrassed to speak up. I covered the bruises and lied when people noticed my anguish and grief. I felt so stupid. I couldn't even tell you what he did to me at the office. If only I had told you…"

Max squeezed my hand. "It's okay, baby, we were in a bad place."

"I don't think he penetrated me with his penis, but he didn't attempt to rape me—he raped me!"

"Gabby, please let me stay with you tonight. I don't want to leave you alone. I'll stay in the guest room or in the corner of our bedroom. Come on baby, I'll do whatever you say, but please let me stay."

"I'm going to need at least another month of separation to get my nerves up to confront Gretchen." I laughed even as I cried.

"That's not funny, Gabby."

River was born less than three months after Makai. I did the Math in my mind, and laughed again. It all adds up to Mommy being right—God gives the toughest choices to us women. We got out of Max's Corvette and crossed our threshold in silence. I retreated to our bedroom and locked myself in. The next morning, I found Max in the den knocked out on the sofa, with an empty Jack Daniel's bottle still in his hands.

Month two and three pasted in a blur. I just didn't have the energy to comfort Gretchen. I just couldn't picture her doing that again, and if she didn't, it can only mean one thing.

37

Makai had been extra good in his father's absence. He helped me with the other kids, and he hadn't been a brat once. I feared that he blamed himself. On the other hand, Melissa was turning out to be a terror. I wondered if it was because Max was absent, or if it was because I had gone to work too soon after she was born. One night I was checking on her when I heard Makai crying. I asked him what was wrong. He wished he hadn't told me about Gretchen.

I hugged him and said, "Sugar, she shouldn't have said those things to you. You did the right thing by telling me."

"Then, why are you so unhappy, Mommy? Why did you make daddy leave?"

"It's complicated, sugar, but it's not your fault." I hugged and kissed him again, and said, "Go to sleep, sugar."

"Mommy, don't you want daddy to come home?"

"Yes," I said and to my surprise I meant it.

"Did you tell him?"

"I wish it was that simple."

"You told him to leave. Can't you tell him to come back?"

Max hadn't asked to come home since his confessions. His eyes still dance when he smiles, but he rarely smiles anymore. He told me to call him whenever I needed him. When I smiled instead of answering, I could see a small glimmer of hope in his eyes.

"You can try, can't you, Mommy?"

"Yes, sugar, I will try."

Max and I had worked out a system where he took the kids to his parents' house every other weekend. He wanted me to have time to think, reflect and heal. He said I needed to know how it feels to miss my family. I welcomed the quiet time, but when I started to think and reflect all my thoughts were about him and our children. We had been happy despite his premarital cheating. It still hurts, but I had gone from feeling silly to downright stupid. I spent my free weekends cleaning and cooking so I wouldn't have time to think and reflect.

Melissa's third birthday was approaching. She is the youngest, but she questions her father's absence the most. She insisted upon Max reading her bedtime story every night. One night he had back-to-back deliveries and he couldn't make it. I tried everything to get her to go to sleep. Nothing worked. I took her to bed with me. We had a blast singing along with the tape Lorna had made her until she finally conked out. She woke up again around midnight crying for Max. I paged him. Melissa was asleep when he showed up an hour later. I asked him to stay just in case she woke up again. We climbed into our bed with Melissa between us.

The next morning Melissa was gone, and I was moaning into Max's neck, and caressing him. He didn't move even though his boner was in my hand. I slipped out of bed, took a cold shower, checked on Melissa, and went to prepare breakfast. Melissa was sound asleep in her bed hugging her *The Cat in The Hat* book. Max hates cold cereal. I made pancakes, eggs, and sausage. He joined me in the kitchen before the kids started to ramble.

"You're up early," he said, and the big smile on his face got bigger when I blushed.

"Melissa was missing. I went to check on her. Did I disturb you?"

"I was enjoying…" He paused and flashed me another sexy smile. "You were knocked out when I read Melissa her story around four, and put her in her bed."

"You know me—when I'm out, I'm out."

"Melissa wants me to buy bunk beds for her birthday. She wants me to have a place to sleep so I won't have to leave." My eyes met his. His looked damp but he continued. "I don't want her to think I don't want to stay, Gabby. I promised myself that I would never be far away from you and our children after I was separated from you and Makai."

A tear escaped from my eyes. Max apologized for upsetting me, but I doubt if he had a clue about how torn I was inside.

"I wanna come home, Gabby. I'm here all the time anyway. I miss you."

I held Max's hand and stared into his eyes. He seemed sincere. He always does. I wanted to trust him again. Damn, I was horny, but I knew I couldn't relent on that alone. I was about to kiss him when Melissa wrapped herself around his legs. One of her Afro puffs was headed north, the other was going west. Her eyes were puffy from the night before, but there was no mistaking the love and excitement in her eyes when she smiled at Max.

"Diddy! You're still here! Did you kissy Mommy and make up?" I couldn't deny the hope in her eyes when she looked from Max to me.

"I made breakfast, are you hungry?"

"Yep. I want frosty flakes." Max's smile turned to a frown. Maybe I should let him come home so he will understand that Melissa gets what Melissa wants, and if I didn't know any better I would swear that she was plotting to get her daddy home.

"Why don't you have something hot with daddy and me?"

"O-tay. Can I have Pop Tarts? Pleeze, Mommy?" She made a piti-ful baby face and signaled for me to pick her up. I did. She gave me a bubble kiss. "Pleeze?" Max took her from my arms.

"Melissa, we're gonna have a nutritious hot breakfast and that is that. Now go and wake up your sister and brothers so we can all eat together." His fingers pressed into her chubby thighs. Melissa hasn't lost her baby fat and her baby charm.

She gave Max a bubble kiss and said, "O-tay, Diddy. Are Pop Tarts and frosty flakes new-tricks-us?" She kissed him again. He put her down. "I be right back. Stay right here, O-tay? Mommy, did you give diddy a happy bird-day kissy?" Max smiled broadly so I leaned over the kitchen island I was using to separate us, and gave him a peck on his juicy lips. It was a lips-only kiss, but I still felt magic that I wasn't prepared for.

Melissa smiled and reached for my hand. "Mommy if you want Diddy to stay you have to kissy long time like on TV." She pulled me in front of Max. "O-tay. Kissy." Max put his arms around me and pressed against me. He kissed me hard and penetratingly deep.

"Diddy, you gonna have a bird-day party at Chuck-E-Cheeses?"

Max chuckled. "If you and Mommy can come," he said. His eyes were glued to mine.

I was still smiling from our first kiss in months. Melissa skipped away singing happy bird-day to Diddy.

We were speechless when we were alone again. I didn't know whether to be happy or jealous about their love for their father, and his for them. I blushed and pretended that I hadn't forgotten that it was his birthday. I should have taken advantage of him when I had a chance.

Max was happy to have breakfast at home, a piece of my home-made chocolate pecan cake, and his birthday celebration at Chuck-E-Cheeses with his family. We ate pizza and made gaga eyes at each other.

Things were intense between us in a nice way after celebrating his birthday together. The Oliver family's Fourth of July picnic had been moved to our house. My brothers and Big Curtis even made Max an official family member by letting him make the hot-dogs and grilled vegetables on his brand new super-duper gas grill while they cooked steaks, chicken, red-hots, deer, and ribs on their homemade barrel grill. Belinda made baked beans, a pot of mixed greens and red velvet cakes. And I made potato salad, macaroni and cheese, and my famous chocolate pecan, and coconut cakes. Everyone filled up on food while the blues blasted from the speakers on the back porch. The kids played games, and swam while Max played poker with my brothers and my father. That made him a double official family member.

I got a surprise call from Gina and Charles. I invited them over. They had two kids Kevin and Myesha. Gina had recently quit her job to do her own thing.

It had gotten too hard to fake married bliss at our family gatherings. I kept myself busy by hiding out in the kitchen. Hope and her boys were still living with my parents. She was doing more man hunting than job hunting. I didn't have the heart to burden my parents with my problems. And I sure didn't need to be that close to Anthony. To my surprise, I've been busting with pent up energy since I woke up stroking Max on his birthday. That kiss had been twenty times more powerful than our first kiss. Gina saw right through my charade. She requested a tour of my house so we could talk. I told her about Gretchen and Max. It felt good to get it out in the open. Gina hugged me and whispered, "It's not the choices we make that count, Gabby, it's the consequences of those choices that make life intriguing. You and Max have a good marriage, terrific kids and a beautiful home. Do what feels right for you and your family, Gabby. Fuck what other people think."

"Thanks, Gina. Well, at least now I know why Gretchen hasn't called since Max and I moved back to Mississippi. I always thought it was because Chance used to be engaged to Lorna, and River had a cleft palate and lip. She said Chance wasn't handling having a less than perfect child well, but you know how conceited Gretchen can be. Have you ever seen River?"

"Not even a picture. I haven't seen Gretchen in years, and every time I call her she seems tense or in a hurry."

"She was at the mall, and she didn't even bother to call and to say hello. Makai said she showed him a picture of her twins, but no little boy about his age."

"That's strange. The cleft lip and palate would have been repaired years ago. Do you think something happened?"

"Not to my knowledge."

"I wonder what she's hiding," Gina said.

"I don't know—I just can't picture her doing that again under any circumstances."

After Gina and Charles left, the heat, too much food and wine, and too many things to think about got the best of me. Max put me to bed and went back to his poker game. He partied into the wee hours of the night. He stayed the night since my brothers had been drinking too much to drive home. Lil' Curtis had won three hundred dollars from Max. He refused to go while he was hot. Max woke me up at five in the morning to tell me what I had missed and how much fun he had hanging out with my family. He yakked until he went to sleep ready-to-roll on top of the covers.

Max and I were forced to spend even more time together as we planned Melissa's birthday party. Third birthdays are important to our family. Melissa can communicate her wishes well, and her number one priority seems to be getting her mommy and daddy under the same roof. Max and I went to every furniture store in the Jackson vicinity before we found the perfect bunk beds for her room. I didn't know if Max's motives were to spend more time with me or to make sure Melissa and his bunk beds were perfect. We were back to having dinner as a family on most days. He seemed to make a point of showing up right on time. He didn't ask if he could come home to stay. He didn't even try to kiss me even though I was openly flirting with my eyes, leaving my hair down, and dressing sexier.

I was nervous about Melissa's party. Both sets of grandparents, Brad and Kelly and their adopted son Brandon were all coming. Brad and Kelly had done everything but stand on their heads trying to conceive a child. Nothing had worked. Tammy and her husband and their two kids, Lil' Curtis and his bad ass kids, and Hope and her boys were also going to be at the party. I had somehow managed to keep my problems a secret from my family, and Max and Anthony out of my bed.

Max took the kids to his parents' house the Friday afternoon before the party. Melissa's furniture was delivered shortly after they left. Max came back home alone to make sure the beds were setup properly. We went through Melissa's baby things and picked out what we wanted to save for her to pass on to her children. Max bought a new copy of her favorite book to save because she wasn't ready to give it up. Every time I looked deep into Max's eyes I wanted him to pounce on me and love me like he used to do before I sentenced us to this farce.

I filled a box with Melissa's baby memorabilia and took it to the attic after Max left. When I put her time capsule box next to Miles's, I saw a box marked: MAX/BOSTON which piqued my interest. I pulled it down and ripped it open. The red silk robe I had given Max years ago was wrapped around several photo albums. I ran my hand over the silky-smooth fabric as the memories raced through my mind. Instead of putting everything back in the box I put the robe on while I examined the black and white photographs Max had taken of me.

The photographs of me pregnant with Makai were especially touching. I cried my way through the pictures. Then I took the phone off the hook while I took a warm bath and pleased myself. We had promised to love each other for the rest of our lives, but Gretchen had made our marriage seem like a big fat lie. And what was I doing with this phony separation? I still love him. I needed to be sure that he didn't marry me just because I had his son. The doorbell rang while I was soaking in the tub. It was nine o'clock on a sultry hot Friday night. I slipped on the silk robe and let my hair down. I peeked out to see who was banging on my door so late. Max was outside rocking on his heels and puffing on a joint.

"Are you in there, Gabby? Let me in. Are you alone? Why didn't you answer the phone?"

I flung the door open. "Are the kids okay? I took the phone off the hook." He smiled and I recognized a familiar twinkle in his eyes through his haze.

"Dammit, Gabby, can I come home, or do you want to be free? I'm not leaving until you give me an answer one way or..." He smiled. "Is that my robe?"

I stared at him and wondered what had taken him so long. I took the joint from his hand and took a long pull. It made me cough. Max came inside and wrapped his arms around me while he patted me on my back.

"Do you know what you're asking for?" I coughed out.

"Are you okay?" he asked. "I want to come home. I haven't cheated since we got married. Baby, I haven't been with anyone since you put me out."

Guilt about my night of closure with Anthony flashed through my mind. I took another pull on his joint. His glazed eyes met my misty eyes as I untied his robe.

"I'm a good husband and father—that should count for something." Max took and exaggerated breath and continued. "Baby, there is too much shit out there these days to mess around. I have a beautiful wife, and great kids. I love you. I want to come home?"

"What took you so long? I wanted you to come home on your birthday."

"I hadn't forgiven myself." I hadn't forgiven myself either.

"I've never broken our wedding vows. I swear. I knew my ass had ran out of *I'm sorry cards* long before you finally said I do. My life sucks without you. I wasn't about to fuck this up. I'm a good husband and believe it or not my mother didn't raise a fool."

We had suffered enough. Self-pleasuring hasn't worked since the morning I woke up caressing him. And fucking Anthony certainly wasn't the answer. Instead of answering I let the robe gap open, and said welcome home with my eyes.

Max took the joint from me and took a long pull. He swept his eyes over my nakedness. Then he dropped the roach on the brick porch and squashed the flame with his shoe. His eyes were dead on me when he bent down. "The first time you smoked pot with me, I got us in all kind of trouble with your father." He picked the joint up and stuck it in his pocket. We stared at each other. "I wouldn't want the kids to find this. Can I come home or do you want to be free?" He smiled sideways, and my stomach tickled on the inside like it was filled with slaves who had just been freed.

"I'll be free when my family is back together," I said. I stammered over my words and my lips quivered, but I was sure of my request.

Max stared into my eyes again. He kicked the door shut and smiled. Then he pulled my body to his and wrapped his large hands around my waist. The sweat on his fingers felt like hot message oil as they floated over my moist skin. I waited for him to kiss me. He didn't.

"Should I go get the kids tonight or tomorrow," he said as our hands continued to probe each other for missed dreams. He had lost his happily-married-with-five-kids gut and was as svelte as he had been at twenty. His hands moved with slow determined ease over my soft mounds of damp flesh. I was still waiting on him to kiss me. He didn't. He moved his hands from my hills and valleys to my butt and pulled my naked flesh against his scratchy linen shorts. He held me there until I understood his needs, then he backed away. Sticky sweat trickled down my thighs with just enough tickle to make me aware of the heat within and without. He played with wayward strands of my hair and stared into my eyes while he waited for my answer. I waited for him to kiss me. He didn't.

"Tomorrow," I finally said. "I never doubted that you love our kids. Tonight, you can show me how much you love me. If you can do that, we can get our children tomorrow together."

"I never ever stopped loving you, Gabby." He scooped me up like a child running into oncoming traffic. I kicked, and screamed, and giggled, and waited for him to kiss me. He didn't.

"If? Proof? I've been giving you proof since we got married. I'll give you more proof than you will know what to do with." He carried me through the house, but instead of taking me to our bed, he carried me outside and threw me in the pool. "I will never stop loving you," he said.

I kicked and screamed when my butt hit the water. It splashed high around me as I sank deeper. The warm water wrapped completely around my nakedness when I touched the bottom. Max was as naked as I was when we came up. His lips covered mine and we suckled desperately for the same air. Then we made love in the murky August heat under the twinkling stars until freedom bells rang in my mind.

After we caught up on our loving, we shared a chaise lounge and the red silk robe I had given him for Christmas nearly ten years ago. He played with my wet hair, and I caressed him.

"Have you made plans for our monthly date next week?" I asked.

"Yep, we're gonna go to Disney World."

"You sound like you just won the Super Bowl."

"I feel like it too. My super sperms have been locked up too long for them not to make a few touchdowns tonight. They're probably making triplets as we speak."

He had done the do, and I had stopped taking the pill a month ago. Everywhere he had kissed was still shouting a song about freedom.

"You're probably getting pregnant as I speak. A brother knows when he busted a nut." Max chuckled and hopped up. He snatched the robe, and ran toward the house. "The camera is in the car. Are you coming? I have some more proof for you."

⚬

The phone jolted us awake around ten the next morning. A crying woman on the line blurted out, "River had an accident and nearly died. He's asking for his father!"

I didn't know but one River. "Gretchen?"

Max sat up in the bed. Our eyes locked.

"I didn't want to bother you and Max, but I promised River that I would call his father."

"His father?"

"What in the hell is she talking about?" Max asked. I signaled for him to be quiet.

"I promised Max but…" She started crying again. "Gabby, I couldn't do it."

"You had Max's baby?"

"What!" Max yelled more than asked.

"Chance was so happy when I told him I was pregnant… I didn't have the heart to tell him it wasn't his." Gretchen's voice changed and I could feel her love for Chance in her voice. "Chance left when River was born. Our sons, can pass for twins."

Max left the room. A few minutes later he was breathing hard into one of our other phones.

"I didn't want to hurt you, Gabby. I swear. I love you."

"Humph! You? Love? Me?" I asked. I chastised myself for sounding like Maryanne. Max didn't say anything, but he looked like he was about to explode.

"I went to Max's to help."

"Baby, I was on a binge—I thought…"

"Shut up Max. Go ahead, Gretchen."

"It will be better if Max tells you. I hope you will be able to forgive us after you hear all the circumstances and match them with the consequences. My little boy thinks he is dying. He made me promise to call his father." She sniffled again.

"Where was River when we came to visit you?" I asked.

"He was with Nana; she died." Gretchen started crying again.

"I'm sorry. Why didn't you call me, Gretchen?"

"River and I took her death really hard. Nana pretty much raised him. It wouldn't have been fair to you or to River to find out the truth at her funeral."

"Damn, Gretchen. How did River find out?"

"He overheard Chance and me arguing. Chance wanted me to tell Max and you the truth from the get-go. When I saw Makai at the mall, I slipped. It is uncanny how much our sons look alike. I was trying to do damage control when I told him I had aborted his brother. I know that is not an excuse, but I'm under tremendous pressure at home." Max grunted into the phone.

Gretchen sniffled and continued, "The truth was only going to ruin more lives. I couldn't do that to you." Max and Gretchen snuffled at the same time.

"It's too late to cry," I said. Max cleared his throat.

"River was angry with me. We think he may have been trying to kill himself. He thinks Max didn't want him, and Chance didn't love him. He was unconscious for a while..." Gretchen started crying again. "He has a concussion, a few broken bones. He is in a lot of pain. When he woke up this morning, he asked me if he could meet his father before he dies... Please help me, Gabby? He's just a baby, and I promised."

"How could you sleep with Max after all I did for you, Gretchen?" She started sobbing into the phone again.

"I'm sorry. I don't blame you if you hate me. I thought I was doing the right thing by keeping my secret. Max didn't know."

All I could think about was the night I found her in the shower at school close to death.

"River wants to meet Max. He..." She sniffled. "He promised to be a good boy so his real father will love him."

"Where is he?" I asked.

"They flew us to UMMC."

Max walked into the room with the cordless phone firm to his ear. His eyes were misty and begging.

"I'm not forgiving you, Gretchen," I said. My icy eyes bored into Max's. He didn't have to say what was on his mind. I didn't have to say what was on mine. "Max is a wonderful father." My eyes never left Max's. "What is River's room number—we will be there soon." Max let out a sigh of relief.

I listened to Max's frantic story about his two-minute slip-up with Gretchen while he rushed us to the hospital to meet his son. We got there in record time. Chance meet us at the door. He pointed me toward Gretchen. Then he wrapped his arm around Max, and led him in the opposite direction.

ACKNOWLEDGEMENTS

Special thanks to my family, friends, book club and readers for encouraging me to continue this wild journey. I hope that you will enjoy *Stay in My Corner* as much as you said you enjoyed *Playing Your Game*. To my children, Alicia and Alfred, this is what happens when you let your positive energy flow, and never ever give up on your dreams.

Shout outs and many thanks to Soul Passages: A Book Club for a wonderful coming out party, and a lively book discussion of *Playing Your Game*. Shout outs to Spice It Up Ladies Book Club for reading my e-book a little bit or a lot before it was finished.

Thanks again to all my writer friends. I try my best to *work* what I learned from you all. Many thanks to my sisters in the Hartford and Waterbury Alumnae Chapters of Delta Sigma Theta for your support. Much love and thanks to my patients for supporting me and my novel—you all are the best. Extra special thanks to Bryan—thanks for drilling me in my first book interview, and for all the other ways you encourage me to dream bigger, work harder, and let go and let God.

Much Love Always,
Gloria
gperryauthor@gmail.com

ABOUT THE AUTHOR

Stay in My Corner (A Consequences Novel) is book two of Gloria F. Perry's three book series. **Playing Your Game** was Gloria's first published novel, and the first book of the series. Gloria has published fiction and non-fiction stories in various local magazines, newspapers, and anthologies. She has earned local recognition for her commentary and non-fiction stories. Gloria attended Tougaloo College in Mississippi where she grew up. Gloria is a proud graduate of UCONN Dental School. Her dental practice received the 2017 Minority Small business of the Year Award from the Middlesex County Chamber. Dr. Perry lives in Connecticut with her family. She is working on the third book of the Consequences series.